EFFECTIVE
Foreign Language
INSTRUCTION
in the
Secondary School

Edited by

GEORGE E. SMITH

and

M. PHILLIP LEAMON

prentice-hall, inc.

englewood cliffs, n. j.

PRENTICE-HALL INTERNATIONAL, INC., *London*
PRENTICE-HALL OF AUSTRALIA, PTY. LTD., *Sydney*
PRENTICE-HALL OF CANADA, LTD., *Toronto*
PRENTICE-HALL OF INDIA PRIVATE LTD., *New Delhi*
PRENTICE-HALL OF JAPAN, INC., *Tokyo*

PRINTED IN THE UNITED STATES OF AMERICA

13-241802-9   B&P

The Editors' Introduction

For more than a decade now, specialists in foreign language instruction in the United States have been working to advance the concept that an effective foreign language program is the planned-for result of a careful and deliberate combination of interrelated factors. Examination of highly successful programs reveals the presence of all, or nearly all of these factors; and, apparently, the degree of program success varies in direct proportion to the extent that each factor has been coordinately included. Since this is so, one might expect that administrators and foreign language teachers would by now be familiar with the most important "components" and their details, and could be concerned primarily with their implementation. However, this desirable goal has not yet been reached. Communication is a difficult art to practice in our society—especially in the educator's many-faceted world.

Establishing an effective modern foreign language program at any level does indeed require attention to and detailed knowledge of a variety of closely related problems. Some of them appear to grow more complicated as time passes. First, in order to initiate, improve, or expand foreign language instruction in any geographic or educational community, it is necessary to establish a widespread, basic desire for change. There must be a suitable intellectual and emotional climate before "new" ideas can flourish. This often means that those working to bring about any change may have to engage first in an intensive campaign of education. This campaign may be simple, involving only a few key people in planned conversation, or it may require the use of all manner and means of communication: public meetings, radio, news press, television, etc. Once the ideas take root, and the newly created interest turns into demand for action, the planners are next faced with a set of questions that are largely administrative and supervisory in nature. These matters then lead to further questions of teaching methodology, materials, and so forth.

Let us assume that an educational entity has decided it wants effective foreign language instruction for its "consumers" and that the community is willing to supply the necessary financial support. Immediately they have created a need for skillful, well-prepared teachers. If the teachers are found, they must be provided with proper tools and equipment. This means development of well-designed texts and materials for all levels, tests for various purposes, electro-mechanical and audio-visual aids, maintenance programs, in-service education, etc. Each of these elements may in turn require additional related activity. At the state level, institutions preparing foreign language teachers must be prepared to do the best possible job; schools with inadequately prepared teachers must find ways to provide in-service education; research on methods of instruction and development of materials must be carried on continuously; and, as the program grows, the community must be prepared to provide increased financial backing. In other words, the desire to establish a single superior foreign language program in even a small community could ostensibly act as a catalyst for a whole series of activities with requirements and demands even at the national level.

One goal of this book is to discuss in a single, ready source, some of the major factors and combinations of elements which now seem essential to the development of an effective program for foreign language learning. Lack of information, or sometimes the dissemination of misinformation, about these building blocks of our specialized profession has resulted in disappointments and persistent problems. The present status of the language laboratory in many of our schools is only one example. In too many instances school administrators have been led to believe that this electro-mechanical aid to instruction would provide nearly automatic, self-contained answers to all questions on audio-lingual teaching. Where this expectation has failed to materialize, the blame has often fallen on the very concept of laboratory work or on the equipment itself. The result is often an idle or misused laboratory.

A good foreign language program is not developed merely by studying for a certain number of years, beginning in a particular grade, or using one publisher's materials and one manufacturer's equipment. The problem of upgrading foreign language teaching and strengthening foreign language programs is much more subtle and complex than that.

A good foreign language program is usually built around good teachers who use the foreign language as the means of communicating in the classroom. It may begin, for example, with four years study in the high school, continue into the community college, and work downward also to insure continuity. This may mean offering third and fourth level classes for only a few students initially, until the "cycle" has had a chance to build. The good program has the support of the faculty, the administration, and the community. It often offers one or two long-sequence programs of languages well taught, where enrollment is limited, rather than weaker offerings in more languages. It normally today encourages students to think of foreign language study in terms of a *minimum* three- or four-year sequence. It insures that teachers are helped to know of new developments in materials, equipment, and teachniques, and provides competent leadership and supervision. There is no panacea or simple answer for achieving these goals. It can be done, however, if "team" effort is effectively used.

Perhaps the *major* objective of this book, then, is to try to provide the three most active members of this "team" (specifically the administrator, the supervisor, and the teacher) with two kinds of help in their important tasks. First, we believe that since success does require cooperative action on the part of several individuals, each should be aware of questions confronting the others. For one thing, teachers should know something of the problems which an administrator faces, and administrators should know what they may do to facilitate the task in the classroom. For this reason we hope that this volume does succeed in addressing itself to both those whose principal responsibility is planning and those who are mainly concerned with practicing their art.

Secondly, we have tried to assemble in one convenient package some of the new, exciting ideas of a group of the most successful educators, teachers, and foreign language specialists concerned with foreign language instruction in the United States today. We have selected specific topics which apply to several major areas of concern: the basic teaching activity, materials and facilities, the new media tools, and administration or planning.

The contributors of these chapters have written specifically for this book with particular goals in mind, and we trust that every chapter will help the reader to achieve his personal goal of becoming a better foreign language teacher, supervisor, or administrator.

George E. Smith
M. Phillip Leamon

Contents

Donald K. Davidson
Harvard Graduate School of Education

Structure of the secondary school • Size and composition • How many languages? • Grouping and tracks • The roles of the administrator • The chairman and the supervisor • The foreign language head and his responsibilities • Selection and evaluation of teachers • Curriculum research and development • Department head vs. the school • New structures and the foreign language program • Ability grouping • The junior high school

Everett V. O'Rourke
California State Department of Education

The state department of education: its function and responsibility • The chief state officer and how he may help • Foreign language leadership in the state office • The state's role in materials production • Teacher certification • Publications

CHAPTER ONE

Teaching
the Basic Skills

by

Jermaine D. Arendt

Foreign Language Consultant, Minneapolis Public Schools

Objectives

The foreign language department
for each school system must establish for itself a set of objectives. Once
in mind, these objectives should determine the selection of curriculum
materials, and of methods and techniques. Objectives should be as
specific as possible in order that the department, through testing or
other evaluative procedures, can determine whether its goals are being
met. Usually it is wise to establish both short-range (yearly) and long-
range (four or six year) objectives. In this way the department is
better able to keep in mind the way that each year or level of learning
contributes to the overall long-term goals. Below is a sample statement
of one state's long-range objectives for a four-year foreign language
sequence.

1

OBJECTIVES OF A FOUR-YEAR LANGUAGE PROGRAM [1]

General Objectives

1. Develop positive attitudes toward FL learning and toward people who speak foreign languages.
2. Develop an understanding of how language is learned.
3. Develop an understanding of the nature of language—its changing character, how it reflects culture.
4. Develop some appreciation of the role that the foreign language can play in achieving the general goals of education (developing salable skills, promoting worthwhile use of leisure time, etc.).
5. Develop an understanding of the life of the adolescent and adult in the foreign country, with special emphasis on alerting the learner to cross-cultural differences.

Specific Linguistic Objectives

1. Develop the ability to communicate with a fair amount of skill in everyday situations typical for the young adult.
2. Develop skill in reading for different purposes the different kinds of materials typically read by the average youth of his age in the foreign culture.
3. Ability to write a simple free composition such as a letter with clarity and correctness in vocabulary, idiom, and syntax, and with a feeling for the level of language appropriate to the task.
4. Begin advanced work in conversation, syntax, composition and mature literature on the basis of sound fundamental knowledge of the language and culture.
5. Begin to devolop an ability to translate (with a feeling for correct interpretation from one language to the other) that material which is within the scope of his knowledge and experience.

Scope and Sequence

Selection and Presentation of Material. Once objectives have been determined, the scope and sequence for the entire language program, and for a particular level or year of study, can be established. In fact

---

1. Adapted from State of Minnesota Department of Education, *Guide for Modern Foreign Languages Grades 4-12,* Curriculum Bulletin No. 27, (St. Paul, 1965), pp. 50-51.

each class period and unit of study should be carefully planned, the teacher considering how best to present a particular element or elements of language. As far as possible, these elements of language should be presented through a situation that approximates real life.

The new language elements may be considered completely learned when the student can use them to express his own ideas in speaking and writing. He should: (1) make the right choice of words, (2) put the words in their proper order, (3) use necessary grammar signals correctly, (4) say the expressions with proper standard pronounciation in suitable patterns of intonation and rhythm, and (5) have an understanding concerning the situation (s) in which precisely this language will be appropriate.

Obviously, sometimes one may be satisfied if the student can get meaning from reading or listening (recognition) without his being able to recall the material for oral or written production. Most basic material, however, particularly in levels one and two, will require the complete mastery described above.

Variety of Activities. One cannot stress too strongly the need for variety in the activities chosen for a foreign language class. No matter how effective a single activity may be, it will stifle learning if it is overused. This is not meant to imply that indiscriminate jumping from one activity to another is necessarily wise. Each class hour, like each unit of study, should represent a cohesive whole, an entity, the parts of which stick together because they are bonded by the glue of common purpose, that of mastering a body of material.

Conserving Teacher Energy. Teaching speaking and listening skills in the modern foreign language class require considerable physical exertion on the part of the foreign language teacher. Because of this, foreign language teachers should be aware of special ways that they can conserve their energies and yet remain effective. Using conservative hand motions to signal desired student responses, using tape programs to present lesson material, employing student aides for taking attendance (where permissible) and reviewing drills, and conducting some activities from a high stool rather than from a standing position are some ways to avoid exhaustion.

The Need for Review and Re-entry. Learning a foreign language requires careful sequencing of elements of instruction, each unit building on previous study. On the other hand, we must resign ourselves to the idea that what is taught is often soon forgotten or at least partially so. Throughout the year—unless the material has built-in, systematic review—teachers should plan for re-entry of material that has been studied earlier. In this way, elements of language, once introduced, are reviewed from time to time and not allowed to fall into disuse and oblivion. An opportunity for re-entry is provided by teacher-led warmup sessions at the beginning of the class hour. In these sessions the teacher uses in natural communication with the class a number of utterances learned earlier. The warmup session is dealt with in more detail below in the section entitled *Speaking*.

Further review should be provided before unit, quarterly, semester and yearly tests, for this will also facilitate learning.

Another kind of highly valuable review is that which begins each school year. Students returning to school in the fall have generally been away from foreign language study for the entire summer. Some of them, perhaps the majority, will have had their previous study in other schools with other teachers and possibly with different materials taught in other ways. It is therefore wise to review material which is basic to that which will be studied in coming months. The review should contain all of the various kinds of activities typical of the previous year in order to include practice in all four skills. The teacher may at the same time prepare students for the new year of work by explaining how it will differ from that of the past.

Developing All Four Skills. A truly modern course in foreign language begins with the understanding that learning all four language skills is important. It does not pay lip service to listening and speaking or ignore them completely as many courses did in the past. At the same time it does not postpone reading and writing overly long or relegate them to a secondary role as some courses in recent years may have done. While the modern course is based on the assumption that there is a natural and appropriate progression from listening and speaking to reading and writing, it recognizes that each of the four skills reinforces the other to a considerable degree. The pre-reading period, a period of time devoted to listening and speaking for the purpose of developing good habits of pronunciation and intonation, is widely accepted as important by the profession. However, in practice the length of the pre-reading period has been shortening in comparison with recent custom which often extended pre-reading into the first three months of instruction and beyond.

Considering the Learner's Age. While audio-lingual methods and techniques have been used successfully with both children and adults, they must be modified to take into consideration the age of the learner. Characteristically very young children are especially adept at mimicry-memorization of sentence patterns. By age 12-14 the child becomes more able to see relationships and patterns in what he is learning. Obviously the secondary school teachers should take advantage of the student's growing ability to symbolize, analyze, and generalize. Thus grammar or, if one prefers, structure, is used to reinforce student learning, to help as he listens, speaks, reads and writes the foreign language. However, learning theory indicates that we will help the student become a more perceptive learner if we make him form his own rules for language phenomena that he encounters. Finally, nothing in the few sentences above is intended to convey the idea that foreign language classes should revert primarily to talking about language instead of learning language. A good rule of thumb is that five minutes of a fifty-five minute period might be devoted to generalizing structure (i.e., discussing grammar patterns). In beginning levels this generalization of structure will normally have to be done in English.

Stressing Learning, Not Teaching. The burden of FL learning should be on the student, for we have no more important responsibility than to teach him to learn on his own—to be a self starter. On the other hand, early learning in a modern foreign language requires that most of the class activity be teacher directed. The teacher (sometimes with the assistance of a tape recorder) presents material, calls for group and individual responses, evaluates the responses and reshapes behavior until the result is natural native-like use of language including appropriate body movement (kinesics). The foreign language teacher is at times a combination of a choir director and a director of a play.

Even in the beginning weeks, however, the teacher must begin building student ability and confidence to function independently in the foreign language and to learn without direct teacher intervention. Students need to be helped to see the characteristics of the language under study and guided how best to learn. They should be taught to judge whether they are performing well or poorly (self evaluation) as they practice, and by self criticism to upgrade their performance.

Worthwhile, satisfying home assignments have a double value. They increase considerably the exposure that a student has to the foreign language and, perhaps more important, they put the student on his mettle to learn alone without a teacher standing by. Step-by-step class activities and home assignments lead him from complete dependence on the teacher to the point that he can use his second language for purposes he considers important and to where he can learn a third language rapidly, employing techniques he learned in second language study.

Summary. The teacher in the modern language classroom has a number of important overall responsibilities. They are:

1. To establish objectives for each year of foreign language instruction and for the entire foreign language sequence.
2. To choose carefully course content and teaching techniques which will enable the instructional program to achieve the objectives.
3. To provide a variety of worthwhile classroom activities that keep the class stimulated and challenged.
4. To conserve his own energies by controlled activity that enables him to achieve the goals of audio-lingual instruction in all his classes each day of the school year.
5. To provide frequent opportunities to review material learned earlier.
6. To promote the learning in all four language skills in a way that each reinforces the other and none prevents growth in any other.
7. To adapt the methods and techniques of foreign language instruction to the age of his students in order to capitalize on their special learning abilities.
8. To promote student responsibility for language learning.

In the remainder of this chapter, attempts will be made to suggest how these responsibilities may be met.

Teaching Listening-Speaking Skills to Beginning Students

Listening to Establish a Model for Speech. Throughout language study the student must hear the foreign language spoken by native speakers so that he may have first-rate models for his own speech. This need to hear the language spoken is never satisfied, not even after a high level of proficiency has been reached, as teachers themselves can testify after having grown rusty teaching beginning level courses over a period of years.

However, the need to hear and pay close attention to native models for pronunciation and intonation is particularly acute in beginning years of language learning, for the student brings only his knowledge of his native language to the task. While it may be that this knowledge of his own language may be used to help him learn a second language, it is often true that the native language may get in the way of learning the second language. For example, new habits of sound reproduction will have to be learned. The need to learn to listen carefully for the purpose of eventual mimicry has given rise to the period of pre-reading instruction, a portion of time primarily devoted to listening to and drilling pronunciation and intonation. During the pre-reading period students are not provided with printed material because the printed page, at least in the use of Western European languages, will suggest English habits of pronunciation which must be repressed in favor of those of the new language. Without the distracting printed page, students *must* listen in order to learn.

Listening activities, then, in early levels of language learning primarily provide a model for student mimicry. However, even at the beginning of language learning the content practiced should be meaningful. Thus, as a rule, pattern sentences are taught in the framework of a situational dialogue usually concerning itself with everyday matters with which the student is familiar. Some such everyday concerns are the home, school, community, and individual and group activities.

In teaching pattern sentences the teacher and tape recorder can operate as a team to promote learning. The tape recorder presents material for student listening, mimicry-memorization and other drills, while the teacher controls the rate of presentation, calls for group and individual responses and supplements the tape program when necessary with extra drills or explanations.

An Audio-Lingual Unit Based on a Basic Dialogue. As indicated above, dialogues based on everyday situations are appropriate material for learning audio-lingual skills through mimicry-memorization and variation. Dialogue text is also suitable for beginning reading and writing practice when students begin to learn these skills.

Component parts of a typical unit will be:

1. The basic dialogue (or basic sentences) for mimicry-memorization.
2. Dialogue variations which make minor changes in the basic dialogue to make it fit different situations.
3. Directed dialogues which enable the teacher (or student leaders) to elicit utterances learned from basic dialogues.

4. Response drills (dialogue adaptions) which provide a stimulus statement or question calling for a given response. Questions may relate to the basic dialogue or to the life of students in the classroom.

5. Recombination dialogues which re-use utterances in new combi-utterances to form new dialogues.

6. Pattern drills for practicing substitution and variation in basic sentences.

7. Narrative recombinations of dialogue materials to give students practice in reading narrative style.

SAMPLE BASIC DIALOGUE

Robert: Hi, Bill! Where are you going?

William: Hi, Bob, I have to go to the bakery.

Robert: Good. I'm going that way. I'll walk with you. I have to go to the store too.

William: Say, who's that cute girl?

Robert: That's Sandra Johnson. She just moved in. Would you like to meet her?

William: You bet I would.

Robert: Hi, Sandy. This is Bill Swanson. He lives in the next block.

Sandra: Hi, Bill. Where are you fellows going?

William: We're going to the bakery. Are you walking that way?

Sandra: Yes, I have to go to the bakery too.

William: Great! Let's all go together.

SAMPLE DIALOGUE VARIATION

Douglas: Hi, Pete! Where are you going?

Peter: Hi, Doug. I have to ride up to the store to get some milk. Do you want to ride along?

Douglas: No, I can't. We're going to eat lunch in a few minutes.

Mrs. Anderson: Doug! Lunch is ready. Oh, hello Peter! How are you?

Peter: I'm fine, Mrs. Anderson. Are you feeling better?

Mrs. Anderson: Yes, I am. Thank you, Peter.

Peter: That's good. Well, I'd better go now. Good-bye Mrs. Anderson. So long, Doug.

Mrs. Anderson: Good-bye, Peter.

Douglas: So long.

SAMPLE DIRECTED DIALOGUE

Teacher: Thomas, greet John and ask how he is.
Pupil I: Hi, John! How are you?
Pupil II: Hi, Bill. I'm fine. How are you?
Pupil I: I'm fine too, thanks.
Teacher: John, ask Mary where she's going.
Pupil II: Mary, where are you going?
Pupil III: I have to go to the office.

SAMPLE RESPONSE DRILL (OR DIALOGUE ADAPTATION)

Teacher: Hello, John. Where are you going?
Pupil I: I'm going to the library.
Teacher: Marie, are you going to the library?
Pupil II: No, I'm going to the office.
Teacher: Where is Bill going?
Pupil II: He's going home.

SAMPLE RECOMBINATION DIALOGUE

Pupil I: Hello, Dolores. Where are you going?
Pupil II: Hi, Sue. I'm going to the beauty parlor. I have a two o'clock appointment.
Pupil I: I'll walk along with you. I'm going to the bakery.
Pupil II: Who's that cute boy across the street?
Pupil I: That's George Nelson. He's a new boy in the neighborhood.
Pupil II: I'd like to meet him.
Pupil I: I'll introduce you sometime. We don't have time now.

PATTERN DRILLS

(See *Grammar* for examples of pattern drills.)

RECOMBINATION NARRATIVE

Bill is leaving the house on his way to the store when his friend Bob comes by. Bob has to go to the store too, and so they set out together. They go only a few steps when Bob notices a pretty blonde girl sitting on the steps of a house across the street. Bill waves to her, smiles, and says hello, but when Bob says he would like to meet the girl, Bill tells him they do not have time and hurries him away. Both Bob and the girl wonder why Bill is in such a hurry.[2]

---

2. Adapted from State of Minnesota Department of Education, *Guide to Instruction in Modern Foreign Languages, Grades 4-12*, pp. 51, 52.

Techniques for Teaching Basic Dialogue Material. Successful teachers of audio-lingual materials vary somewhat in their approaches to teaching. However, with some variation owing to individual preference, the procedures indicated below are typical.

STEP 1. The teacher gives his students a short summary of what occurs in the dialogue. While the summary is generally in English, sometimes depending on the inventiveness of the teacher and the difficulty of the dialogue, the summary may be in the foreign language.

Note—Many teachers prefer to introduce new vocabulary and structures that students will meet in the dialogue before the dialogue is played for the first time. Usually meaning of new lexical items is established through use of pictures, real objects and teacher gestures, actions and facial expressions.

STEP 2. The teacher plays a recording of a part or all of the dialogue while students listen. Dialogue meaning may be established by simultaneous showing of a film strip, through blackboard drawings, transparencies, or use of posters depicting the course of dialogue action. The teacher may point to individual speakers in the visuals as the tape is played to help students follow the development of the situation.

STEP 3. To determine whether all students understand the dialogue, the teacher may ask questions concerning the content.

STEP 4. Following several playings of the tape for listening only, group mimicry of the model voices begins. Performed with textbooks closed, repetition concerns one complete utterance at a time. Ideally the lesson source (tape recorder) is operated with a manual pause button or foot pedal so that the teacher can create a pause of proper length. If the student response is poor, the teacher may break the utterance down into smaller units (sounds, words, phrases) and then rebuild element by element until students can repeat the entire utterance. Many authorities feel that building up a phrase from the end is most suitable because the elements are more likely to retain natural stress and inflection.

SAMPLE BACKWARD BUILDUP

> *Teacher:* I have a cat, but I don't have a dog.
> *Teacher:* .... a dog.
> *Pupils:* .... a dog.
> *Teacher:* .... I don't have a dog.
> *Pupils:* .... I don't have a dog.
> *Teacher:* I have a cat, but I don't have a dog.
> *Pupils:* I have a cat, but I don't have a dog.

During initial mimicry-memorization the teacher calls for both group and individual responses and is especially attentive for unsatisfactory pronunciation and intonation patterns. If necessary she may describe the position of tongue, lips, teeth, and direct students to watch as she pronounces.

Intonation patterns that present difficulties may be presented visually through the use of a musical staff or a line depicting the flow of speech. See Intonation and Rhythm below.[3]

STEP 5. The teacher and class take dialogue roles in an attempt to reproduce a part of the dialogue from memory. This whole class memorization involves beginning with the first few lines, then adding a line at a time, each time repeating all previous material until the part of the dialogue is memorized. Teacher-class practice may be followed by having parts of the class (halves or rows) take roles. Next, the process is repeated with reversed roles (i.e., class-teacher, ½ class-½ class, student-teacher, student-student).

STEP 6. Procedures in 2, 3, and 4 are followed in succcessive parts of the dialogue until the whole dialogue has been practiced and memorized.

STEP 7. The teacher and student(s) present the dialogue before the class using appropriate gestures.

STEP 8. Groups of students present the dialogue from memory acting out the parts before the class.

---

3. Repetition may be accomplished in a somewhat different form by cuing with (a) teacher questions regarding dialogue content, (b) directive statements (i.e., Tell John your sister isn't well.), (c) the immediately preceding statement from the dialogue (i.e., *Teacher:* I'm going swimming today. *Student:* How nice. What time are you going?).

Pronunciation. In the past we have generally settled for poor results in the area of pronunciation. Using modern methods and materials we have every right to expect that our students will develop pronunciation which will be perfectly acceptable to the native speaker. First of all, however, our students must have good models to imitate. The teacher, himself, must have near native pronunciation. Furthermore, additional voices using native pronunciation should be heard in class each day. As a general rule students should hear and practice language orally before they see it in print. This order of presentation is particularly important in beginning levels of instruction.

However, simple imitative repetition is not enough. Beginning students need teacher supervision to help them determine whether or not they are reproducing correctly the sounds of the new language. In class, individual responses must be called for and reinforced when correct, or corrected when wrong. In the language laboratory student mimicry of pattern sentences should be monitored for the same reason. Teachers must insist on good pronunciation and work throughout the language sequence for constant improvement in this area. Before students try to produce new sounds or combinations of sounds they should hear the utterance modeled a number of times. Studies have indicated that a crucial factor in learning to speak a foreign language is the quality of the sound reaching the student's ear.

1. If a taped voice is used, the quality of the recording and the tape player must be high.
2. The foreign language classroom should be acoustically treated and properly located to limit extraneous noise.
3. If the teacher himself is providing a model, he should move about the room to make sure that students in all parts of the room can hear equally well.
4. When a language laboratory is used, all components should provide for good transmission of sound.

Students may also benefit from watching the teacher's face as he produces the sound and from hearing a description of the position of the articulators.

Many newer courses being developed have as elements special pronunciation materials which isolate difficult sounds and provide drills for their massive practice. Under development are materials which will teach students to discriminate and therefore perform more self-correction during mimicry of utterances in the foreign language. In the meanwhile teachers will have to continue to help students with pronunciation. Special attention must be directed to sounds which are particularly difficult for American students. Four such problems deserving special attention are: (1) familiar sounds coming in unfamiliar positions in words, (2) sounds which have some similarity to sounds which the learner uses in his own language, (3) completely new sounds, and (4) sounds which make a phonemic distinction in the foreign language, but not in English.

Drills to combat the above problems may include the following procedures.

FAMILIAR SOUND IN UNFAMILIAR POSITION

1. The teacher points out that the approximate sound occurs in English.
2. The teacher may model the sound in isolation for student repetition.
3. Word partials, and words containing the sound are modeled by the teacher for student mimicry.
4. The teacher models the sound as it appears in a phrase or short sentences. Students imitate the sound.
5. The complete basic utterance in which the troublesome sound appears is presented by the teacher for student repetition.
6. Other sentences containing the sound are practiced.

PRONUNCIATION CONFLICT POINTS BETWEEN ENGLISH AND THE TARGET LANGUAGE

1. The teacher points out that the apparently similar sounds are really different and models the difference.
2. The articulation of the English sound is contrasted with that of the sound in the foreign language.
3. Other words in which the new sound appears are modeled by the teacher and repeated by the students.
4. The teacher models and students repeat the phrase and basic sentence in which the sound appears.

COMPLETELY NEW SOUNDS

1. The teacher explains how the articulators are positioned to form the sound.
2. The sound is modeled for student repetition.
3. The sound is presented in a number of word partials and word mimicry.

4. Various phrases, and utterances containing the sound, are modeled and imitated.

SOUNDS THAT MAKE A PHONEMIC DISTINCTION (e.g., in English pin-pen, pitch, peach)

1. The teacher explains articulation of the two sounds.
2. The sounds are modeled for student repetition.
3. Other words in which the sounds appear are modeled by the teacher for student repetition.
4. Phrases or short utterances containing the contrasting sounds are presented by the teacher for student repetition. The teacher may wish to cue the utterances with pictures to stress differences in meaning conveyed by the single sounds.

Intonation and Rhythm. Two other important elements of oral languages which have often been poorly handled or ignored in the classroom are intonation and rhythm. Unfortunately, unfamiliarity with melody patterns of language is likely to result in complete lack of aural comprehension even where the non-native "knows all the words." Furthermore he may fail utterly to communicate when speaking or may communicate a message he did not intend.

Like pronunciation, intonation is primarily taught by imitation. The model voice presents an utterance which is then repeated by the learner. When all students perceive the pattern without difficulty, no special measures need be employed. However, generally some students will repeat the pattern without difficulty while others will not. Oftentimes the teacher need not discuss the pattern, but can represent it pictorially on the chalkboard. Most commonly used to represent the flow of language is a line.

Is he imitating the /teacher?
I want to be a/lon/e.

The height or depth of the line depicts the relative voice level.

Another similar device is the representation of the speech pattern on a musical staff.

He took a train not a bus.

Finally, some energetic teachers direct the student response in a manner similar to that of a choir director, representing the voice pitch and inflection of each syllable with arm movements.

Memorization of Dialogues. Most of the foreign language texts ·written in recent years include at least one dialogue per unit of instruction. Usually the dialogue is the vehicle for presentation of basic sentences, but sometimes its introduction follows intensive practice with individual pattern sentences in mimicry-memorization drills, substitution and transformation drills and directed dialogues. Whether or not dialogues should be memorized has at times been hotly debated. Actually there are good reasons for at least occasional memorization of dialogues. In the first place the student practices the language in the context of a typical situation, a "slice of life" so to speak. He takes a role in this little play, not only delivering the lines but acting them out, living the culture. Second, he must learn this limited amount of language exceedingly well with corresponding automatic control of kinesics and paralanguage. Third, he gains in confidence in the use of the language by presenting a portion of the dialogue before his classmates.

Dialogue memorization should probably be a regular practice in the first year of language learning, but may be only intermittent after that.

Grammar. A great deal of misunderstanding has arisen in recent years about the place of grammar in foreign language instruction. Modern theorists and practitioners of foreign language teaching agree with their predecessors that a knowledge of the structure of language is basic to second language learning. It is in the way that grammar is taught that present-day teaching varies from that of the past. While in the past, structure was taught through rules, today's modern language teacher places his emphasis on practicing language. Through mimicry-memorization drills, response drills and recombination dialogues the student progressively gains control over the basic sentence patterns.

Dialogue utterances will, however, be of little use to the student unless he can vary them to fit the specific needs of a given situation. Thus an important part of each unit of work (some say the most important part) is intensive practice in manipulation of the basic patterns. Variation drill is performed through directed dialogues, substitution drills, transformation drills, and translation drills. Directed dialogues were shown earlier. Samples of the other drills will be illustrated below.

SUBSTITUTION DRILLS

Substitution drills are of many types and may provide practice in manipulation of many different aspects of language structure. A few types of substitution drill are shown below.

1. Item substitution

Teacher	Student
I see a cow.	I see a cow.
He _____.	He sees a cow.
We _____.	We see a cow.

2. Item substitution (by analogy)

Teacher	Student
Robert speaks French.	
And they?	They speak French.

3. Item substitution (moving slot)

Teacher	Student
Bill wants a new bike.	Bill wants a new bike.
Mary and Joe _____.	Mary and Joe want a new bike.
new bikes	Mary and Joe want new bikes.
bought	Mary and Joe bought new bikes.

TRANSFORMATION DRILLS

Transformation drills may require one of a number of changes in a pattern sentence: (1) a change in word order, (2) expansion of original elements, (3) contraction or reduction of original elements, (4) combination of several utterances into one.

1. Question to statement or statement to question

Teacher	Student
Is she going? (Yes)	Yes, she's going.
The class has started.	Has the class started?

2. Expansion

Teacher	Student
He's going.	He's going.
in the morning	He's going in the morning.

He's going in the evening.	He's going in the evening.
at six o'clock	He's going at six o'clock in the evening.

3. Contraction or reduction

Teacher	Student
He swears that he saw the crime.	He swears that he saw the crime.
to it	He swears to it.

4. Combination

Teacher	Student
The train had just arrived.	The train had just arrived.
The station was crowded.	The station was crowded.
Because _____.	Because the train had just arrived, the station was crowded.

TRANSLATION DRILLS

Translation drills are particularly useful for teaching what we usually call idiomatic expressions, that is, constructions in the target language which are considerably different from those used to say the same thing in the learner's native language.

Sample Translation Drill

Teacher	Student
Es gefällt mir.	Es gefällt mir.
He likes it.	Es gefällt ihm.
We like it.	Es gefällt uns.
We like the house.	Das Haus gefällt uns.

Generally speaking students should not be expected to work longer than twenty minutes of the class hour in pattern drills. Because the practice is very intense, students tire of the drill quickly, and when boredom sets in, learning stops.

For the most part modern texts provide the tape drills necessary for pattern practice. These drills are generally excellently done and deserve to be used. Sometimes, however, special drills not provided by the publisher will be needed to insure learning of a difficult structure. In that case the teacher herself will have to construct drills to overcome the problem that her classes are having. Probably most teacher-made drills should be presented live by the teacher since making high quality recordings is a difficult and time-consuming job.

After some practice the class may take a brief amount of time to discuss a pattern it has been working on, but it will be assumed that students learn to control structure not through discussions but through drill. Generalizations regarding structure (i.e., grammar discussions) are best reserved until the end of the foreign language class period and confined to about five minutes. Such discussions regarding patterns of language are more helpful to older than younger students and more beneficial to intelligent youngsters than to those of lesser ability.

In using pattern drills teachers should remember that (1) presentation should be lively; (2) reinforcement is necessary—that is, after the student has given what he believes is the correct response the teacher or tape should provide the correct answer to confirm or correct; (3) drills should be of different kinds to provide novelty; (4) during teacher-directed drill there should be a mixture of group and individual responses; and (5) drills should not be continued beyond the point that fatigue sets in.

Songs, Poems, Rhymes, and Proverbs. All through language learning the student can benefit from memorization of some material. Songs, poems and rhymes are particularly valuable material for memorization for a number of reasons. For one thing the selection may have some intrinsic value as cultural material. Even popular songs of the day, however transitory, tell us something of the current culture. Folk songs, sayings, short poems, and rhymes may have more lasting worth.

In the second place rhythmic material has a charm for most students. They enjoy singing particularly, and the story that a song tells.

Finally, songs and other rhymed material help teach intonation and pronunciation because melody forces students into an intonation pattern, and rhyme gives clues to pronunciation.

SUGGESTED PROCEDURE FOR TEACHING A SONG

1. New vocabulary and structures are introduced.
2. Orientation to the song's content is given.

     a. Kind of song (popular, folk, etc.)

     b. Point of view

     c. Background of song, if pertinent

3. A recording of the song is played while students listen. The melody may be played on a piano or other instrument if a recording is not available.

4. The teacher reads the text or part of the text aloud to students.

5. The teacher reads a line at a time as the class repeats. Rows of students may be called upon for repetition after whole class response. Finally individuals repeat the lines alone.

6. The teacher reads two lines at a time for student repetition.

7. The teacher reads the first two lines, then first three, then first four for student repetition. (The first word of each line may be written on the board as a cue.)

8. When the verse has been learned, students sing with the recording or instrumental (piano, guitar, etc.) accompaniment.

9. The procedures in 4-8 above are repeated with subsequent parts of the song until the complete song (or a desired number of verses) has been mastered.

Games. Foreign language games provide another opportunity for highly motivated use of language once the necessary sentence patterns have been mastered. Normally the game would be one of a number of culminating activities of a unit of study and would grow naturally out of that study. Below are a few possible games and ways in which they may contribute to learning.

Game	*Description*
Spelldown	Two teams of students spell words read to them by a game leader. The game is useful in beginning weeks of instruction for reviewing alphabet learning and to focus attention on spelling of the foreign language.
Bingo	This is the well-known game available in any department store. The game is useful for reviewing numbers in the foreign language.
Crossword Puzzles, Scrabble, Keyword	These games reinforce vocabulary learning. Crossword puzzles may be worked

individually or in teams. Word games of the Scrabble type may pit individuals or teams against one another.

Twenty questions

This game requires students to use complete utterances as they ask questions trying to identify an item that is in the mind of the game leader. The game leader begins by indicating whether the "thing" is "animal," "vegetable" or "mineral." All questions are answered with a simple yes or no. Students get practice naming colors and using comparatives. After students have learned more than a handful of verbs, teachers may wish to have students play the game without the verb "to be."

As useful as games may be in instruction, they have not always been wisely used in the past. Therefore it may be well to suggest some ground rules for their employment.

1. Teachers should be alert to the fact that the game may require some vocabulary and sentence patterns beyond what the student has already learned. Even if the new vocabulary and structure load is minor, time must be taken to teach it before the game is begun.
2. The game should not be continued as a class activity beyond the point that it functions as a worthwhile instructional activity. We are, of course, teaching a foreign language, not running a recreational program.
3. Leadership for games should be provided by students whenever possible. Once the teacher has taught the game, student leadership should be encouraged to take over.

The Use of the Target Language. One of the problems of learning a foreign language in one's own country is the lack of adequate opportunity to use the language to communicate wants and ideas, that is, for real communication. Conducting foreign language classroom affairs in the foreign language is one highly effective way to insure that meaningful material is communicated in the foreign language. Many classroom expressions may be taught in the early weeks of a beginning class. Others can be introduced as needed. Once taught, the expressions are used over and over by the teacher and the students in the normal course of classroom operations. Students should understand from the beginning that they are expected to use the foreign language, except perhaps at certain times designated by the teacher. Generally the last five minutes of class might be designated for questions and discussion which cannot be conducted in the foreign language. Occasionally the teacher may wish to present and discuss with students in English certain cultural material relating to life in the foreign country. However, the first purpose of the foreign language class is foreign language learning, and only by directing major efforts to this goal will teaching efforts be successful.

Learning to Use Language Independently and Meaningfully. It is the major job of the foreign language teacher in early years of foreign language instruction to guide students from total dependence on the teacher to the point that they can select language appropriate to a given occasion. This gradual transition is accomplished by careful planning which leads the student through many steps, one at a time. Recombination dialogues and narratives present already learned material in a new format. Directed dialogues and response drills provide closely controlled practice in inter-student communication. Substitution and transformation drills help the student learn to make changes in basic sentences in order to use them in new ways.

An extremely useful device for realistic use of the foreign language is the warmup period. This is a short period at the beginning of the class hour. In the warmup the teacher uses previously learned material to converse with students about themselves, their families, friends or any topic within their ability to discuss and of interest to them. The following sample warmup is an indication of what might take place in one such conversation. However it is important to remember that while the teacher may have an outline that she expects to follow for the warmup conversation, the student is speaking "extemporaneously." Thus the warmup retains a flavor of spontaneity and the teacher must be alert to unexpected turns in the conversation. The warmup will benefit if occasional utterances from previous units are mixed with more recently learned material.

SAMPLE WARMUP— (ON THE PHONE)

The teacher provides the student with a mock telephone and has one for her own use.

Ring ————

Student: Hello.
Teacher: Is this George?
Student: Yes, this is George.
Teacher: Hello, George. This is Miss Adams. How are you?
Student: I'm fine thanks. How are you?
Teacher: I'm very well, thanks. George, may I speak to your mother?
Student: I'm sorry she isn't at home. May I give her a message?
Teacher: Yes. Would you ask her to call me?
Student: Yes, I will. What is the number?
Teacher: 731-8270.
Student: 731-8270. I will tell her you called.
Teacher: Thank you. Good-bye.
Student: Good-bye.

Many other activities for encouraging relatively free use of language are possible at the beginning levels. Some are listed below.

1. The teacher provides a series of statements to which students are to add the words "because," "when," or "so," plus a clause of their own choosing.

Sample — add "because" plus completion clause
   Teacher: I was sick.
   Student: Because I was sick, I didn't go to school.
   Teacher: I was hungry.
   Student: Because I was hungry, I went home to eat.
   Teacher: I was tired.
   Student: Because I was tired, I went to bed.

2. The teacher displays a picture in which much activity is portrayed. Students volunteer statements describing parts of the scene.

3. A Few introductory dialogue utterances are provided. Students are assigned roles and are expected to add additional ad lib utterances to complete a dialogue.

4. The teacher chooses a question or statement for which many previously learned responses are possible. Students volunteer or are called upon for responses.

Sample

What are you going to do this weekend?

5. A familiar story is retold. Then the teacher chooses a point

from which students are to proceed in developing a different ending. She may ask a question to start off discussion.

Example

What might have happened if the woodsman had not heard Red Riding Hood's cries?

SUMMARY

1. Students may have to be taught the importance of listening, as well as what to listen for, as they begin foreign language learning.
2. A pre-reading period of language study is important so that students may give their undivided attention to the sound system of the new language.
3. The teacher and the tape player operate as a team in teaching basic sentences.
4. The steps of each unit of language learning are:
   a. Recognition (i.e., understanding) through identification of the language's system of signaling meaning as well as learning the meaning of vocabulary.
   b. Imitation of basic sentences presented by native speakers.
   c. Repetition of basic sentences in memorized dialogues, directed statements, etc.
   d. Variation of basic sentences through substitution and transformation drills and other conversational practice.
   e. Selection of language suitable for use in a given situation.
5. Learning the sound system of a language is an important long-term task requiring continued guidance by the teacher. It can benefit from regular use of high quality recordings played on equipment capable of transmitting high fidelity sound.
6. Grammar is an integral part of audio-lingual instruction. In fact, vocabulary learning is held in check in beginning levels in order that students can focus their attention on language structure.
7. Learning of foreign language games and songs can be a highly motivating and worthwhile activity in foreign language classes. However it must be apparent that they are really contributing to language learning.
8. Foreign language class activities should be carried on in the foreign language. The teacher must provide leadership by constantly using the foreign language himself if the linguistic island is to be maintained.

9. Even beginning students should be given the opportunity to use the language naturally for communication.

Teaching Listening Skills

The Importance of Listening. Throughout his years of study, the foreign language student should have daily opportunity to hear the target language. Listening to the foreign language may have one or more of the following purposes: (1) To provide a model for later speaking practice: (2) To practice understanding ever more difficult oral language, both informal and formal: (3) To gain useful knowledge.

Good teaching requires that the teacher will explain at the beginning of the first year of study the way he intends to teach the foreign language. He will have to clarify the need for students to listen carefully in order to learn. They should know that not since their early school years have they been expected to learn so much by listening. In the course of time they will have to be reminded again and again about the importance of listening.

Recombination Dialogues and Narratives. Especially in beginning levels of foreign language learning, as we have seen, listening will usually be for the purpose of later modeling. Students will listen to pattern sentences introduced randomly or in dialogue form. Their first assignment may be to get the sense of utterances and to determine who is speaking. Next, they will listen to one utterance at a time for the purpose of immediate imitation and memorization. As they proceed, the teacher may direct class attention to special sounds with which he anticipates they will have difficulty. Finally, students may listen to new dialogues or narratives that recombine the utterances they have learned. Recombination dialogues, narratives and descriptions are valuable for listening practice in that the student hears the basic sentences in somewhat changed form and in new context.

SAMPLE EXERCISE—RECOMBINATION DIALOGUE OR NARRATIVE

1. New vocabularly and structures (if any) are introduced and clarified orally.
2. A brief description of the setting and characters may be provided.
3. Students listen to the tape recording of the dialogue.
4. Depending on the character of the listening selection, level of

student language proficiency, and the objective of the lesson, students may be asked to do one of the following:

a. Summarize the recording in English.
b. Summarize the recording in the foreign language.
c. Answer, in the foreign language, written or oral questions regarding the content. (Questions may have been provided and previewed before listening.)
d. Answer questions requiring drawing inferences, or make generalizations from evidence provided.

Practice Using Context Clues

STEP 1 The setting of a fable is supplied in English.

STEP 2 Students preview five written questions concerning the content.

STEP 3 Students listen to the fable.

STEP 4 Students answer orally the questions relating to the fable.

STEP 5 Students again listen to the fable, discussing new words as they appear to insure that they know the meaning. Each new word is written on the board.

STEP 6 As homework, students write answers to the five questions, using at least some of the new words in their sentences.

Films. Foreign language films can be highly worthwhile for class use if that use is planned carefully. Because they combine both visual and audio stimuli, films generally have unusual appeal for students. Furthermore, the visual aspects provide clues for aural understanding and broaden and deepen meanings.

A Sample Exercise—Viewing a Film

STEP 1 Students view the film.

STEP 2 Students listen to a tape recording of the sound track as they read silently the written text.

STEP 3 The class studies the new vocabularly and structure.

STEP 4 Students view the film for the second time.

STEP 5 The teacher asks questions about the film content. Points of misunderstanding are cleared up at this time and students encouraged to ask about points they do not understand. Particular stress may be laid on comparing and contrasting the students' native culture and the foreign culture as seen in the film.

STEP 6   Students are assigned a dictation for the following day.

or STEP 6   Students write answers to questions about the text.

or STEP 6   Students are assigned the writing of questions about the text. Next day they ask each other their questions.

or STEP 6   Students rewrite the film text changing the point of view (person or tense) or changing selected statements to questions.

Listening at the Intermediate Level. After beginning levels of foreign language learning, some objectives for listening activities change. Two objectives now predominate:

1. To enable the learner to understand an ever more difficult body of spoken material including language suitable for a wide range of purposes and on an increasingly wide range of topics.

2. To gain useful information.

Occasionally the purpose of a listening activity may be to entertain.

Listening assignments are best if they grow naturally out of other class activities. Thus, generally a recording will be used because it promises to contribute something to the topic under study. Teachers should plan for specific listening activities as a part of every unit of work. Recordings of lectures, poems, operas, plays, radio programs, newscasts and films are suitable fare.

Recordings should feature a variety of voices speaking the foreign language at the normal rate in a variety of situations. Male and female voices of various ages speaking with some dialect differences is appropriate.

Follow-Up for Listening Activities. Any listening activity must have a purpose which is obvious to the student. Furthermore a listening assignment should be followed up quickly by oral and/or written discussion of the content in a fashion similar to that suggested below.

SAMPLE EXERCISE—LISTENING FOLLOW-UP

STEP 1   Questions may be posed orally by the teacher or by students.

STEP 2   After such audio-lingual practice, questions may be dictated to the class and then written on the board by individuals for group correction.

STEP 3 All students correct their own dictation and finally write answers to the questions either in class or as homework.

For students who are not rank beginners in language learning, re-telling the content of the material they have just heard can be a challenging and worthwhile assignment. Re-telling may take the following forms:

1. Re-telling in oral and/or written form in one's own words.
2. Re-telling the story changing the person or tense.
3. Re-telling and changing to another format (i.e., dialogue to narrative).

At all levels of instruction a true-false or multiple choice quiz may have the virtue of providing motivation (when students have been forewarned) or review for a listening assignment. It may, as well, provide the teacher with an immediate check of student comprehension. Normally, listening assignments should not be dismissed with a short quiz but rather provide subject matter for discussion, just as reading matter may do. Furthermore, just as the listening activity grows naturally out of other activities, it in turn provides new information which leads to further discussion and reading.

SUMMARY

1. In beginning levels of foreign language instruction listening practice is primarily for the purpose of establishing a model for student speech.
2. Increasingly during the language sequence, listening activities should be introduced for other purposes. These purposes are:
   a. To review in new form material already studied.
   b. To practice using context clues to aid understanding.
   c. To gain new understandings relating to levels of language appropriate to various situations.
   d. To gain factual information particularly for the purpose of making inferences and forming conclusions.
3. Listening activities must have a purpose evident to the student and one that he can accept.
4. The student must be involved actively, either because the material is extremely interesting in itself or because it will help him achieve some immediate goal.
5. Listening periods should be of moderate length.

Teaching Speaking Skills

Transition from Mimicry-Memorization. Early speaking practice, as was indicated earlier, has as its primary objective learning the sound system and intonation patterns of the new language. Throughout language study, review of pronunciation and intonation will have to be undertaken to counteract any tendency for these important skills to deteriorate. However, there comes a time that intensive daily mimicry of word partials, words and phrases is no longer necessary except possibly for short periods after extended vacations.

Mimicry-memorization may continue but it will primarily be for the purpose of practicing new language patterns and learning new vocabulary and idiomatic expressions. Much of this material will continue to be presented through recordings, but more and more, reading will become the source for material to be discussed. Substitution and transformation drills will continue to provide extensive and intensive drill in varying the basic patterns.

It is important that throughout language study there be increasing opportunities for less controlled use of language and for increasing student responsibility for learning.

Controlled Oral Narratives and Dialogues. Students may be assigned the composition of oral narratives or dialogues carefully directed so that the learner will make use of language previously learned rather than get bogged down in concocting original language of his own.

SAMPLE CONTROLLED NARRATIVE

Tell a friend about a letter you got from a German pen pal. Relate what he told you about his family. Give the father's profession and daily activities of mother and older brother.

SAMPLE CONTROLLED DIALOGUE

Rosemary, a friend of yours, stops you in the hall. She was absent yesterday and wants to know the assignment for today. You say that a dictation is planned on the dialogue for lesson five. Tell her that you forgot your pencil and would like to borrow one from her. She thanks you and says that she will lend you a pencil.

Students may prepare skits based on legends, fairy tales or other sources. These skits can be presented to the class as a culminating activity of a reading and/or listening assignment.

Picture-Story Presentations. Pictures or slides may be used along with tape, as we have seen, to present basic dialogue utterances. They may also be used to review basic utterances in slightly changed form or as cues for storytelling. Three possible uses of these visuals are suggested:

1. The teacher announces the roles for the dialogue and appoints students to the roles. Students then provide appropriate dialogue as the teacher holds up each picture depicting the cause of dialogue action.

2. The students engage in cooperative storytelling. As the teacher holds up successive pictures, students take turns telling parts of the story in their own words. Initially students may have to have a story suggested to them by the teacher before they try to tell the story themselves. Later on, after students are accustomed to this kind of assignment, they may just preview picures without teacher commentary before they attempt to relate the story.

3. Students may bring their own pictures to help them present descriptions, and relate stories or other narratives.

Question-Answer Practice. A familiar and valuable type of class exercise is that in which the teacher or students ask questions relating to material read or monitored. The language learner gains practice in rephrasing (transforming) questions into statements with minimum need for recall. Furthermore, he is helped to learn new vocabulary as well as idoms and structure. Through the review he is aided in learning new information contained in text materials. Finally, at upper intermediate levels he may be guided in making inferences and judgments.

Semi-Controlled Dialogues. As students move from beginning levels of instruction, we have noted, they will be reading more and more. They will need practice in discussing the material as one adult might discuss new information with another. Yet, at the same time, some reign is held by the teacher to insure that discussion does not break down. A semi-controlled dialogue is useful in providing some guidance and yet allowing some creativity in dialogue building. In a semi-controlled dialogue the students are provided with the first part of each utterance upon which they build to compose complete statements.

SAMPLE SEMI-DIRECTED DIALOGUE

Student A: (Introduces topic) I was interested to read in the paper this morning that . . . .

Student B: (Agrees and adds a point) I found it interesting too. It also said that . . . .

Student C: (Asks for more information) Who? . . . . What? . . . . When? . . . . Why? . . . .

Student A: Answers

Student C: Asks another question

Student B: (Answers) I believe that . . . .

The above pattern and other similar formats may be used to talk about many different subjects.

Structured Class Discussion. Beginning and maintaining a stimulating discussion in the classroom is an art. To be really successful the discussion should primarily involve students and not require constant questioning and commenting by the teacher. However, students at the intermediate level may not feel as free to join in a discussion as they would in other classes in which English is the means of communication. Advance structuring of the discussion can help to insure that it will go smoothly. Students should be alerted beforehand to the contributions that members of the group can make to begin a discussion and keep it moving. The following outline suggests a pattern for group discussion:

1. An idea or topic is introduced.
2. Agreement with the idea is expressed.
3. Disagreement is expressed.
4. Additional information is asked for.
5. Additional information is provided.
6. The idea is illustrated through an anecdote from personal experience.
7. A new person is drawn into the discussion via a question.
8. The subject is changed to a related topic.

Besides alerting students to the mechanics of discussion, the teacher will have to concern himself to see that topics are of interest to the students. Discussons might initially center around current teen-age idols, political campaigns, teen-age drivers, or the choice of a career. Later on, topics introduced through reading may lead to controversial areas which lend themselves to discussion. For example, reading about

World War I might trigger a discussion regarding the effect of the Versailles Treaty on international affairs.

Teachers should not be discouraged if the first attempts at discussion are not particularly successful. Eventually students will get the idea.

Suggested Procedure for Introducing Structured Class Discussion

STEP 1. The outline for the discussion is presented and explained to the class.

STEP 2. A complete prewritten sample discussion is studied to illustrate how the discussion works.

STEP 3. The teacher now indicates that the class is to try a discussion. He introduces an idea, for example, "The Dog is Man's Best Friend" or "A Cat is a Better Pet than a Dog." Students volunteer statements according to the outline.

STEP 4. The teacher now forms groups within the class with the responsibility of composing their own discussions for presentation the following day. He may wish to suggest topics for the discussions.

STEP 5. In succeeding days the teacher introduces one topic per day for extemporaneous discussion. The outline remains on the chalkboard for reference.

STEP 6. When students seem relatively familiar with the procedure, the discussion format is applied to listening and reading materials under study.

Oral Reports. Another excellent controlled speech exercise is the preparation and presentation of oral reports modeled after previously studied narratives, descriptions and dialogues. In the beginning it must be possible for students to give personal presentations by making minimal changes in the text.

Sample Model for Oral Report

My father is 53 years old and my mother is 45. My father was born in Los Angeles and my mother in Chicago. My father is a carpenter. My mother was formerly a secretary. . . .

Reporting will be enhanced if reports are related to topics under study and if students use pictures and articles to illustrate their reports.

By the intermediate level, students should be able to make short reports on independent reading and listening activities. To be most effective, such assignments should appear to evolve naturally out of class discussion. Individual reports will appear important to all when they are assigned to clear up a question asked by a member of the class or the teacher, or when they add interesting additional information to that provided by the basic set of learning materials. Obviously, special reports are an excellent way of providing for individual abilities and interests of students.

Other individual in-front-of-the-class presentations that can be made are: telling a joke, explaining a word, trying to sell a product or a service, describing an incident or a thing, telling a story, presenting a newscast and giving a "how to do it" demonstration.

Group Presentations. Students will often eagerly spend many hours preparing material for eventual class presentation. They especially like writing and presenting satires or parodies of radio and television programs. Presenting a commercial, professional lecture, magic act, a quiz program, a sportscast or a newscast are types of activity they may enjoy from time to time. Original skits may be dialogue versions of material found in reading assignments. When the class reads a play, the teacher might determine whether some portions of the play should be performed by class members. Normally such performances would not require memorization of parts of the play.

Memorization. Though dialogue memorization will be less common at the intermediate level than in previous levels, memorization of portions of various written materials continues to be an effective learning activity. Memorization of dialogues and portions of great plays, poems, songs, and narrative text will continue to give students material upon which they can build speaking skills. Important quotations from literature, proverbs, poems, and songs may deserve student memorization.

An Interview. Class visitors who are native speakers can provide the basis for a highly motivated series of class lessons. Before the visit, the class will spend time discussing appropriate questions to ask the visitor. These may then be organized by topic. To provide for individual differences, slower students may be assigned to ask these questions and better students told to develop questions of their own and/or to be alert for opportunities to ask questions which may arise spontaneously out of the discussion. After the visit, students may be asked to write a report summarizing the discussion. Obviously the visitors may be asked general questions by elementary students (i.e., What school subjects do students take in your country?) while more advanced students may ask technical questions dealing with the visitor's specialty.

SUMMARY

1. Mimicry-memorization at intermediate levels maintains pronunciation and intonation skills and provides practice with new language patterns and vocabulary.
2. Carefully structured speaking activities at intermediate levels provide controlled practice in use of oral language for conversations and reports.
3. As students progress there should be opportunities for increasingly freer use of speech in the foreign language classroom.

Teaching Reading Skills

The Place of Reading in Foreign Language Learning. Learning to read a foreign language was for many years almost the sole objective of foreign language learning in the United States. Other skills were usually justified in an instructional program according to the degree they were supposed to aid the reading skill.

Learning to read continues to be a primary objective of foreign language instruction. It will be the means through which students ultimately gain most of their knowledge of the foreign culture. In addition, the written word reinforces learning in other skill areas.

However, it is important to observe that foreign language classes in the past often seemed predicated on the idea that there was no difference between learning a foreign language and learning to read a foreign language. Students primarily learned, or failed to learn, through the printed word. Now we know that most students will benefit from some pre-reading instruction stressing listening to and speaking the foreign language.

In the past we also usually assumed that the student would transfer those reading skills he used in his own language to the second language that he was studying. Today we recognize that he may need some specific instruction in the second language similar to that which he received as a beginning reader in the primary grades. In fact we know

now that some of this instruction is necessary to counteract habits
learned with the native language.

Pre-reading Instruction. Much discussion has revolved around the
length of period between the beginning of language study and the
introduction of the written word. Actually the length of the pre-
reading period should be determined by several factors:

1. The course objective
2. The language being learned
3. The age and intelligence of the learner

Obviously if the primary objective is learning to get meaning from
a printed page of scientific prose, very little, if any, time may be spent
on developing pronunciation and intonation skills. On the other
hand, if the objective is receiving an aesthetic experience from a poem
or work of prose, there may be ample justification for devoting an extended period of time to study the melodic aspects of language in
order to help the reader appreciate the artistic skill of a writer.

Different languages seem to require pre-reading periods of varying
lengths. Spanish and German as a general rule do not seem to require
as long a period before the introduction of reading as does French.
Chinese, Russian and Arabic, which are taught less commonly in the
schools, do not use the Latin alphabet to represent sounds. Thus they
present fewer conflicts with written English. However this is more
than compensated for by basic differences in signaling meaning (i.e.,
involved ending systems, pitch), so that, as in other languages, a
strong audio-lingual base should be built before reading is begun.

As a generalization, younger students can endure and benefit from a
longer pre-reading period than older students. (Many adults require
a visual handle which they can grasp as they venture into the murky
and forbidding waters of language study.) Young students usually
enjoy simple repetition, mimicry and memorization of much of the
language they are exposed to; while older students need plenty of opportunity to master the sound system of the new language, they
share the teacher's desire to see it written and benefit from independent study in class and at home.

One might say that a formal reading program should begin when
it will have the most helpful effect upon the whole instructional program. In typical beginning courses at the senior high school level, the
following length is suggested for pre-reading programs:

1. German, Spanish, Italian, Russian, Chinese—3–4 weeks
2. French—4–6 weeks

The assumption is that a number of readiness activities will be introduced during the pre-reading period. These will be suggested below.

The Pre-reading Period. In learning to read a second language, students will transfer successfully many techniques which they have used in reading their native language. On the other hand some habits will have to be unlearned if they are to be successful in the foreign language.

During the pre-reading period, as has been pointed out, students will be concerned primarily with learning a new sound and intonation system. Such practice will establish somewhat the same foundation that every young child brings with him to school when he first learns to read. Establishing such an audio-lingual base means that the student has some established habits on which he may superimpose the writing system.

At the same time that this intensive oral-aural practice is going on, some specialists feel that students may be introduced to the graphemes which make up the writing system. With the European languages, this means that the alphabet and its sounds are practiced. New graphemes particularly are noted, and students should practice printing them to focus the learner's attention on the differences in sound between them and other similar letters.

SAMPLE EXERCISE—ALPHABET LEARNING

STEP 1. A section of the alphaget (5 or 6 letters) is introduced in correct order. The teacher writes the letters on the chalkboard, places them on overhead projector or shows flashcards pronouncing letter names and signaling student repetition.

STEP 2. Letters are again exposed for students to name chorally. The teacher then repeats the correct letter name and students say the name again.

STEP 3. Letters are exposed or pointed to for individual student naming. The teacher then says the name and the whole class repeats.

STEP 4. Letters are exposed out of order for class and individual naming.

STEP 5. Unfamiliar graphemes are written by the teacher as students watch. Students then practice writing them.

STEP 6. In subsequent periods additional segments of the alphabet are practiced until students can say the alphabet in order and name letters out of order.

STEP 7. Students write the letters of the alphabet as dictated by the teacher.

Common alphabetical abbreviations for longer names are excellent for use in practicing alphabet learnings. Normally students should practice alphabetical designations that are commonly used in the country or countries speaking the language they are learning. A few typical examples for practice are:

EU	French
NU	French
VW	German
DKW	German
PEMEX	Spanish

In using these combinations of letters, the teacher may list them on dittoed sheets for distribution to the class or write them on the board. Students, in turn, practice calling the letters.

Many teachers, perhaps most, like to assign names typical of the foreign culture to their students. When this is done, the names may provide excellent pre-reading practice in the foreign language. If foreign names have not been assigned, well known words, product names, or geographical names from the foreign language may be chosen. Some such words are:

Volkswagen (May be broken down) Volk (s) Wagen	German
Mercedes	German
Champagne	French
Normandie	French
España	Spanish
Méjico	Spanish

SAMPLE EXERCISE—READING NAMES

STEP 1. The teacher writes the name on the chalkboard and says the name. Students repeat in chorus.

STEP 2. As the teacher points to the letters, students call names of the letters.

STEP 3. Several more names are written on the chalkboard, repeated and spelled.

STEP 4. The teacher points to names out of order. Students chorally, then individually, read the names.

STEP 5. If necessary, students are asked to sound out the words, noting particularly beginning and ending letters and letter combinations.

Beginning Reading Instruction. Even though students have intensively practiced the spoken patterns of language and also drilled on sound-letter correspondencies, many teachers note some retrogression in oral production when reading begins. This backsliding is natural as students focus their attention on meaning instead of the mechanics of production. To minimize deterioration of pronunciation and intonation, students learn to read material they have practiced orally.

SAMPLE EXERCISE—READING BASIC SENTENCES

STEP 1. Words, phrases, and a complete utterance are read from chalkboard, overhead projector or textbook by the teacher (or taped voice) and then by the students in unison.

STEP 2. Difficult letter combinations are isolated, contrasted with similar sounds in the students' language or in the second language.

STEP 3. After a number of basic sentences have been read, students practice reading in unison words, phrases and sentences pointed to out of their normal order. Individuals are called on intermittently to read.

After all basic sentences have been practiced, students read recombination dialogues and narratives. During this reading, the teacher will be advised to note errors for remedial practice. Rereading will follow remedial practice.

SAMPLE EXERCISE—READING RECOMBINATION DIALOGUES AND NARRATIVES

STEP 1. The teacher previews pronunciation and meaning of new vocabulary, if any.

STEP 2. The setting is indicated and the content may be summarized.

STEP 3. Students listen to a tape recording of the text, as they read silently.

STEP 4. The class reads the text aloud with the taped voice.

STEP 5. Individuals are assigned parts in the dialogue for oral reading. If a narrative is being read, students may be called upon in turn to read a few sentences aloud.

Other activities for beginning readers are possible.

Jumbled Sentences. A number of cards containing words of an utterance are placed along the chalkrail at the front of the room. Students go to the board and put the cards into correct order. Or mimeographed work sheets containing the jumbled sentences may be distributed. Students may be assigned the rewriting of the sentences as "seatwork" or homework.

Answering Questions. Written or oral questions require the student to find and copy the sentence which contains the information asked for. Instead of writing the answer, he may read it.

Special Problems. There are essentially three problems to deal with in teaching students to begin to read a foreign language. First of all, students must be taught to deal with regular patterns of the writing system. These regular patterns refer primarily to letters and sounds with a one-to-one relationship. Letters which have more than one sound can also belong to regular patterns if the sound can be predicted by position in a word. (Example: German "d" in initial position is voiced (Donau), while in final position (und) it is unvoiced.) Most of these regularities will be learned easily from the reading of basic sentences. Occasional generalizations may be necessary, for example, when the sound of a letter varies according to the position of the letter in the word.

More persistent and deep-rooted problems are those caused by interference from the first language. There are, for example, the following common types of conflicts between the first and second language:

1. Difference in sound represented by a grapheme or combination of graphemes.

2. Difference in intonation patterns.

3. Difference in reading direction (i.e., right-to-left in Arabic and top-to-bottom in Chinese).

Generally, interlanguage conflicts can be anticipated by the teacher. When such problems are encountered, it is not enough to have students practice a single example of the conflict. Other words illustrating the foreign language pattern should be written on the blackboard or displayed via overhead projector, and then students should try to form a generalization regarding the pattern. Teachers should not despair if errors result from these conflicts. The student's native language habits and the fact that he is surrounded by English speakers for most of his waking hours will contrive to have a deleterious effect on his pronunciation and intonation patterns. The foreign language teacher will have to combat this tendency all through the foreign language sequence.

A third type of special problem for the beginning reader is that caused by inconsistencies within the foreign language itself; that is, problems caused by multiple patterns of fit between sounds and symbols. Fortunately for the speaker of English most languages are more regular than English in this respect. ("Bough," "though," and "through" illustrate irregularities in English.) Inconsistencies may often have to be dealt with separately as they appear in basic sentences. If possible they, like interlanguage conflicts, should be taught as patterns.

Supplementary Readings. Already in the first year of instruction some material which is similar in vocabulary load and structural difficulty, but not identical to that learned in basic dialogues, should be read. Song lyrics, simple poems, and other simple cultural readings are particularly suitable. The class may read most of these materials together and should practice intelligent guessing (using cognates and context) about word meanings and the general meaning of sentences, paragraphs, and whole selections—*not* making translations. Readings may be followed by a true-false or multiple choice quiz on content, or a writing or speaking exercise. (See speaking and writing sections for possible activities.)

In addition, even in the second semester some students will be ready for graded independent readings. Extensive readings of this kind are highly valuable in fostering student independence and responsibility for learning. Reports should be kept to a minimum to avoid discouraging an otherwise enthusiastic reader. A simple form for the student to complete in English may suffice to help the teacher determine whether the student has understood the material he read. Some books contain simple content questions that students may answer. Answers are then turned in for credit.

Supplementary readings should continue throughout foreign language study. Often such readings can be related to basic course content and lead to special individual or group reports. Teachers should seek opportunities to request that individual students look up the answer to a question that has come up in class. Of course, teachers should also suggest possible sources for the information. As students grow in reading power, special interest reading should be promoted. Teachers will need to inform themselves regarding student interests to stimulate learning. Information about student interests can be gathered through questionnaires and class discussions. Of course the classroom or school library will have to be supplied with supplementary reading material on a wide range of topics.

Systematic instruction in reading techniques should be worked into most reading with the objective of making the learner an intelligent, resourceful reader. Intelligent guessing about the meaning of unknown constituents should be encouraged as students are taught to use the following to get at the meaning:

1. Grammar clues—
   What do word order, endings, accent marks, gender, etc. suggest?
2. Word roots, prefixes, suffixes—
   Have we encountered any of the word elements before?
3. Knowledge of the topic—
   Considering the meaning of known elements in the passage, what does our knowledge about this topic suggest regarding meaning of the word, phrase or sentence?
4. Knowledge of usual human, plant, animal and other natural behavior—
   What behavior may we naturally expect in this situation?

Reading at Intermediate Levels. In the intermediate levels, reading is an important nucleus for course work. Selections will be made carefully to stress the importance of learning to read different kinds of materials, for different purposes.

Selections will include contemporary literature suitable to the maturity of the learner:

1. Drama
2. Short stories
3. Historical text
4. Articles from newspapers and magazines
5. Advertisements
6. Comics, jokes, cartoons
7. Poems
8. Essays
9. Short novels

In addition foreign language encyclopedias, atlases, and dictionaries should be available for reference.

At the beginning of the intermediate level (i.e., third year of high school) the foreign language program should continue to place emphasis on comprehension rather than style or literary analysis. The teaching program should give students the opportunity to read with the following objectives in mind:

1. To get the general idea of the passage
2. To note details
3. To find a specific piece of information (skimming)
4. To follow directions
5. To predict outcomes
6. To form sensory impressions
7. To read critically
8. To organize what is read

The increased emphasis on reading demands careful teaching techniques to avoid overburdening students. The teacher may find it advisable to use carefully graded material in the beginning (of Level III), with the transition to normal prose being made gradually during the school year. Even afterward he should choose carefully to avoid stepping into the abyss of highly stylistic, technical or otherwise highly erudite writing.

Furthermore, new words and expressions will generally have to be previewed if students are going to learn to enjoy reading. Glossaries and foreign language dictionaries may be used in such word study. If the class is supplied with dictionaries for each student, all students can look up words together. When only one or two dictionaries are available, students should in turn be delegated the responsibility of looking up words and their meanings.

SAMPLE EXERCISE—DICTIONARY STUDY

STEP 1. The teacher lists new words and idioms on the chalkboard and pronounces them for student repetition.

STEP 2. Students copy the words in their notebooks.

SEPT 3. Students look up meanings and copy definitions into their notebooks.

STEP 4. Individuals look up the words and write definitions on the chalkboard.

STEP 5. With especially difficult words or expressions, the word is then studied in the sentence in which it appears in the text.

Another technique for helping students, as they read ever more difficult material, is systematic practice in using context clues. Such practice may take the form of previewing selected sentences from the passage to be read for class analysis. However such preview has an obvious limitation in that students are working only with clues provided by immediate sentence constituents, rather than those provided by the entire selection leading up to and following the troublesome passage.

Systematic study of word families will not only provide 'students with noun, adjectival, verbal and adverbial forms of words studied, but provide students with the key to discovering meanings of many new words they encounter. Such study should note characteristics of various parts of speech, root words, and common prefixes and suffixes. Then just as systematically the teacher must guide students to apply their knowledge to new words they meet.

Another type of orientation which may be helpful to the reader is that which provides him with background information about the subject treated in the selection. Such orientation may deal with setting, characters, plot, and even the author of a work of fiction. It may provide introductory material about the person treated in biography or information essential to student understanding of an unfamiliar topic.

Plays. While dialogue materials are not usually appropriate for intermediate levels it continues to be important for students to be exposed to the language of speech in the course of their study. Plays, particularly modern ones, are excellent for this purpose. Text should be available for study in both printed and recorded form for mimicry-memorization and for dramatic presentation.

1. Recordings of parts of plays may be listened to as students follow in their texts.
2. Students may be assigned parts for class reading.
3. Students may read parts of the play at home for in-class discussion.

Sight Reading. As students grow in their ability to understand written text, some sight reading should be built into class activities. Materials read should of course be intrinsically interesting (to the student as well as the teacher). Furthermore, the material should usually relate to a larger topic under study. Journalistic writings lend themselves particularly well to this kind of reading and often have the added virtue of timeliness. Material that is read by sight should, like all other material, be discussed, written about, and tested. Even when high-interest, humorous material is read it may be beneficial to discuss such questions as: How does the author achieve the humorous effect? How would you compare this humor with that in American stories you have read? Is there any purpose other than to make the reader laugh?

SAMPLE EXERCISE—READING A NEWS ARTICLE

STEP 1. New vocabulary and structures are previewed.

STEP 2. The news story is presented for study on the overhead projector or through individual newspaper copies. Ordinarily the teacher reads the article aloud the first time through.

STEP 3. The teacher or students ask questions regarding the content of the selection.

STEP 4. The format is studied. Does the organization of the selection differ from that in American newspapers?

STEP 5. Students are called upon in turn to read parts of the article aloud.

STEP 6. Further discussion may revolve around the significance for the future of the information contained in the article.

Students and teacher may discuss how the point of view expressed or implied in the news article differs from that current in American news sources.

Students may be provided with a number of facts which they are to incorporate into an original news article.

Correlation with Other Subjects. At the upper end of the intermediate level (Levels IV and V) there are more opportunities to correlate foreign language learning with other subjects in the school curriculum. Correlation offers an excellent opportunity to compare contemporary cross-cultural viewpoints on great questions confronting mankind and to note that men of all nations have contributed to our world civilization.

Fostering Independent Reading. By Levels III and IV, much reading should be done independently outside of class. When students are using reading texts, teachers may find it helpful to intersperse in-class reading and discussion between out-of-class reading assignments with follow-up discussion in class. The closely supervised reading and follow-up discussion should insure that independent study will result in understanding at the same time that the student is gaining confidence in his ability to read without immediate teacher help.

The school library and public libraries should also be the source for individual interest and assigned reference reading. Students need to learn how to use community resources to find out what they want and need to know.

SUMMARY

1. Reading continues to have an important place in the foreign language program.

2. Pre-reading activities are carefully planned to benefit the reading program as well as listening and speaking skills.

3. Systematic drills accompany the introduction of reading. These drills are particularly designed to counteract conflicts caused by the similarity of graphemes used in English and the foreign language and to foster true reading as opposed to decoding.

4. Differentiated reading assignments may be used to provide for individual interests and abilities.

5. Reading materials should be chosen because of their intrinsic worth and because of their appeal to the student. Reading should excite the student to be interested in more reading.

Teaching Writing Skills

Writing in Beginning Foreign Language Classes. Like reading, instruction in writing is postponed in beginning foreign language classes until students have developed a measure of audio-lingual skill. However once reading is introduced, writing may also begin. As was noted previously, reading and writing letters of the alphabet is begun in the early weeks of pre-reading instruction. Students may be asked eventually to write letters of the alphabet in order, from memory and to write the letters as dictated by the teacher.

When the pre-reading period ends, writing exercises will take the form of copying dialogue material that has been heard, spoken and read. This exercise forces students to observe carefully each word in order to reproduce it. Copying establishes accurate habits of transcription if the teacher insists that practice exercises be carefully done.

In the case of most languages commonly taught in American high schools, cursive writing may be taught immediately. However with Russian, printing should be taught first to reinforce learning of the new printed alphabet; then the transition to cursive writing may be made.

There are a great number of simple writing assignments possible for use with beginning students. They are listed below in approximate order of difficulty:

1. Copying work which has been mastered audio-lingually in class.
2. Labeling maps, charts, classroom objects, showcases, and bulletin boards.
3. Working a crossword puzzle.
4. Filling in missing words or phrases on worksheets containing dialogue sentences.
5. Writing a cued response to a statement or question.
   Example: Hello, how are you? *Cue* (fine)
   I'm fine. How are you?
6. Unscrambling sentences.
   Example: going town to I am
   I am going to town.
7. Writing a dictation.

8. Writing a transformation of a basic sentence.

Example: (Change to a question) I am going to town. *Cue*
(who)

Who is going to town?

9. Writing a random replacement drill.

Example: *Teacher:* John is going downtown.
Student: John is going downtown.
Teacher: went
Student: John went downtown.
Teacher: to Evelyn's party
Student: John went to Evelyn's party.
Teacher: detested
Student: John detested Evelyn's party.
Teacher: fish
Student: John detested fish.

10. Writing directed dialogue type sentences.

Example: *Teacher:* Tell John to get a book.
Student: John, get a book.

11. Using basic sentences to label a picture or cartoon story
provided by the teacher.

SAMPLE EXERCISE—WRITING A DICTATION AT THE
BEGINNING LEVEL

STEP 1. Students are told to prepare at home for a dictation
which will be given the following day. Material should
be taken from that which has already been copied or
otherwise written in daily assignments. More material
should be assigned than will actually be written.

STEP 2. If the material is used in a new context, as in a recombination dialogue or narrative, it may be wise to review
the setting and characters before the material is read
aloud. Then the selection is read once through for sense.

STEP 3. The material is now dictated. Short sentences may be
read only once in their entirety. Longer sentences may
be broken up into thought units.

STEP 4. The selection is read a third time to enable students to
make a final check on their work.

STEP 5. Papers are exchanged for checking. Student checkers

should circle all errors and write the total number of errors at the top of the paper.

A final simple activity which many students enjoy is locating magazine pictures and labeling them with basic sentences they have learned. Many students are usually imaginative in their matching of pictures and utterances. The result can be highly motivated, good fun suitable for bulletin board display.

In all of the above exercises the teacher should insist on accuracy in spelling, punctuation, capitalization and paragraphing.

Before long, beginning students can engage in other carefully controlled writing practice. Short descriptions such as "My House" or "My Family" and diary type narratives ("My Day" or "Excursion to the Beach") are possible, particularly when they can be modeled on previously read selections. Other possibilities are: (1) writing answers to questions about dialogues and narratives, and (2) correcting false statements about text content.

Many of the exercises suggested above can be used well beyond the first year of language study with increasingly difficult text materials.

For example the "My Day" assignment, suggested above at Level I, will probably feature simple sentences in the present tense relating to daily events.

Example: I get up at 7:00 o'clock. I go to the bathroom. I brush my teeth. I get dressed, etc.

At more advanced levels students' diary writing might follow reading such material as the *Diary of Anne Frank.* Students would be expected to show considerably more sophistication in use of tenses, in subordination of ideas and varying sentence length.

Other writing activities will provide opportunities for increasingly independent writing. One possible activity provides the student with a topic sentence and asks him to write three or four sentences to complete the paragraph. If the teacher desires, cues may be provided to guide the composition.

Example: Topic sentence: Tomorrow I am going swimming . . . (At what time?) (With whom?) (Where?) . . . (How will you get there?) . . . (Who is going with you?) . . . (Do you like to swim?) . . . (How well do you swim?) . . . (What time will you get home?)

Writing at Intermediate Levels. As students advance to intermediate levels copying continues on a much smaller scale than before. In fact, copying, if done at all, will be for the purpose of storing exact information of some intrinsic value. Thus students may be told to locate in their reading a statement or statements which prove a point and to copy it for later class discussion. Sometimes they may be told to locate and copy topic sentences in order to summarize the main thoughts of an essay. If the teacher desires, these sentences may then become the main points in an outline.

Dictations will be continued at intermediate levels to stress preciseness in writing but only on a limited scale. Occasional simple dictations of the type used with beginners will be supplemented by modified dictations.

1. Some elements such as words and phrases may be omitted from the passage dictated. Students add the missing material.
2. One half of the passage may be dictated. Students complete the passage with their own original material.

Many teachers have found that carefully conceived questions dealing with previously studied text can elicit written answers that in turn become topic sentences for a composition.

Other possible writing activities are the following:

1. Sentences or paragraphs are rewritten in a different person or tense.
2. Sentences are combined, simple to compound or complex.
3. A title is supplied by the teacher. From this the student writes a topic sentence. Then he writes three sentences to develop the topic. Finally he adds a concluding sentence.
4. The student relates an incident based on a personal experience. Usually this will follow the reading of a short narrative that may be used as a model.
5. The student reports on a school event such as an athletic match.
6. The student expresses an opinion or preference on an issue.
7. A picture is displayed for all the class to see. The student writes a description of the picture. In time students may become increasingly imaginative about the pictures.
8. Students take notes in the foreign language on class discussions, reports, and lectures. They may then put the mate-

rial into an outline or a summary and submit it for teacher evaluation.

9. Students are assigned the writing of sentences, paragraphs or short themes in which they are instructed to use certain vocabulary items or structures.

10. The first part of a story is provided for student reading. Students are told they are to complete the stories as homework. Sometimes it is wise for the class to develop a possible ending in discussion before the assignment is made.

11. Only the ending for a story is supplied. Students are assigned the task of writing the part of the story leading up to the provided conclusion.

Grading Compositions. In grading student compositions five factors are suggested for teacher consideration.

1. Total output—number of words
2. Range and diversity of vocabulary
3. Accuracy in spelling, capitalization, and punctuation
4. Correctness in language usage
5. Quality in sentence structure (i.e., variety in type and length)

Pen Pal Letters. Writing pen pal letters is a lesson in highly motivated guided composition. It is especially effective in secondary school foreign language instruction. Letters may be individual or whole class efforts. The procedure described below is for individual letters. Some changes in procedure will be necessary if letters are whole class tasks. While it is assumed here that an actual letter exchange will take place, letter writing exercises may of course be used without posting the letters. Instruction should pay attention to correct use of grammatical structures, letter form, paragraphing, placement on the page, punctuation and appearance of the letter.

Sample Exercise—Writing Pen Pal Letters

1. Topics for the letter are selected in a whole class session and arranged in logical order.
2. The class studies the format of a friendly letter.
3. A model letter is then written using the blackboard and revised as necessary.
4. Each student then writes his own letter following the model and substituting data that applies to himself (changing age,

address, information on the size of the family, subjects he takes in school).

5. The first letter may include information on name, age, subjects being taken in school and other interests and hobbies.
6. Preparation of the second letter includes study of replies received.
    a. The class notes format, particularly the salutation and complimentary close.
    b. The class discusses characteristics of foreign youth as evidenced in the letters.
    c. A list is composed of questions to be answered and model answers are composed.
    d. Some additional model comments are suggested as well as questions that the American students can ask of their pen pals.
    e. A sample paragraph may be composed illustrating how the student may describe his family in further detail.
7. Class planning similar to (6) above precedes the writing of the third letter. Already by this letter some students will be using the model letter only to a small degree. Others will continue to depend largely on the model.

Interpretations. As the student becomes more mature and also grows in control of the language, writing exercises should begin to ask him to do more than recall facts from material he has studied. Now he should begin to make inferences and judgments. Questions on the text should not only ask him what happened but why it happened. He should be called upon to characterize important figures in the text. (i.e., What kind of person is Hans? What factors led to the hero's downfall?)

Advanced Level Writing Assignments. Only a few secondary school students are presently in sequences extending beyond four years of high school study or its equivalent. As more and more students begin second language learning in the 7th grade and below, they will be capable of handling writing assignments far more complex than any common at present.

Furthermore even now, because of outstanding ability and motivation, some students are ready to undertake compositions that are more difficult than any outlined above.

Advanced level writing assignments for advanced classes should stress to a considerable degree writing compositions that require the use of levels of language appropriate for various situations. For example in listening and reading assignments students should direct their attention in their own writing to style, nuances of language as well as expressing ideas in a clear, logical manner.

Suggested for advanced students is the writing of the following:

1. Various kinds of letters
2. Playlets
3. Essays including simple critical essays on literature read
4. Short stories
5. Poems
6. Research papers on subjects chosen by students

Naturally any of the above assignments should be undertaken only after students have read and discussed a number of writings of the type they are attempting. They should follow a model very closely several times before they are given freedom to go it alone. When they no longer use a model they will continue to need an outline to follow if they are to produce worthwhile compositions. Pre-composition instruction may need to review the organization of a paragraph, the use of connecting words and phrases, organization of ideas, as well as introductions and conclusions. Acceptable form and neatness should, of course, be stressed.

SUMMARY

1. Writing assignments in the beginning are designed to insure that the student can transcribe only that which he can understand, speak and read.
2. Models continue to be provided for writing as students begin writing simple compositions.
3. Even at advanced levels translation should have only a minor part in the writing program.
4. As they learn to write, students need to learn the situations in which a given level of written language is acceptable in the foreign culture.

CHAPTER TWO

Culture and Literature
Through Language

by

Robert L. Morgenroth
Northern Illinois University

Language and Culture: Their Relationship

While the culture and literature of
a people may be studied by persons with no knowledge of the
language of that people, the foreign language remains a lifeless and
occasionally meaningless code until it is understood and appreciated as
the manifestation of a specific culture.

Edouard Herriot, in a now-famous phrase, once defined culture
as that which is left when all has been forgotten: "La culture, c'est
ce qui reste quand on a tout oublié." This describes the culture of
the individual, that hard-to-isolate element that distinguishes the
"cultivated" man. One long-range aim of the foreign language
teacher is to transmit to the student the target country's conception
of the "cultivated" man; paradoxically, then, the teacher must actively
teach those elements which the "cultivated" man has forgotten, elements which exist for him at the subconscious level.

From the practical standpoint, however, defining the "cultivated"
man is an enterprise fraught with obstacles. Which man? From

which part of the country? Of which period? Isn't the "cultivated" man in part born and not made? Wouldn't it be foolish to assume all students capable of comprehending such a concept?

For the anthropologist the concept of culture is exceedingly complex and eludes simple definition. Edward T. Hall concluded his excellent study, *The Silent Language,* with the following statement:

> Probably the most difficult point to make and make clearly is that not only is culture imposed upon man but it *is* man in a greatly expanded sense. Culture is the link between human beings and the means they have of interacting with others. The meaningful richness of human life is the result of the millions of possible combinations involved in a complex culture.[1]

Culture is communication simultaneously carried on at many levels, conscious and unconscious, informal, formal and technical. Since the comprehension of one's own culture is already a gargantuan enterprise, how presumptuous the undertaking to acquire total anthropological understanding of two cultures. Extremely useful for the teaching profession would be a series of contrastive cultural studies similar to the Contrastive Structure Series being published by the University of Chicago Press.

But until such research is available, where should the teacher begin? For the purposes of this chapter "culture" will be defined according to the teacher standards established by the Modern Language Association. The three gradations of "culture," contained in these qualifications for secondary school teachers, read as follows:

Minimal: An awareness of language as an essential element among the learned and shared experiences that combine to form a particular culture, and a rudimentary knowledge of the geography, history, literature, art, social customs, and the contemporary civilization of foreign people.

Good: Firsthand knowledge of some literary masterpieces, an understanding of the principal ways in which the foreign culture resembles and differs from our own, and possession of an organized

---

1. (New York: Fawcett World Library, 1966), pp. 166-67. This fascinating book, first printed by Doubleday in 1959, is now available in inexpensive paperback. It should be on every language teacher's bookshelf.

body of information on the foreign people and their civilization.

Superior: An enlightened understanding of the foreign people and their culture, achieved through personal contact, preferably by travel and residence abroad, through study of systematic descriptions of the foreign culture, and through study of literature and the arts.[2]

Thus "culture" (henceforth the term will be used without quotation marks) includes the ways and attitudes of a people as well as their history, geography, social structure, art and literature.

Literature Expresses Its Culture. Literature, the written transcription of man's thoughts and aspirations, is the expression of the culture to which it belongs. Thus, while cultures exist without developed literatures, literature could not exist without the culture which gave it birth.

Many aspects of a literary work survive translation, and happily so, for few are the people in the United States who read Russian, Swedish, Italian, Greek and Chinese with ease, but in their own native language these same people can discover Tolstoy, Ibsen, Dante, Sophocles and the Wu Ching. Nonetheless, the student of German, for example, who possesses a near-native command of the target language, gains a marked advantage over his colleague who either must rely on translation (many of which are very good) or slowly work through the text with dictionary in hand. That student has it in his power *to appreciate the untranslatable:* the lyric poetry and the rhythm, the flow, the precision of the author's expression.

This is why a good translation is a work of creation. It first involves perceiving and understanding the ideas, attitudes, and the cultural allusions and other elements of style of the original author in the original language. It is a problem of creation to bring out these same ideas and attitudes, with comparable allusions taken from the treasury of the second language, along with the flavor and feeling of the first culture, the style of the first author, and inevitably the style of the author who brings them into being in the second language, where they become part of that culture.

Truly a good translation requires understanding not merely of lexical equivalents, but of two cultures. Where there are no cultural

---

2. *PMLA,* vol. 70, no. 4, pt. 2 (Sept. 1955), pp. 46-49.

equivalents, as for instance the "Close, but no seegar" of the country fair sledge hammer trial, there are no lexical equivalents and the item belongs to the *untranslatable* and to the person who knows that culture.

The study of literature as an art form, as a style, as a means of personal expression can only be approached through language. First the student must be aware of the conversational, the expository, and the formal variants of the language in order to perceive the author's individual characteristics and the effects his style produces. How can the student appreciate the *tâches de douceur* of Supervielle's description of "L'Enfant de la Haute Mer" unless he is familiar with the French expression *taches de rousseur* (freckles)?

Problems of Teaching Culture

A recent observer of the American educational scene has remarked: "The American wants to conquer knowledge, but has less taste for learning on its own account. His education as well as his whole life is a race against the clock." [3] Presented with the wide spectrum of courses and course content offered in the secondary schools and colleges the students automatically question the validity of specific subject matter: why this and not that?

Many are the reasons that can be advanced in defense of the study of foreign cultures. The rapid growth of technology has so increased the contacts between countries and peoples that mutual understanding and tolerance are becoming important requisites for human survival. The study of a foreign culture affords the opportunity to get rid of the cliches and prejudices we have of foreigners and their ways.

The study of culture presents us with new extremes which, like most of reality, seem improbable. People all over the world come into focus as distant relatives of the same family. We receive a new awareness of the world, even though friendship with the foreign people should never be postulated as the guaranteed outcome of study—there are many around us who speak our own language and with whom we are not friends!

But, the alert prospective language student will be quick to point out that the foreign culture, its ideas, its history, its music, its geog-

---

3. Juliette Decreus, "A Practical Approach to the Teaching of Modern Language," *Advances in the Teaching of Modern Languages.* p. 34, ed. B. Libbish, McMillan Company, New York (1964).

raphy, all these elements may be profitably studied in English. Moreover, given the wide diversity of cultures in the world, this education might more efficiently be undertaken only in the student's native language.

Why approach a foreign culture through its language? Language provides the key to culture. Even if the student cannot presume to study as many languages as he may cultures, the acquisition of a second language provides valuable insights into the role of language as a cultural conditioning factor.

Languages differ among themselves in many ways:

1. Verbal expression: The richness of vocabulary in certain areas and the lack of precise terminology in others indirectly reflects the preoccupations and needs of the culture; Eskimos have several words to describe different kinds of snow. Structure reveals the existence of varying types of thought processes. French and Spanish, for instance, use the subjunctive to express nuances which generally pass unnoticed in English.

2. Literary expression, particularly poetry: The rhythmic stress patterns of English are essential elements of poetry to the American nurtured on nursery rhymes and later on Shakespeare and Longfellow. In comparison, French verse seems artificial, contrived, a mere counting of syllables. Haiku appears even less natural, less "poetic."

3. Power of abstraction: When richness of vocabulary is combined with flexibility of structure the result varies from language to language. Consequently each language favors certain types of mental operations which are not the same for all cultures. A culture whose numerical system includes only *one, two,* and *many* cannot handle higher arithmetic manipulations without modifying its language.

4. Power of persuasion: Oratorical devices differ. It has been jokingly remarked that German lends itself well to dictators because the crowds must remain attentive until the end of the phrase in order to catch the verb, the meaning.

Language does not exist independent of culture. How, for instance, do you explain to a Fiji Islander the meanings of the word *bourgeois* without portraying the society it fits into? For the Frenchman the word possesses somewhat different meanings than it does for the American or the Britisher. Fitting a word accurately into a variety of grammatical patterns does not guarantee communication—your foreign interlocutor may understand something quite different from what you intended to say because you misinterpreted the meanings given to specific words or structures.

Once the student knows a second language well and realizes the role it plays in expressing and shaping the culture of that country, he will be more conscious of this "missing link" in studying the cultures of other peoples "in translation."

Language vs. Literature. Language and literature do not exist apart from one another regardless of their separate listings in a college curriculum. Structure and vocabulary are the building blocks of any literary work. Even the sounds of language persist as internal vocalizing when the student is reading to himself. For this reason, *control of the sound system is central to all reading but especially to literature* where the choice of sounds is an element of the author's artistry and the reader's appreciation.

The conflict, when one exists, is not so much one between language and literature, as one between teachers of "language" and "literature" courses. How often have teachers' meetings at the undergraduate level, and often in the high schools, reverberated with considerations such as: "We can't let our students graduate as majors unless they have taken coursework in the Renaissance and the nineteenth century!" "How can they possibly fit advanced composition into their schedules if they are required to take the course in the Enlightenment?" Curiously enough the greatest concern is over authors or periods, knowledge of which could be more rapidly gained by reading the works in translation, as opposed to additional practice in conversation or composition. How much more appropriate to ask how well students can *read* the works and express their conclusions fluently in the language under study? How much more to the point to question not how much the students have read (and often the students, frequently the better students, procure translations in order to understand what they are assigned to read) but how *well* they have read, to what degree they are appreciating the untranslatable.

Literature in the High School. Handing the intermediate level high school student a foreign literature for discussion and analysis is like handing a child a sealed jar of candy. He may see what is inside and like what is inside, but he is less likely to get fed than frustrated and disgusted. Teaching him to open the jar lets him get at the contents, sort them out and appreciate the quality of the mixture.

In selecting reading material the teacher must seek the rich mixture that best presents the culture: current, contemporary, formal and informal language found in fiction, short stories, plays, novels, newspapers, magazines, even captions under cartoons. It is no small series of problems to select authentic material, graded to the student's abilities, varied to his tastes and maturity, and stimulating to his interest. The experienced teacher knows that growth follows motivation, be it implanted by the comics, football scores, James Bond or Dostoyevsky.

Means and Methods

Culture via Language. The new audio-lingual materials offer the students their initial taste of the culture of the country. In the course of the dialogues which form the basis of the first year of language study the student learns about forms of address, polite expressions, eating and drinking habits of the country under study, social customs and various aspects of daily life. These topics are closely linked to the language activities of the classroom, thus integrating culture in the anthropological or sociological sense with speech and movement.

Throughout the formal sequence of language study the student grows to appreciate the similarities and differences between the target language and his native English. Gradually he becomes intimately involved in the thought processes of a different people, their sense of humor, their view of life. Those students who are fortunate enough to continue their course of study for more than a couple of years, and who are given perhaps the opportunity to travel and live in a foreign country, will experience the epitome of cultural identification—the curious phenomenon of dual personality. In English they will react and express themselves as Americans; in the target language they will speak and feel more like natives of the foreign country.

CULTURE IN THE CLASSROOM. Since the language experience of most students becomes closely identified with the classroom and, where applicable, the language laboratory, a wealth of realia may be displayed and employed to increase student interest in the culture of the country under study.

1. *Visual appeal.* If the classroom is a colorful, cheerful place, the students will be more eager to learn. If the walls are decorated with colorful posters which can be varied from time to time,

the inevitable moments of daydreaming may be subconsciously oriented toward the foreign culture. Similarly, effective use may be made of reproductions of appropriate works of art and architecture, particularly if these reproductions are accompanied by large attractive captions giving the artist, his dates, and the name of the work. *Students should in no direct way be held responsible for the information thus displayed,* but the more curious would have their questions answered and unknowingly be introduced to the "refinement" culture of the country. Like the posters, these reproductions, too, could be changed at certain intervals, perhaps with the teacher enlisting the aid of interested students.

2. *Calendar.* A large calendar showing the national holidays of the foreign peoples may prove a valuable asset. The calendar can furnish the point of departure for brief questions and answers at the beginning of the language class. As holidays occur, they may be illustrated pictorially or through actual objects (a *piñata* in a Spanish class, for example). In elementary classes where students would be unable to follow a description of the festivities in the target language, a few moments at the beginning of the period could be devoted to a brief discussion in English.

3. *Maps.* Most classrooms are equipped with wall maps of the countries in which the target language is spoken. While nothing can be so dull as having the students memorize lists of geographic features for written tests, geographical elements can be naturally incorporated into the language-learning activities. Many pattern drills lend themselves to the use of place names: instead of verbally giving the element for substitution or transformation the teacher can direct the students' attention to the map and point out the new places to be employed in the pattern.

Later when the students begin reading original texts, the teacher, in each selection, can point out on the map the places where the action is occuring. Most textbooks have at least one lesson about travel; here the map can offer a point of departure for a series of directed dialogues and dramatized purchase of tickets in which the students work out their own routes according to the map.

4. *Periodicals corner.* One designated area of the classroom may become a display area and shelving corner for foreign language

periodicals. Illustrated magazines may even be loaned out overnight as homework in the intermediate and more advanced classes. The text serves as preceptor of both language and culture, and at a level of style that is likely to reflect the colloquial language. Moreover, the pictures are instantaneously and richly translated into the viewer's native—and personal— language yielding yet another introduction to the foreign culture. Some magazines, in covering a range of subjects that cater to a variety of tastes, may include articles on the United States. This look at ourselves through foreign eyes, through a foreigner's camera and in foreign words, provides another facet in learning the new culture. A sharper, more objective understanding of America and Americans is necessary if we are to appreciate the differences of a foreign culture.

Advanced classes can benefit from a group subscription to the weekly airmail edition of a foreign newspaper. Once students possess the requisite command of the language, they cannot but profit from both feature articles and straight reporting on actual current events interpreted from a foreign point of view.

5. *Displays*. One small corner of the classroom could be utilized for changing displays. Students could be encouraged to take charge of preparing a small exhibit incoporating their own particular interests: a foreign doll collection, stamps, coins, works of a particular artist, postcards. Others interested in other fields, such as music, history, archeology, physics, astronomy, could organize displays showing the foreign country's contribution in a particular area.

6. *Scrapbooks*. Students, either in groups or individually, could put together scrapbooks by collecting newspaper clippings about the people and culture under study. Not only current events, but concerts, exhibits, films, and scientific achievements could be included.

CULTURE THROUGH PERSONAL CONTACT

1. *Visitors*. Since many students will not have the opportunity to travel abroad, those native speakers who live in the area should be invited to the class individually or in small groups over a period of time. Their presence confirms more than any other realia that the foreign language and the culture are living. In addition to each student's having the opportunity to make

personal contact, by questions and answers, with the representative of the foreign culture, a tape could be made of the
interview, for later study of the differences in speech of the
speakers. In speaking to a beginning class, the guest will be
most effective when he has been given the known vocabulary
list beforehand and urged to resrict himself to the list as
much as possible.

While the teacher can point out later which of the accents
heard are considered the most "cultivated" and perhaps the
best to imitate in an approach to the standard language, a
variety of accents and the inevitable variety of viewpoints
will enlarge the student's aural and cultural range, and help
clear up false and stereotyped concepts.

Exchange students brought to this country by such groups as
the Experiment in International Living, Rotary International, and the American Field Service afford an opportunity
for contact with foreigners close in age and interest. These
are likely to be the most satisfying of all such contacts.

2. *Correspondence.* Correspondence with foreign students should
be encouraged at all levels of language proficiency. Beginning
students would first write in English; as their control of the
target language improves, they could be encouraged to write
the salutations and, gradually, a few controlled sentences in
the new language while putting the body of the letter into
English. The teacher must try to avoid the danger of indiscriminate use of the dictionary and the inevitable "fractured"
results. Advanced students could correspond by letters in the
target language.

Regardless of the language used, the student writing of his
own activities may begin to see them objectively for the first
time. In his correspondent's reactions he will see his culture
through foreign eyes. The views of a representative of a foreign
culture have value as those representing one of many people.
They have even more value as views of an individual of a
foreign culture, for any communication between people must
immediately, as well as ultimately, be between people considered "foreign" or "countrymen" not because of their origins
but by virtue of their personal tastes and values. Most professional organizations such as the AATF (American Association of Teachers of French), AATG (German) and AATSP
(Spanish and Portuguese) can supply information as to how
to obtain lists of international pen pals.

3. *Field trips.* While the classroom may profitably be viewed as a "cultural island," the students will increase their appreciation of language as a living phenomenon by hearing the language spoken naturally in a variety of situations. In many instances appropriate field trips and visits may be arranged: perhaps there is a foreign restaurant nearby where the waiters speak the target language; perhaps there is a section of the city where the language is spoken. In college or university communities, high school teachers might establish contact with the various language departments and keep informed about lectures, films and plays sponsored by the college and open to the public. The teacher may arrange to have more advanced students invited to foreign language club gatherings on the college campus: most high school students enjoy an opportunity to visit a campus and are enthusiastic about speaking a new language with interested college students.

4. *Travel.* The fitting reward and logical culmination of careful study of language and culture is the trip abroad. Given the opportunity to stay in different parts of a country for periods long enough to become acquainted with its people and customs is valuable for removing misconceptions, acquiring a firsthand, accurate knowledge of the culture and the language, and, finally, for bridging the space between the imagined and the real.

The teacher should have at his disposal information on student exchange opportunities, foreign study, work-abroad programs and scholarships. Whether the program covers the academic year (sometimes available to high school students), a semester, or merely the summer, all aspects should be considered. Many foreign study programs provide effective combinations: courses that meet American students' needs, foreign professors offering a foreign specialty such as *explication de texte,* American professors or foreign professors oriented to or complementing the United States approach, through classroom discussions, term papers and final examinations, not necessary features of the host country's own schools.

With a view not only to the eventual evaluation of foreign study by a registrar in the United States, but also to the effect such study, residence, and travel abroad will have on the student's development, the programs of the various study abroad groups should be carefully investigated.

The Contribution of Audio-Visual Resources. With the technological advances of American society, more and more teachers find they have access, even if this must be carefully planned in advance, to a multitude of audio-visual aids. Such aids, if properly incorporated in the coursework or imaginatively introduced as periodic supplements, contribute immeasurably to the teaching of culture even though their use in teaching language per se may be more restricted. Let us examine several of the possible uses of the more common equipment.

1. *Recordings.* Most schools, if not eqiupped with language laboratories, at least have at the disposition of the teacher a tape recorder or record player. For beginning students, the sound equipment fulfills the primary function of providing acceptable native models to develop proper listening habits in the students; the role of culture is secondary, limited to an introduction of certain social customs and conversational formulas. After some training and experience in listening to textual, controlled material in the language laboratory, or over records, the students are exposed to non-textual material such as transcriptions of foreign language radio broadcasts, taped interviews with native speakers, operas and plays recorded by foreign companies, including national opera companies and national theater companies, all of which are preparing more and better cultural material for the educated listener.

   Very soon even beginning students can appreciate short folksongs, and at the appropriate season, Christmas carols. Particularly in the elementary schools, songs and dances become vehicles for teaching the new language. Junior-high and high school students enjoy learning current song "hits" in the foreign language.

   The possibility of presenting the sounds of typical foreign scenes is being investigated. Recordings could be made of marketplace activity, cafes, busy intersections, country fairs, train stations, and the like.

   At a more advanced level, literature students may go to the language laboratory to hear lectures which they missed or on which they took imperfect notes; they can stop the "teacher" and make him repeat material they have imperfectly understood. Thus they grasp more of the content, increase their active vocabulary, make themselves more effective and free more time for valuable discussion in class.

2. *Films and television.* One of the most valuable aids to the teacher is the film. Here care must be exercised to exclude the film that does not teach because the speech is too fast or too advanced for the student (however delightful to the teacher), that is poorly done technically, i.e., in acting, photography, or sound, or that is so long the passivity in film viewing leads to apathy and boredom.

Let us use the one great power of television common to all films: seduction. It is almost impossible to be in the same room with a television program and not watch it, however slyly. We are thus drawn into watching trivialities and trash, even commercials we have seen a dozen times already, without any conscious desire to do so. The proper film, properly used, may employ this same hypnotic power, and achieve language and cultural learning without conscious effort on the part of the student. Whenever possible, the teacher could describe the film in advance. Certain recurrent, and unfamiliar, vocabulary items could be presented beforehand. When feasible, the entire script should be previewed orally. The problem to the student is not visual understanding and visual recall, but auditive understanding and auditive recall. In presenting the script before showing the film we will be going from the known (audio) to the unknown (visual) and further reinforcing the audio associations after having first required concentration on the audio functions alone.

Similarly, cultural films may be presented over classroom television. The shortcomings of television arise primarily in teaching language usage. The difficulty in eliciting (and the near impossibility of evaluating) student responses and the fixed pace of presentation regardless of student differences in ability are obvious drawbacks to language teaching. Geography, dress, housing, eating, and most of the behavior that makes up sociological or anthropological culture can be effectively presented whether live or taped. Many art forms, comprising the "refined" culture, lend themselves well to filmed presentation. Video tape and video machines have become drastically cheaper and far easier to operate.

3. *Still projectors.* With the increased availability of films and particularly of audio equipment the projectors have fallen into disuse in the language classroom, and this is unfortunate. The opaque projector in particular provides a versatile addition to the language classroom. From the very first weeks of language

instruction the projector can be put to effective use in the class-room bringing together culture and language. The teacher can collect postcards, magazine clippings, photographs and the like showing the people of the foreign country engaged in daily activities, depicting street scenes from villages and cities, show-ing "fashionable", middle-class, and peasant interiors. Since the classroom need not be darkened while the projections are being used, questions and answers as well as other pattern drills can be constructed around the pictures. The students will be en-couraged to use structures and vocabularies with which they are familiar while broadening their concept of the culture of the people under study. A wide variety of pictures about a specific topic will be most effective in preventing the unfor-tunate formation of stereotype impressions.

4. *Slides.* Slide projectors are most effective when fidelity in color is high, particularly in presenting the art masterpieces of the foreign country. When possible, native speakers should be in-vited to the classroom for special art programs followed by questions and answers. The students would be presented with special vocabulary in advance, in order to be prepared for the lecture.[4]

The slide presentation could be linguistically and culturally reinforced by preparing a follow-up session in the language laboratory. As the same slides are shown, the students repeat parts of the presentation and answer questions about particu-lar features of the slides.

Slide projector and recordings can be combined to permit special programs on specific periods of history combining music, art, and perhaps brief literary selections. The history of the period: its personalities, its events, attitudes, philoso-phies, its social and economic structures, types of dress, all lend themselves to a more animated presentation when ac-companied by the arts and customs of the period.

Through Language to Literature. Traditionally the sequence of foreign language courses progressed *from* language courses *to* litera-ture courses; the latter were the more difficult, presumably, and car-ried the greater prestige. The unfortunate result is that "liteature" is offered to students so dependent on their pocket dictionary that pre-

---

4. See Mary M. Hamilton, "Teaching a Foreign Culture: New Help," *French Review*, vol. xxxviii (April 1965), pp. 645-49.

paration becomes an exercise in deciphering a new code. Language majors often progress through an entire language program without ever acquiring ease in expression and confidence in their reading ability. Time limitations are such that once the student has passably understood the plot and the characterizations, little time is left for more critical reading. The majority of the "New Key" audio-lingual materials try to remedy the situation by postponing the introduction to literature until the student has developed the reading skill and acquired equivalent fluency in listening, speaking and writing. But the progression has remained the same: *from* language *to* literature.

Yet that which is unique about a literary work is precisely that indefinable quality linked with the writer's vehicle of expression: the language. The "untranslatable" lies in the author's particular choice of sounds, of words, of phrases which somehow cast a particular spell, a glow. Every language possesses brief works of literary art, be they poems, excerpts from plays or novels, or lyric passages, which utilize a fairly restricted vocabulary and a limited number of grammatical patterns. Thus, in a natural manner, the teacher can introduce brief selections of true literary merit to elementary and intermediate students who often crave something more substantial than drills and dialogues. The selections are brought into the classroom for their own sake: they are neither abridged nor edited (if the whole poem, verse or paragraph is for some reason not suitable, then another should be found); nor are they turned inside-out in pattern drills. The literary excerpts are illustrations of the heights to which the target language can rise, of the diverse means of expression representative of the culture being studied.

Through language the student is introduced to literature. His appreciation of the target language and the target literature develops and matures simultaneously. The culture of the foreign peoples, in the anthropological and sociological sense of the word, is presented concurrently with the cultural achievements attained by that country. The unity of culture, in all its aspects, must be maintained.[5]

---

5. The teacher will discover a wealth of ideas concerning various ways of incorporating literature and the arts into the study of the language itself in the MLA Conference *Newsletter: Teaching Language Through Literature.* (Address correspondence to General Editor, *Newsletter,* 501 Philosophy Hall, Columbia University, New York, New York 10027.)

The Role of the Teacher

The success of any particular method of teaching culture rests ultimately on the teacher. The competent language teacher, besides knowing his own and the foreign language well, besides having learned a certain amount about language laboratories, tape recorders, and programmed materials, must also know the culture of the two countries: literature, history, geography, politics, education, fine arts, science and technology, and at the same time manners, customs and attitudes of the foreign people.[6] These qualifications can be gained through reading and by speaking with foreign visitors to our country, but hardly so intensively or thoroughly as they can through extended residence and travel abroad.

But, formal qualifications, however excellent, do not guarantee a fine "performance." The teacher should strive to impart to the class a feeling of understanding, if not some identification, with the people of the foreign country. Student motivation will increase proportionately. An enthusiastic presentation of the *Oktoberfest* will ever be preferable to a dull account of Bismarck's achievements; and enthusiastic reading of Prevert is more profitable to the students than an erudite but monotonous analysis of *Le Cid*. Particularly among pre-college students, the teacher's enthusiasm is contagious. For the majority of the students, the teacher and classroom offer the first contact with the foreign culture. It should be a fruitful one.

The Challenge

Of what value is learning German, for example, and finding ourselves assigned to Italy, or touring France? The answer is simply that having learned to make one's way in a culture other than one's own, a person is far less likely to experience antipathy towards an unknown culture simply because it is foreign. This does not mean that because we speak English we are necessarily more sympathetic to the British, nor even more friendly to our compatriots of the South, the West, the neighboring town or across the street. But one barrier, the often un-

---

6. A "must" for teachers is the *Publications of Interest to Teachers of Modern Foreign Languages*. This brochure is available free from the Materials Center, Modern Language Association, 62 Fifth Avenue, New York City. The Materials Center distributes the useful selective and annotated bibliographies entitled "Six Cultures" and "Four Cultures".

conscious resentment for what we do not understand, has been re-moved. And apart from the probability that, having learned a second language, a third will be easier, we will find that our cultural aware-ness is likely to be much greater, and the prospect of our understand-ing and tolerance increased. For the teacher, a new dimension or new dimensions will be added to his classroom contribution.

What needs to be done is to write better texts and to train our present students who will become teachers to program materials that will hold interest—they are close enough to the learning experience, they will know the target culture—and to transform the target lan-guage into an irresistible target.

The teacher must never be a "slave" to his media any more than a student should become a "robot" in the language laboratory or in the classroom. Learning a language is still hard work. The demands on the teacher are to be a craftsman, an artist, and, above all, an en-lightened human being.

CHAPTER THREE

Developing Effective
Practice and Study Techniques

by

Donald R. Iodice

Oakland University

Control over the four language skills cannot be accomplished through self-instruction at home. Although the *passive* skills might be developed to some degree, a trained teacher is certainly responsible for development of the *active* skills. Such may not always be the case in other disciplines, but a modern language teacher *teaches* during most of her classroom hour. Her classroom is a *learning* session where the student first encounters and partially masters new structure, form, and idiom. Then, he *practices* these at home, rather than solving problems or "getting it by himself." His homework done, he returns to class for perfecting, polishing, expanding, and varying what he has practiced, and he learns to use these structures, forms, and idioms in creative situations.

For the learner of a modern language, the relative roles of classroom recitation and homework have thus been considerably altered from the common pattern. Although the purpose of the recitation and homework may have changed, we still retain the sound pedagogical principles of the past: appropriate homework should be assigned from the first week; and new techniques, approaches, exercises, and skills should be practiced in class before the student attempts them at home for the first time.

Some confusion seems to exist, however, as to the content of recitation and homework for each skill at the various levels. Two sources *(1959 Northeast Conference Reports,* and *Connecticut Curriculum Bulletin No. V)* offer the following percentages:

Level	Hearing	Speaking	Reading	Writing
I	40%	30%	20%	10%
II	30%	20%	40%	10%
III	20%	20%	40%	20%
IV	20%	20%	40%	20%

Neither source indicates that much of the reading and writing of levels II, III, and IV would be done outside the classroom nor that the major classroom activity would still involve oral recitation, manipulation, questions and answers and, when appropriate, oral exercises on the reading. It becomes self-evident that extensive use of classroom time for writing practice is less than efficient.

By virtue of the preceding interpretations, the type of material used at home will also vary from the conventional. The student is practicing, rather than solving problems. There is no need to withhold the correct answers to prevent him from copying his homework—the *bête noire* of all teachers! If home-study practice is to be effective, he *must have* the "answers," so that he can immediately verify the accuracy of his work. This implies use of a text, ditto sheets, or a workbook in which all the answers are supplied. Such teaching materials are a rarity in most institutions and courses. In fact, an approach of this type might be considered highly suspect by teachers and students: what *would* prevent the student from copying? In truth, nothing except proper orientation and occasional reminders of the reason for homework.

If the class is a display-testing situation, the student cannot be blamed for copying and thereby assuring himself of the desired approval during recitation; he can prove that he is able to solve problems. But in the audio-lingual classroom, he is quite honestly perfecting drills, dialogues, etc., that he has encountered in class and then practiced at home. The answers in the book simply save precious time, allow him to correct his own mistakes and identify his weaknesses, and give an accurate model. Nevertheless, he and his parents have had quite a different educational experience, and by the time he reaches high school our student is accustomed to certain types of homework in his other courses. His parents and counselors may judge a class by the number of pages read, exercises written or problems solved. The first few weeks may be the crucial turning point for the neophyte. This segment of pre-reading instruction (the precise length depending upon frequency of class meetings, level of the class, and other factors) is a necessary part of an audio-lingual course. Unfortunately, the lack of conventional homework may set negative attitudes: a "no-homework" course may be quickly classified as Fun-and-Games or worse. The student may judge the class by a conventional yardstick and decide that this unconventional modern language class is unworthy of his esteem. Some teachers anticipate this reaction and spend the first day or two specifically describing the course: what will be done in class, how the four skills will be tested, what type of homework is involved, and how to practice effectively at home. They may even send a short statement home to the parents describing the course and giving the rationale of the pre-reading phase.

Homework During the Pre-Reading Phase

It is self-evident that virtually all homework during the pre-reading phase will be oral: practice and overlearning of high-frequency small talk, dialogues, dialogue line variation, simple structural and morphological drills, and contrastive phonology drills. Yet the student cannot practice correct foreign language without a model; non-controlled practice might bring about the learning of incorrect forms, structures, and pronunciation. He is not ready for practice with a book, and most likely does not have a native tutor at home. One common source of an authentic model is the practice records that accompany several audio-lingual texts now available. Although they are often limited to the basic dialogue and do not include dialogue line variation and structure drill, these discs are an invaluable aid. They sometimes receive rather brutal treatment, however, and should be checked periodically for scratches and other imperfections. Still another means of providing audio models at home would be through the use of miniature reels of tape and inexpensive tape recorders now flooding the retail market. While audio quality is not the best, it would probably not be any worse than some of the home phonographs used with home-study records.

Yet a third possibility for homework would be the language labora-tory. These electronic installations have become an integral part of the classroom and lesson plan, but few are used as a *homework center* to which students may come during free hours and after school. Two arguments are offered against such a suggestion: students come to school by bus and leave according to a fixed schedule; and, it is ad-ministratively impossible to have "library-type" laboratory schedules. A quick glance at the size of the school parking lot will invalidate the first objection. The second misconception is not dispelled so easily. A few schools with modular scheduling or evenly balanced study halls have nevertheless managed to establish an independent-study schedule for the language laboratory. Administrators have justified the pro-cedure by maintaining that time alloted for independent study during the day should be spent where it will be most effective: in the library, seminar rooms, or language laboratory, depending upon the subject matter involved.

Nevertheless, this type of oral homework is at great variance with the established pattern of most educational institutions. Seven or more years of "book" homework, and generations of prejudice, will cause even the forewarned student and parent to doubt the seriousness of purpose of a course that minimizes reading and writing at home. Perhaps we can turn this prejudice to our advantage, using this pre-reading phase to introduce concepts concerning the contemporary folkways and mores of the people who speak the language we teach. A language should not be divorced from the contemporary culture of its native speakers. We know that Americans often have unusual, pre-conceived notions concerning the life, customs, and mentality of a typical Frenchman, German, or Spaniard. One of the first assignments —in English—could be a short essay giving the student's impression of a typical person who speaks the foreign language. Some teachers ask for a similar essay at the end of the first year, and students are sur-prised to discover the degree to which their ideas have changed.

Cultural orientation need not be limited to just an essay or two; it involves a systematic presentation of the similarities and differences between the two cultures. During the first two weeks of an audio-lingual course, when the new type of classroom recitation is demand-ing and fatiguing, some teachers have effectively set aside a ten-minute segment at the end of the hour during which the foreign culture is discussed in English. With this additional type of classroom activity, it is then consistent to assign short, interesting reading, in English, about the foreign culture, limiting the topics to a few given in the listing by Brooks' *Language and Language Learning* (2nd ed.), pp. 88–96. Students will welcome the change of pace, find the topics interesting, and feel more secure with what appears to be brief, conventional homework assignments. As they progress to the reading-writing phase of the course, their assignments in English can be replaced by the types described below.

Homework for the Neophyte During the Reading-Writing Phase

While it is generally agreed that reading should precede writing, most statements concerning the time gap involved seem rather subjective. Personal experience with audio-lingual teaching has led many of us to feel that it is not necessary to postpone reading until the end of the fourth unit and writing until the end of the fifth, for example. Rather than considering the precise timing involved, we would prefer to limit our present dscussion to home study activities once these skills have been introduced.

As the student begins each of these new phases, it may be wise to review the ground rules of the class. He has spent virtually all his time on oral practices and may now consider this to be the only requisite of the course. He needs to be aware of the type of material he will be using and what he is expected to do with it at home. At first, his reading will essentially be limited to dialogue, dialogue line variation, and drills that he has *already learned to handle orally* in the classroom. The purpose of the first printed material is not to test his reading comprehension, but to provide graphic representations of familiar utterances, forms, and structures. It allows him to practice reading aloud—a perfectly valid endeavor, though usually overemphasized in conventional classrooms. The printed text also allows him to drill the form and structures not usually available on discs and sometimes omitted from tapes. If well prepared, an audio-lingual text permits practice without the risk of learning incorrect foreign language. Some formats lend themselves to immediate self-correction: on one side, each set of clues is listed vertically under the model sentence; on the other side, each correct response is given. However, unless the student is shown how to use the text correctly, he will simply read the responses aloud—a practice of questionable value at most. Simply parroting answers will not prepare the student for the type of manipulation required in class and on tests. The instructor should demonstrate how to study: use a four-by-six card to cover the right-hand column; look at the cue, try to give the answer; then drop the card to check his answer. If the student has difficulty with a particular response, he checkmarks the cue for additional practice. After the first few assignments have been given, it may be wise to ask an average or less-than-average student to demonstrate how he drills himself. Teachers are often shocked to discover that a drill lasting fifty seconds in class may take several minutes at home if the learner stumbles, hestitates, or is not demanding of himself. He must be taught to pace himself with the rapidity of the classroom and laboratory drill.

Not all printed materials will be of the drill-practice variety; even the neophyte should be exposed to some reading comprehension lessons. During the first year these will probably be recombinations of previously learned structure, idiom, and vocabulary, carefully seeded with a limited amount of new material. As in the case of drills, students need to be shown how to work with this kind of home study material. We would assume that the selection has been introduced and read aloud in class, and that new structure and vocabulary have been paraphrased by the instructor. As they prepared their homework, students would then be cautioned against translation, and would be encouraged to: (a) read the selection aloud, grouping the words in thought-phrases; (b) read for meaning and sequence of ideas; and (c) compose questions on the reading of the who-what-when-where-how variety or of the yes-no type. Evidently, the last activity cannot be done until the students have learned the various types of questions, but they seem more capable of answering questions in class if they have practiced asking and answering the questions themselves.

Finally, the newcomer begins to write, and he experiences yet another trauma. The reasons for his reaction are several: he may be completely unaware that there are two language systems, a written and a spoken; he may seem oblivious to the need for accuracy in the written language as well as in the spoken; or, he may have been encouraged by other teachers to be creative at all costs, regardless of structure, idiom, or nuance. If he falls into the first category, he may be confused; if he is in the last, he may be bored by the necessary first steps of learning to write a language—copying, subsitutions, simple manipulations, and paraphrasing. Our audio-lingual instructor will stress the need for accuracy and precision as the key to effective written practice at home, with particular emphasis on punctuation, capitalization, elision, letter configurations representing certain sounds, accentuation, and the graphemics of non-Roman alphabets.

The first written homework will probably be copying a well-known dialogue five or ten times, paying careful attention to the phenomena given above. It may be wise to caution the student against recopying his first copy in the series: any errors in the first would be repeated in subsequent versions. Spot, full, and recombination dictation are usually included in first-year classroom work. To help prepare for these, some schools encourage students, to give themselves dictation on familiar dialogues and narrations, using their home study discs or lab tapes and stopping the machine after every utterance while they write.

The language learner should be able to use the written forms of the structures he has been using orally. To this end, his practice at home with patterns should now include two phases: the oral, described above; and a written, following the same general procedure. With a self-correcting text of the type previously mentioned, students should again be cautioned not to *copy* the responses, but to compose the response from the cue and then check their accuracy. But writing drills is not an end in itself, and the recent convert to audio-lingual teaching sometimes forgets that patterns are just one of many steps in the process of teaching active command of a language. He should include some homework in the form of *exercises* that recapitulate the forms and structures taught in the drills. We do not mean to imply that translation is necessarily appropriate; we would rather include exercises involving recombination, re-statement, expansion, contraction, tense shift, etc., to evaluate the effectiveness of the drills.

Homework for Intermediate-Level Students

As students progress from dialogue to narrative material as the point of departure for each unit, some change in the orientation of their homework would be appropriate. We must assume that classroom procedure still follows the underlying philosophy of the New Key: new structures and vocabulary are introduced in class prior to encountering them in the homework. Before assigning the reading, our instructor will have identified the new structures and forms, and will then teach them in the form of drills to be practiced orally and in writing at home. She will have also identified the new, high-frequency vocabulary that should become part of the student's active repertory, and she will present this vocabulary in the form of a foreign-language-to-foreign-language dictionary, with the items listed in order of occurrence in the text rather than in alphabetical order.

Once the structures and forms are under control, the class is ready to do the reading selection. Near the end of one particular class hour, the instructor could present orally the sections of the dictionary corresponding to the section of reading to be done that evening. Students might then have the following assignment:

1. Memorize the specific section of the "dictionary"—synonyms, antonyms, simple paraphrasings necessary to understand the lexical items or the reading itself.
2. Read the selection assigned, in conjunction with the *questions précises* that correspond to the reading.
3. Practice both oral and written answers to these questions.

With advanced second-year and with third-year classes, a brief oral or written resume would be basic phrases, vocabulary, and structures taken from the selection.

In addition to writing practice based upon reading selections, questions, drills, etc., students must gradually be weaned away from the strict controls of earlier writing experience and be led methodically to creative composition. They will welcome written homework involving narrative tense shifts, stylistic transformations from dialogue to narrative and the reverse, parallel writing, the "dehydrated sentence" or string of words, composition from a detailed outline, and composition from a brief outline. Sequences appropriate for written homework are well described in the *1963 Northeast Conference Reports,* pp. 63-81, and are exemplified in Beaujour and Relgado's *R.S.V.P.—Invitation à Ecrire* (Harcourt, Brace and World, 1965).

Homework for Levels IV and V

As the focus of the modern language class turns increasingly to a preoccupation with literature, the amount of oral homework required of the student will diminish. Even at this level, however, some oral practice is still advisable in the form of advanced structure drills and exercises, remedial phonology drills, and intonation patterns. Nevertheless, the great bulk of homework will involve the reading of literary selections, and the way in which students do their homework will have an appreciable effect upon the course. Many high school students are not sufficiently mature to delve into the mysteries of literary appreciation, stylistics, genre, and the many topics dear to the heart of the literary scholar. A few schools have tried a daring new approach, rather than attempting to imitate the college survey courses. In these schools students are encouraged to read for meaning, to look for lines typical of the main characters, to summarize scenes, acts, and chapters, to associate the words of main personages with the thought and circumstances of the times. Written work also tends to avoid literary interpretation, since this would require a vocabulary and sophistication of structure and background well beyond their experience. These language students are encouraged to write essays of several hundred words on topics within the scope of their general education and specific language experience.

How Much Homework?

The realities of public schools militate against more than forty-five minutes to one hour of homework each night. In some ways this is fortunate: it requires us to *teach* in class, rather than merely test. However, we often fail to calculate the amount of time necessary to cover the homework carefully with a sufficient amount of practice. We need to ask ourselves, "How long *will* it take to copy the dialogue ten times and practice five pattern drills?" Moreover, as students begin to work with reading selections, we should calculate the amount of time necesary to handle the "dictionary," *questions précises,* oral and written answers, and resumes discussed briefly above. A segment of several hundred words might provide enough material to keep them busy for an hour, depending upon vocabulary density, idea content, thought sequences, and associated exercises. It seems preferable to concentrate on quality rather than quantity, by reducing the total corpus of homework and encouraging our students to strive for perfection through overlearning, manipulation, and practice.

Bibliography

New York State Education Department. *French for Secondary Schools* (German, Spanish, etc.). Albany, New York, 1960.

O'Connor, Patricia. *Modern Foreign Languages in High School: Pre-reading Instruction.* D. H. E. W., P. E. 27000. Bulletin No. 9, 1960.

CHAPTER FOUR

Measuring Achievement
in Language Skills

by

Rebecca M. Valette
Boston College

Testing in the Classroom

The teacher who sets out to "measure achievement" has already, though perhaps unknowingly, made two assumptions: first, that during the course of instruction the students have mastered a new skill or acquired a new body of knowledge; and, second, that this skill or body of knowledge may be defined in quantitative or measurable terms. Thus, before developing even the most informal testing program the foreign language teacher must consider the objectives of the class and how these may best be evaluated.

Determining the Objectives. In many recently developed audio-lingual materials, levels one and two emphasize the acquisition of structure rather than rapid vocabulary development. After all, the structure of the language indicates the relationships among the parts of the sentence. A single unfamiliar word can be looked up in a dictionary, but a new construction generally poses greater difficulty. The spoken language is transmitted by a system of sound, intonation and stress; thus, in audio-lingual classes, phonology is indirectly introduced in the very first lessons.

Two groups of skills are taught to enable the student to use and understand the foreign language. The receptive (or "passive") skills (that is, listening and reading) prepare the student to receive the message sent by another. The productive (or "active") skills (that is, speaking and writing) enable the student to give expression to his own thoughts. These various elements, all components of a sound language program, may be schematically represented:

DIAGRAM I

	RECEPTIVE SKILLS		PRODUCTIVE SKILLS	
	Listening (oral)	*Reading* (written)	*Speaking* (oral)	*Writing* (written)
Content				
Phonology				
Structure				
Vocabulary				

Achievement in each of the above areas should be evaluated, even though a certain amount of interaction between areas does exist. Whereas it is possible to perfect the receptive skills in relative isolation, the productive skills are intimately related to the receptive skills: it is in listening to himself that man controls his speech; it is in reading what he has written that man continues his composition. The oral skills of listening and speaking may be taught without reference to the written skills; many are the languages with no written forms. To a lesser extent, reading and writing may be taught separately from the oral skills.

Incorporating the Objectives. The students themselves draw up their version of course objectives primarily according to the types of tests, both informal and formal, that the teacher gives rather than according to the teacher's verbal description of what is to be learned. Consequently the teacher's objectives can be met only if the testing program specifically measures the degree to which each student attains the objectives. For example, high school and college students will fail to develop the desired oral proficiency in the language if the classroom tests utilize only skills of reading and writing.

The teacher should examine his course in the light of the above considerations while planning an hour classroom test or final examination. On a chart (see Diagram II) he would indicate the percentages allotted to each skill and caleulate the appropriate number of questions.

DIAGRAM II

(Spanish Level II, first semester, 50 items)

	Listening	Reading	Speaking	Writing	Total %	Total No.
Phonology					25	13
Structure					50	25
Vocabulary					25	12
Total %	30	20	30	20	100	
Number	15	10	15	10		50

As the items are prepared the teacher enters a mark in the appropriate box.

For brief quizzes given in the classroom or in the laboratory, the teacher would prepare a large sheet of paper under similar headings. Here, however, the procedure is the reverse. After each quiz is given, the 10 or 20 items are analyzed and the appropriate ticks entered in the outline. As the semester progresses, the teacher can tell at a glance if any areas are being overemphasized or neglected and remedy the imbalance in subsequent quizzes.

The Function. The primary function of the classroom test as distinct from a final examination is to contribute in a positive manner to the learning process. Since time given to testing could, at the discretion of the teacher, be devoted to other activities, tests can only be justified if they directly or indirectly enhance language instruction.

First, a well-designed testing program should reinforce the objectives of the instructor. If the entire class is conducted in the target language, then English should only be used for the instructions (the student is not being tested on his ability to understand directions). The test items, however, appear entirely in the foreign language. Mixed sentences, partly in English and partly in the target language, are eliminated as inconsistent with the aims of the course. If an English equivalent must be included to clarify the meaning of the item, then two entire sentences should be used. Thus, whereas homework sentences or test items once read:

Où est Pierre? Je veux— (him) voir.

such questions now appear as:

Où est Pierre? Je veux—voir.
Where is Pierre? I want to see him.

With parallel sentences the student sees that there is no consistent one-to-one or word-to-word correspondence between English and French. In the above item the questions used identical word order, but the second set of sentences point up differences in vocabulary and structure between the two languages. In the audio-lingual classroom tests, only correct forms are used. Consequently on a multiple-choice test all choices are idiomatic and properly spelled, although only one choice constitutes an appropriate answer. If language is to be considered a habit, then only correct habits should be presented as models, even in classroom tests. Finally, audio-lingual examinations include only natural constructions. Contrived sentences containing pitfalls which would confuse even the native speaker are eliminated.

Second, the testing program should stimulate student progress. The test allows the pupil to demonstrate what he has learned; there should be enough easy questions that even the poorer student can gain a certain degree of satisfaction from his performance. If the questions are arranged in order of increasing difficulty, student confidence is built up at the beginning of the test and each student is encouraged to try the next item. The stopping point of the weaker students will, moreover, serve as an indication of their ability. For older students, announced tests provide particular incentive for more conscientious study. From the pedagogical point of view, the classroom test is effective to the degree that the student can learn from his mistakes. If the test can be reviewed immediately after it has been administered, the students remember the items more clearly and are more eager to have their correct responses reinforced and the incorrect responses explained. For longer written tests, the teacher should make every effort to return the papers the following day.

Third, the testing program should help the teacher. Most schools demand some sort of report card, and well-constructed tests facilitate the objective evaluation of student performance. The tests play an even greater role as diagnostic instruments: By studying student performance, the teacher can assess the relative effectiveness of different teaching methods and at the same time discover areas in which the class as a whole, or certain students, may need additional work.

Common Types of Informal Achievement Tests. In the course of instruction the foreign language teacher will be employing three types of informal tests: the unit test or more comprehensive exam, the classroom quiz, and the language laboratory quiz.

The unit tests and comprehensive examinations should be announced in advance. The material covered may be described so that the students may orient their attention to the features on which they will be tested. When an advance description is given, it is quite important that the teacher include all the proposed elements in the test; some students tend to become discouraged and feel cheated if they have spent time mastering points which do not appear on the test. If all skills are being developed, then the test should include both oral and written sections.

The classroom quiz, which may be distinguished from the test because of its brevity, is generally unannounced. Often teachers of older students feel that optimum performance is maintained when the students expect a quiz at any time. The quiz may be given at the beginning of the period, to encourage careful preparation, or towards the end of the period, to stimulate attentive participation in class activities. In either case, it is advisable to allow enough time after the quiz so that the answers may be reviewed, good performance reinforced, and errors corrected. The feature of immediate reinforcement is one of the prime assets of the classroom quiz.

The language laboratory quiz is generally spliced onto the end of the lesson tape and covers the specific elements which have been drilled during the lab period. The primary function of most lab quizzes is to encourage active drill during the laboratory session. The drawback of lab quizzes is the general impracticability of immediate reinforcement.

More comprehensive listening tests and speaking tests may also be administered in the language laboratory. For the latter group, recording facilities of relatively high fidelity are essential.

THE CORE TEST AND THE CONCEPT OF TOTAL MASTERY

It may well appear in retrospect that the most important contribution of the audio-lingual method to the domain of foreign-language teaching was the introduction of the concept of total mastery. The acquisition of a second language was acknowledged to be a cumulative process. No longer did the first-year course present the student with a two-thousand word vocabulary and all the basic structures of the new language and no longer were the second- and third-year texts review grammars designed to present again that material which the student failed to grasp the first time around. On the contrary, at the first level of an audio-lingual course the student would be introduced to a vocabulary of about five-hundred words and a limited amount of structure (present and past tenses of the regular and some irregular verbs, determiners, adjectives, and noun forms), but he would be able to control that material both orally and in written form. Level Two would continue to build on the solid foundation of Level One.

The effectiveness of the audio-lingual materials ultimately depends on the implementation of the total mastery concept at the unit level. The failure of audio-lingual materials in certain classes or school systems can be linked to a disregard for (or ignorance of) the necessity of total mastery. In some cases mastery is falsely equated with the memorization of a dialogue and the recitation of the drills in the book, when in truth these are but the first steps toward mastery, i.e., the complete assimilation of all the structures, lexicon and sound features included in the unit. In other cases the whole class is expected to continue through the course at the rate set by the *A* students who alone have mastered the unit. The disadvantage of the *B, C* and *D* students is aggravated with time; soon the position of the *C* or *D* student becomes just as difficult and illogical as that of the piano student who still has trouble reading the bass clef and who is given a simple Mozart sonata to play at sight.

The core test or mastery test is an essential component of classes built on the total mastery philosophy, for unless the student actively controls the material in Unit X, he should not proceed to Unit Y. Through the completion of Level Two, all performance on tests is scored on a pass/fail basis with a cutoff point of 95%. The core test of Unit One provides a balanced sampling of the lexicon, structure and sound features in that unit. If a student scores 95% or better, he is allowed to continue to Unit Two. If he scores below 95%, he must continue working with the material in Unit One (preferably in a somewhat different format) until he can pass the

Unit One core test. When the student has in this manner worked his way through Levels One and Two, he has acquired a solid foundation in the foreign language.

In the future let us hope that all students will reach Level Two mastery in a foreign language. This will require different amounts of time for different students, depending on their abilities and on the age at which they begin foreign language study. And let us also hope that colleges will demand a certain level of language mastery rather than a given number of years spent sitting in the language classroom.

"Objective" Testing Techniques. The teacher should make every effort to perfect the objectivity of his testing techniques. An objective test or an objective test item is one in which a precise answer is expected; consequently the student's performance can easily be classified as right or wrong. True-false questions and multiple-choice items possess high objectivity. Yet even essay questions, notorious for their subjective scoring, may be rendered more or less objective if the teacher takes the time to think out the desired responses and plan a tentative scoring system.

The two primary attributes of a good test are reliability and validity. The *reliable* test is dependable: Student scores obtained one day are almost the same as student scores obtained on a second administration. All students perform the same tasks; thus, on an oral quiz, each student is asked the same questions (as is possible, for example, in the language laboratory), or all students are asked similar questions and the responses graded in an identical manner. All students are given the test under similar conditions; if a student is ill, his performance on that test is an unreliable indication of his capabilities. All papers are identically scored: Multiple-choice tests and written tests requiring specific responses enjoy high scorer reliability. Finally, the test is long enough so that the items offer a good sampling of the body of knowledge or skill to be evaluated. An item is reliable if the better students answer it correctly and the poorer students incorrectly. Reliability may be expressed statistically in terms of correlation coefficients comparing two variables such as alternate forms of the same test, alternate items, performances on the same group of students on different days, or test scores and teacher grades; item reliability compares the performance of the better students with that of the poor students on a given item.

The test is *valid* if it measures that which it is purported to measure; language tests must be primarily checked for content validity: Are the items representative of the course objectives? A written Spanish-English vocabulary test may possess extremely high reliability, but it is valid only as a test of ability to pair items of Spanish-English vocabulary; it does not assess student ability to write or speak Spanish, and not even the ability to use the vocabulary correctly in natural utterances. The various components of language and the four skills must all be the object of specific tests if a valid and comprehensive testing program is to be instituted.

The foreign language teacher by experience is very conscious of the efficient use of available time. If daily quizzes and weekly tests are given, however brief the quizzes and tests may be, they must be graded outside of the classroom. Thus, for most teachers, scorer economy is a consideration of utmost importance. Fortunately the first levels of foreign language instruction lend themselves to multiple-choice tests which can be administered with teacher-made answer sheets. Listening comprehension tests, reading comprehension tests, reading tests of vocabulary and structure all may be effectively adapted to the multiple-choice framework. Once the teacher has punched the answer grid for a quiz, even one-hundred papers can be graded in a matter of minutes.[1] Although the score on any given multiple-choice quiz may be influenced by guessing on the part of students, the total performance on a series of daily quizzes yields quite a reliable evaluation of student achievement in the areas being tested.

Evaluating the Listening Skill

The listening skill is the first to be developed in the audio-lingual sequence. All students, except those with physical deficiencies, are able to "hear" languages, but in the foreign language classroom, students learn to "listen," to attach meaning to what they hear. The initial training in discriminating among the sounds of the target language prepares the student to check his own performance as he repeats dialogues and responds to structure drills. Let us examine the attributes typical of the listening skill.

1. For a description of answer sheets to be used in conjunction with multiple-choice listening comprehension tests, see R. Valette, "Oral Objective Testing in the Classroom", *German Quarterly*, Vol. 38, No. 2, March 1965. A more detailed presentation is given in R. Valette, *Foreign Language Tests* (New York: Harcourt Brace & World, 1967).

One problem in listening comprehension is presented by what the linguists call "minimal pairs," words that differ only by one phoneme. An English example may clarify this concept. Many foreigners learning English have trouble distinguishing the vowel sounds in "ham," "hem" and "hymn." A listening comprehension item testing this problem would read:

Directions: Choose the logical rejoinder:
Example: She has prepared ham.

      A. Well, let's sit down to eat.
      B. And Mother has offered to sew it for me.
      C. So let's sing it through to see how it sounds.

Correct Answer: A

Had the student understood "hem," the completion mentioning sewing would have seemed plausible; had he understood "hymn" he might have imagined a choir rehearsal.

A second problem unique to the listening skill is the comprehension of rapid conversation. To understand longer sentences, the student must increase his retention span and learn to pick out key words. Moreover, he must recognize reduced forms, such as "jeet jet?" for "did you eat yet?", "chepa" for "je ne sais pas," and "jachaps" for "ja, ich habe es." Recorded listening comprehension tests, presenting a quick dialogue followed by clearly enunciated questions and multiple-choice responses can validly measure the student's ability to understand rapid speech.

Many other types of listening tests exist. Inasmuch as they measure comprehension of a distinctly recorded conversation or passage which is not built around minimal sound distinctions, such tests primarily evaluate student acquisition of structure and vocabularly via the listening skill. Even students with poor discrimination and no training in rapid conversation will do well on such examinations if they are familiar with the content of the items.

So far we have discussed pure listening tests, those in which the entire examination is recorded and the student indicates only a letter response on an answer sheet. In the 1930's phonetic accuracy tests were developed in a multiple-choice format. Since the skills of reading and writing were receiving greater emphasis in the classroom, the student's listening discrimination could be reliably measured in relation to the printed word. Were such a test given in English, the recorded voice would state once, "He's sleeping." The student would select the proper phrase among the following:

A. He's sleeping.
B. He's slipping.
C. He's leaping.

In the audio-lingual classroom, where the spoken language is presented before the written language, such items at Level One tend to become spelling tests in that they measure the relationship between the sounds, which are already familiar, and the printed word.

Some commercial listening tests, currently in use, are administered with an answer booklet. The student hears a recorded conversation or passage and then answers either spoken or printed questions by indicating his selection among the suggested responses he reads in the booklet. The student who reads with difficulty and is more at ease with the spoken language will be at a disadvantage in this type of "listening" test. (The first standardized listening examinations, employed in the 1920's, avoided this possible danger by presenting the printed section entirely in English.)

SAMPLE LISTENING TEST ITEMS

1. Discrimination of sounds

An initial step toward the evaluation of student proficiency in the mechanical aspects of the spoken language is verifying the student's ability to differentiate between the phonetic features (sounds, stress patterns, intonations and rhythm) of the target language and those of English. Variations of the following types of items may be employed:

1.a. Same vs. different

Directions: You will hear three words (or phrases). Indicate on your answer sheet which word or phrase is different from the other two.

Example: (Italian) A. il   B. eel   C. il
Correct Answer: B

Directions: You will hear one word. After a slight pause you will hear two more words. Listen whether either or both of the two words are exactly the same as the first word. Indicate your answer as follows:

A. Word (1) only is the same as the first word

B. Word (2) only is the same as the first word

C. Words (1) and (2) are both the same as the first word

D. Neither word is the same as the first word

Example: (French) as-tu vu? (1) a tout vu? (2) a tout vu?

Correct Answer: D

1.b. Rhyme

Directions: You will hear one word. After a slight pause you will hear four more words. Indicate which of the four words rhymes perfectly with the initial word.

Example: (German) Tur A. view B. fur C. nur D. Ruhr

Correct Answer: B

1.c. Meaning

(Such items are built around familiar minimal pairs; a change in one phonetic trait produces a change in meaning.)

Directions: You will hear two short sentences. Select the one which describes the picture in your test booklet.

Example: (German) A. Das ist eine Kirche.

B. Das ist eine Kirsche.

Correct Answer: B

Directions: You will hear a single sentence followed by sentences A and B. Select the sentence which best completes the idea expressed in the initial sentence.

Example: (French) Robert habite au quatrième et les Dufour habitent au-dessus.

A. Alors l'appartement des Dufour est au troisième.

B. Alors l'appartement des Dufour est au cinquième.

Correct Answer: B (implicit discrimination between *au-dessus* and *au-dessous, above* and *below*)

Directions: You will hear a sentence. In your test booklet you will see two interpretations of the sentence. Select the most appropriate description of the sentence you have just heard.

Example: (Spanish) Sí, ésta.

A. Yes, this one.

B. Yes, it is.

Correct Answer: A (recognition of stressed syllable plus meaning of stress)

2. Listening comprehension: movement

In the elementary school, and often in the secondary school, listening comprehension may be informally tested with commands requiring movement. The students perform the acts requested by the teacher.

Example: (French) Mettez-vous debout.

                   Pierre, lève la main droite.

                   Anne, met l'horloge à deux heures dix.

3. Listening comprehension: drawing

In this type of listening comprehension test, the students are asked to draw specific pictures (a house, a flower, etc.), to use specific colors, etc. Instructions are in the target language. (A similar type of item has the students draw a certain number of objects, or even write down the numbers in arabic numerals.)

4. Listening comprehension: discrete items

Discrete listening comprehension items, for which the student indicates his response on an answer sheet, are extremely versatile. They may be used with both beginning and advanced students to test simple comprehension, comprehension of rapid speech, vocabulary, structure, and even intonation and stress. The student papers can be scored objectively and rapidly. Several days before giving the test, the teacher prepares the test script; the day before the test the script is reworded, ambiguous items are revised, and, if the test is to be given in the laboratory or over a tape recorder, the script is recorded. Only two or three of the following types of items should be employed on a given test in order to minimize the time necessary for instructions and to allow the students to concentrate primarily on item content.

4.a. True-false

Directions: If the statement is true, blacken space A on your answer sheet.

                If the statement is false, blacken space B.

Example: (French) La neige est rose en hiver.

Correct Answer: B

4.b. Question-answer

Directions: You will hear a question followed by a series of responses. Select the most logical answer to the question and mark the corresponding space on your answer sheet.

Example: (German) Wann essen Sie?
    A. Um sechs.
    B. Auf der Strasse.
    C. Mit meiner Familie.

Correct Answer: A

  4.c. Statement-rejoinder

Directions: You will hear a sentence followed by a series of additional sentences. Among the group of sentences, select the one which would most obviously be made by another person who wanted to continue the conversation along the same lines.

Example: (Italian) Parlo con lo studio del dottor Rossini?
    A. Guardo l'agenda.
    B. Buona sera, dottore.
    C. Si, dica pure.

Correct Answer: C

  4.d. Completion of thought

Directions: You will hear a sentence followed by a series of sentences. (Alternate version: You will hear a partial sentence followed by a series of possible completions.) Select the sentence (or phrase) which most appropriately completes the original sentence (or phrase).

Example: (French) Quand j'ai faim je vais
    A. à l'école
    B. au restaurant
    C. le commencement

Correct Answer: B

  4.e. Adapted structure drills

The directions for a structure drill are given. At the discretion of the teacher, a model may also be included. For each item the cue is read followed by three (or more) possible responses. The students indicate the correct response by blackening the corresponding space on the answer sheet.

4.f. Identification of forms

Students are given a key and asked to indicate, for example, whether the subject of the sentence is singular or plural, or whether the action occurred in the past, in the present, or will occcur in the future.

5. Listening comprehension: passage items

Students hear part of a dialogue or a prose passage. Length of the material and speed of delivery will depend on the level of the class. For a pure listening comprehension test, related oral items of the true-false or multiple-choice variety ask students to identify speakers and situations, and to answer questions about the test they have just heard.

The skills of reading and writing can be introduced into such listening comprehension tests by using printed question and/or answers, or by having students give written responses to questions. Such mixed tests evaluate the student's familiarity with vocabulary and structure but do not offer a reliable assessment of proficiency in a given skill.

Evaluating the Speaking Skill

Development of the speaking skill has become a fundamental aim of audio-lingual language programs. The student who can speak the target language fluently, can normally understand what others say and, with an introduction to the spelling system of the language, learn to read and write the language which he commands orally. In the speaking skill, two levels of language are most apparent: the mechanical level requires accurate pronunciation and intonation, proper use of stress, and fluent expression; the understanding level is mastered when the student can formulate his own ideas, and express them in the target language so as to be understood by his listeners. Within his own experience, each teacher probably knows people of foreign origin who communicate in English but have little notion of the pronunciation features of the language. On the other hand, he may have had students who were able to recite dialogues and respond to patterns with near native fluency and yet could not communicate in less structured surroundings where the stimulus of familiar cues was lacking. Both levels must be developed.

Student mastery of the mechanical level of the spoken language can be evaluated quite objectively, although grades based on a subjective appreciation of the student's class performance are highly unreliable. In recent years testing methods have been improved; trained scorers, often working in groups, have demonstrated the possibility of rating student performance in a reliable fashion. Specific aspects of each utterance are scored, but the student does not know in advance what the examiner will listen for in a given statement.[2]

If students are to be evaluated on their pronunciation of a certain sound or on the intonation pattern they give a particular phrase, then all must utter the same sentence. It appears almost impossible to utilize a pure speaking test to elicit such a response. Consequently other means are employed: The student recites or records a memorized passage or poem; the student repeats a sentence he hears on the tape; the student answers a specific pre-recorded question according to a model response; the student reads a printed passage or sentence. In the audio-lingual curriculum, spoken cues or directions seem preferable at the elementary levels. Advanced students more familiar with the printed word may record sentences read from a test booklet. At this point in their training they are less likely to allow the written forms to interfere with their pronunciation. Tests in which students read aloud have the advantage of cutting the scoring time in half since the judges need not listen to spoken cues. Student performance can be reliably judged on passages as short as four to six lines.[3]

In a pure speaking test the student is asked to talk about a suggested topic, to describe a picture, or to give directions according to a map or diagram. Such tests, scored on fluency and overall quality, are generally administered as the final section of a longer examination.

SAMPLE SPEAKING TEST ITEMS

1. Mimicry and memorization

In the mimicry or memorization speaking test the students speak predetermined sentences. In the mimicry test the student repeats a sentence after a model. In the memorization test he recites a dialogue, passage or poem which he has prepared in advance; dialogues may be

---

2. For suggestions on objective scoring of speaking tests, see R. Valette, *Foreign Language Tests;* G. Scherer and M. Wertheimer, *A Psycholinguistic Experiment in Foreign Language Teaching* (New York: McGraw-Hill, 1964), Chap. 5; E. Stack, *The Language Laboratory and Modern Language Teaching*, rev. ed. (New York: Oxford, 1966), Chap. 11.

3. See Scherer and Wertheimer, *ibid.*

recited between two students. The teacher has prepared a scoring sheet which lists the features being evaluated in the speech sample; for dialogues the teacher must establish parallel grading systems so that both participants are graded on the same features.

2. Lightning translation

Some teachers of the modified audio-lingual method obtain good results with lightning translation tests. The emphasis is on rapidity and fluency and not on "translation" of the word-by-word or phrase-by-phrase variety. The teacher gives an entire English sentence once and the student responds immediately with the target language equivalent. Such tests, primarily used with older students (high school and college), are based on dialogues, pattern sentences or variations of the two. If a student cannot give the entire sentence in the target language right away, he receives no credit. If many students have trouble, further drill on the patterns is needed.

Example: (Spanish) When he wasn't teaching, he would pass the time whittling with a pocketknife.

Correct answer: Cuando no enseñaba, pasaba el tiempo tallando con un cortaplumas.

3. Visual cues

Visual cues may be effectively used to elicit spoken responses. Dates, numbers, arithmetical operations and the time of day may be indicated on flashcards or, in the latter case, on a clock with movable hands. Composite pictures may be used together with a series of appropriate questions utilizing known structure and vocabulary.

4. Pattern drills

Oral structure drills lend themselves automatically to oral testing. For the teacher, the prime consideration will be the preparation of a scoring sheet which indicates the aspects of the performance to be evaluated.

5. Directed speech

In directed speech a conversational stimulus is used, but the students are told beforehand how to respond. The simplest version of this type of speaking test utilizes questions to be answered affirmatively or negatively with whole sentences. Within the classroom, directed dialogues may be used; one student is told to ask another a question and the second is told how to respond. Students may be evaluated on use of modified structure and word order as well as fluency and pronunciation. To insure scorer reliability and objectivity, a scoring sheet should be prepared in advance so that all students are graded on the same features of their performance. The difficulty level should be kept constant.

6. Reading aloud

Reading aloud is a special skill which is generally not introduced until the later levels of language learning. Nevertheless, the reading of a short paragraph of four to six lines provides an identical basis of judgment for the teacher eager to evaluate the pronunciation of intermediate and advanced students. The text should be familiar or use familiar vocabulary and structure. The students are given a short time to prepare the sentences and told to read them as if they were talking to a friend. (The use of new words and complex structures will inhibit student performance and the reading aloud test will no longer be as valid an instrument of student speaking ability.)

7. Free responses

Once the students have mastered the mechanical aspects of the spoken language, aspects evaluated in the above types of tests, the teacher may wish to see how well the student can use the language as a means of communication. In a free response test, the student is encouraged to formulate his own ideas and to talk about whatever subject interests him. Sometimes teachers present a picture to stimulate the less imaginative students; merely a description is acceptable. An unrehearsed conversation either with the teacher, or, preferably, with another native speaker (so that the teacher can judge student performance more objectively) gives the student an opportunity to show how well he can use the spoken language.

Evaluating the Reading Skill

The reading skill is characterized by speed and the recognition of structure in long or complex sentences. Reading comprehension, in this sense, is similar to reading comprehension in English, an area in which not all American students attain equal proficiency. The speed with which a student reads the foreign language can be measured by timing student performance on a reading comprehension test, or, more objectively, by administering a long test which the students are unable to finish within a given period of time.

When it comes to reading, the advocates of the New Key insist on no more "decoding." If the student is really to *read* the foreign language without mentally translating, new words should not be introduced too frequently at the early levels. In accordance with these objectives, reading comprehension items in the early levels should hinge primarily on structure and assess student ability to recognize the key structures of the language.

SAMPLE READING TEST ITEMS

1. Pre-reading items

For languages using an alphabet which differs from the Roman alphabet used in English, pre-reading instruction becomes a necessity. Pre-reading quizzes, which break the monotony of the instruction, are usually timed: The student compares two or more words or sentences to decide which are identical.

2. Discrete reading items: vocabulary

Individual reading items may be built to evaluate primarily comprehension of vocabulary. Completion and question-answer items provide a convenient multiple-choice framework for vocabulary tests which comply with the requirements of the audio-lingual method. Lists of words are avoided and vocabulary items are presented in a natural context.

2.a. Direct vocabulary item

Directions: Select the phrase closest in meaning to the underlined words.

Example.   (French) Marie assiste au cours d'espagnol.

  A. est présente
  B. aide le professeur
  C. est professeur
  D. regarde le professeur

Correct Answer: A

2.b. Indirect vocabulary item

Directions: Select the appropriate completion among the choices given.

Example: Espérate. Tengo que _____ el coche.

  A. aterrizar
  B. entender
  C. anunciar
  D. estacionar

Correct Answer: D

3. Discrete reading items: grammar

Multiple choice items utilizing the reading skill can also effectively test the student's knowledge of the structure of the language. Completion items lend themselves particularly well to the testing of grammar.

Directions: Complete the following sentences by selecting the appropriate word or phrase.

Example 1: (French) J'ai beaucoup de travail _____.
      A. faire
      B. à faire
      C. de faire.

Example 2: (German) Die Frau sucht _____ Hund.
      A. der
      B. des
      C. dem
      D. den

Correct Answers: 1: B, 2: D

4. Discrete reading items: general comprehension

A single reading item can incorporate both vocabulary and structure; the choice of the correct response depends on the general comprehension of the item. Here is one type of multiple-choice item:

Directions: Among the choices select the sentence which best explains the initial sentence.

Example: (English): I went to bed at eight-thirty last night.
      A. I was very tired.
      B. Nine would be too many.
      C. They serve excellent pizza.

Correct Answer: A

5. Passage comprehension

The traditional type of reading test, and the mainstay of commercial standardized tests, is the passage followed by comprehension items. In the classroom the teacher may either compose a paragraph or take a section from assigned outside reading. The accompanying question could be based on grammar, vocabulary or general comprehension; true-false items may also be used. If both reading and retention are being evaluated, the students are allotted a specific time to read the passage; then the passages are collected and the reading questions distributed afterwards.

6. Reading speed

Since one of the characteristics of the reading skill is speed, some teachers may wish to assess how fluently their students are reading the foreign language. A relatively easy but lengthy passage is selected; nonsense words are inserted at irregular intervals and the modified passage is mimeographed. The students are given a specific period of time to read the passage. As they read they are to cross out the obvious nonsense words. When time is called, the score is based on the number of nonsense words crossed out correctly. (Not only do the better students read faster, but they recognize the nonsense words more rapidly.)

Evaluating the Writing Skill

The student learning a foreign language passes through a series of steps in order to develop the writing skill. The mechanics, the spelling, the grammatical correctness of a sentence, the construction of a paragraph must all be mastered before the student can aspire to precision, fluency and style. Classroom tests must consequently be structured so as to measure student progress toward the acquisition of this fourth skill.

Historically, writing was first a system of visual communication utilizing first pictures and then characters. Syllabaries (such as Hebrew and Arabic) brought writing closer to the spoken word; Greece gave civilization the alphabet which facilitated the transcription of both consonant and vowel sounds. As written forms developed, each language modified the system of punctuation so that certain aspects of speech, transmitted by intonation patterns in the spoken language, could be transcribed. But the written form of language was never meant to be a faithful rendering of speech. Written language developed its own conventions and, particularly since the invention of printing, has exerted a conservative influence on further language development.

Even now, in languages possessing a written and a spoken form, native speakers will tolerate a certain "foreign" accent if it does not interfere with communication. But the margin of tolerance as regards written language is narrow. The emphasis is on accuracy in spelling and grammar. In presenting the writing skill, teachers should emphasize perfection: Students are encouraged to write only structures they can handle with relative fluency; spelling is systematically introduced.

Forty years ago almost all extramural language tests were written tests. The advent of the standardized language examination brought with it the introduction of completion items. Soon the recognized ease and economy of mechanical scoring relegated writing tests to the classroom. Currently, the MLA tests and the experimental Pimsleur tests are reintroducing writing samples, which generally evaluate the student's active knowledge or recall of foreign language usage and structure. Since objectivity requires that a single specific response be elicited, such tests may assume the form of fill-in-the-blank passages or sentence transformation exercises. The authors of "New Key" materials, trying to avoid translation by elementary and intermediate students, have popularized two new types of writing tests: the "dehydrated" sentence and the structure retention item.

SAMPLE WRITING TEST ITEMS

1. Pre-writing tests

For languages whose written forms are built on a different alphabet or system of characters, early instruction is in pre-writing, that is, copying words and sentences. In Russian, since the written script differs from the printed form, a pre-writing test may consist of having students copy by hand a printed dialogue. To encourage fluency, pre-writing tests may be timed; student performance is graded both on accuracy and on the amount of material transcribed.

2. Dictation

If the writing skill is introduced after the listening skill has been presented, material to be transcribed can be dictated by the teacher or pre-recorded on tape for use either in the classroom or in the language laboratory. At the elementary level the teacher may wish to assign a text for dictation in advance and then read the material a whole sentence at a time; at the time of the test the material is neither repeated nor read in short breath groups. For all dictations it is important to announce in advance how the material will be presented and to refuse to repeat any sections or phrases at student request.

3. Patterns

Almost all pattern drills can be adapted for writing tests. Substitution drills, transformation drills, question and answers, and directed sentences can be used. The stimulus can be oral (utilizing the listening skill) or written (using the reading skill). Connected paragraphs (printed stimulus) can serve as the base for general transposition exercises: present to past, direct discourse to indirect discourse, singular to plural, etc.

4. Fill-in-the-blanks

In the audio-lingual classroom, traditional fill-in-the-blank exercises with the key words given in English have been discarded on linguistic grounds. The juxtaposition of English and the target language negates the aim of coordinate bilingualism, that is, the coexistence of two distinct linguistic systems. In a modified form, however, fill-in-the-blank items can be effectively used for testing purposes. The blanks represent "little" words, whose meaning is abundantly clear from the context in which they occur: articles, subject pronouns and auxiliary verbs, for example, can be omitted from the paragraph.

Examples: (Spanish) Neustras ventanas daban _____ plaza. (a la)
(German) Die Katze schläft neben _____ Hund. (dem)
(French) Jean-Pierre partira _____ Canada. (au)

5. Structure retention items

The student is given a model sentence. Below this sentence some new words, such as nouns, adjectives and verbs, are given. The student reconstructs another sentence using the new vocabulary but retaining the structure of the original sentence.

Example: (English) The children don't like the older boys.
                    Mary / sell / good / painting
Correct Response: Mary doesn't sell the better paintings.

6. Dehydrated sentences

The student is given a series of words with which to write a sentence; he will add the necessary articles and prepositions and modify the key words in order to construct a fluent sentence. This type of presentation may also be incorporated into completion items in order to test sequence of tenses.

Example: (Spanish) Mientras / viajar / ponerse / enfermo
Correct Response: Mientras viajaba, me puse enfermo
Example: (French) Je quitterai Paris quand Allemands / venir.
Correct Response: Je quitterai Paris quand les Allemands viendront.

7. Composition

The composition, first of paragraphs and later of longer essays, may be considered the epitome of the writing skill. For elementary and intermediate students, composition tests are to some extent directed by the teacher: Not only is the grading more objective but students are encouraged to remain within the limits of known structure and vocabulary.

7.a. Suggested sentences

Students are informed, either orally or in writing, what to say in each sentence. Such instructions may be given in English or in the target language. Direct translation, however, is avoided.

Example: Write a letter to Paul who is in New York. Tell him you arrived in Madrid two days ago and that the weather is warm, even a bit too warm. Let him know that you visited the Prado Museum yesterday and were particularly impressed by the El Greco collection. Tomorrow you plan to take a trip to Toledo and that you will send him a postcard from there.

7.b. Resumes

Students are asked to write a brief resume (the teacher may wish to indicate the approximate length) of a selection read and studied in class.

7.c. Suggested vocabulary

Students are given a list of words which they are to incorporate into a brief paragraph. In addition, they may be asked to write the paragraph about past events or about a future project. Such a test allows the student to exhibit his originality and creativity within the limitations of his language ability.

7.d Suggested topics

The topic for a composition may be suggested orally or in writing. To facilitate scoring, a number of questions or aspects of the subject may be mentioned. Some teachers select a picture representing a subject corresponding to the students' vocabulary. The students may be asked to describe a picture, to tell a story about the picture, or both.

Commercial Tests: Their Uses and Limitations

Commercial tests fall into two general categories: tests distributed by textbook publishers (often with taped listening tests included) and the standardized tests designed for larger student populations.

Many publishers are now advertising test programs to accompany specific textbooks. Some of these programs have been put together quite hurriedly and the teacher would do well to examine the tests in the light of his own particular objectives. The teacher may wish to utilize some of the items and add supplementary questions. With older students the danger exists that over the years the content and answers to the textbook tests may become general knowledge; student performance would then be an unreliable reflection of true ability.

Teachers and students are familiar with the wide variety of standardized tests administered from time to time during the student's career from elementary school to college. Most of these tests use a test booklet and a machine-scored answer sheet on which the student indicates his choice of responses. In the foreign languages additional elements are introduced. Listening comprehension tests require a tape recorder or sound system to present the spoken language. Speaking tests necessitate the existence and proper functioning of recording equipment: Objective scoring is attained by means of a carefully planned scoring sheet and careful training of the scorers. Writing tests must also be hand-scored; again objectivity requires that a precise system of scoring be drawn up in advance.

In the following sections we will describe briefly a few of the current language tests grouped acording to categories: prognostic tests, achievement tests and placement tests.

Prognostic Tests. Prognostic tests are used to assess student aptitude, an elusive quality at best. Two performance factors which the most successful students usually possess are a high IQ and high motivation, although great strength in one area can counterbalance lesser strength in the other. For the majority of the students, however, guidance counselors often utilize an additional instrument to help decide whether a particular student should take foreign languages. Here are two current language aptitude tests designed for guidance purposes:

• John B. Carroll and Stanley M. Sapon, *Modern Language Aptitude Test* (New York: Psychological Corporation, 1959). Used with tape recording.

- *Pimsleur Language Aptitude Battery* (New York: Harcourt, Brace & World, Inc., 1966). This prognostic test covers six factors: grade point average, interest, vocabulary (as an indicator of verbal intelligence), language analysis, sound discrimination and sound/symbol association. For use with students grades 6–12.

Achievement Tests. Standardized foreign language achievement tests are available in the modern languages most currently taught in the high schools. Here are some of the more recent language achievement tests which reflect to a greater or lesser degree the changes wrought by the introduction of the audio-lingual curriculum:

- *MLA Cooperative Foreign Language Tests* (Princeton, N.J.: Educational Testing Service). The tests are available in French, German, Italian, Russian, and Spanish for Level "L" (one or two years secondary school) and Level "M" (three or four years secondary school). Each test contains four sections: listening, speaking, reading, and writing. Tapes are used with the listening and the speaking tests.

- *College Board Achievement Tests* (Princeton, N.J.: Educational Testing Service). These tests are administered around the country at afternoon sessions about five times a year. The tests are composed by a rotating committee of high school teachers and university professors. Achievement tests are available in French, German, Hebrew, Russian and Spanish. The difficulty range is wide enough to challenge fourth-year as well as second-year language students. The general types of questions (all incorporating the reading skill) include situation questions, usage questions, vocabulary questions and reading comprehension.

- *College Board Supplementary Achievement Tests* (Princeton, N. J.: Educational Testing Service). These tests are made available to secondary schools for administration on a single date in February, and they may be taken only by students who have registered for one or more College Board Achievement Tests. Supplementary Achievement Tests exist in Italian, French Listening Comprehension, German Listening Comprehension, Spanish Listening Comprehension, Russian Listening Comprehension and Italian Listening Comprehension. The listening comprehension tests are based on taped material; the tests run approximately 30 minutes.

- *Pimsleur Proficiency Tests* (New York: Harcourt, Brace & World, 1967). These tests are designed for use in the first three levels of foreign language study. Proficiency tests are available in French, German and Spanish. Four separate tests evaluate achievement in the different language skills; the listening and speaking tests are tape-oriented.

• *New York State Regents Examinations* (New York: Department of Education). These achievement tests are given in secondary schools in New York. The tests, primarily reading comprehension, exist for the following languages: French, German, Hebrew, Italian, Russian and Spanish.

• *Affiliation Testing Program* (Washington, D. C.: Catholic University of America). These achievement tests each cover a two-year secondary program of studies. The fields included are French, Spanish and German.

• *MLA Foreign Language Proficiency Tests for Teachers and Advanced Students* (Princeton, N. J.: Educational Testing Service). These confidential tests are available only to university department chairmen, educators and NDEA Institutes for the purpose of evaluating the proficiency of language majors and teacher candidates. The tests, available in three equivalent forms, consist of seven parts: professional preparation, and, for each of the languages, culture, applied linguistics and four tests in the skills. The tests exist in French, German, Spanish, Russian and Italian.

• *AATG Cooperative Tests* (American Association of Teachers of German). German tests at two levels: lower level (two years high school or one year college), higher level (four years high school or two years college). These reading tests cover grammatical skill, structural recognition, and general comprehension.

Placement Tests. Placement tests are primarily employed by colleges and universities to place incoming students with language training in the appropriate courses. Generally it is advisable for a school to develop its own placement program in the light of its specific requirements. The following tests may be used for placement purposes:

• *College Board Achievement Tests and Supplementary Achievement Tests* (see above). Schools may buy retired copies of the achievement tests for local administration. (Since the tests are recent, it is possible that some incoming students will have already taken that particular form of the test and obtain a higher but unreliable score.)

• *College Board Advanced Placement Tests.* (Princeton, N. J.: Educational Testing Service). These tests, available in French, Spanish and German, are administered to students who have taken a specialized course of study in secondary school. The emphasis is literary and a reading list is communicated in advance.[4] Participating universities interpret the scores in relation to their own course offerings.

The Misuse of Commercial Tests. It is unfortunate that in our test-oriented society, pressures from parents and administrators can mount to such a point that teachers and students, often in connivance, try to outwit the "system."

One potential danger of commercial tests is that the teachers tend to modify objectives to coincide with the areas covered in the commercial test. Were the commercial tests perfect instruments of evaluation which adequately sampled proficiency in the four language skills in the areas of phonology, structure and vocabulary, such a tendency could even be beneficial for the weaker teachers. However, time limitations governing standardized examinations are such that some areas receive increased emphasis while others are skipped over. It is the responsibility of the teachers and the schools to class objectives to reflect the needs of the community and the ability of the students.

The College Boards and the New York Regents are printed objective tests. Many of the items on these measure grammatical usage and vocabulary rather than general comprehension. A surprisingly large percentage of items on the MLA Cooperative Tests and the Pimsleur Reading Comprehension Tests also hinge directly on vocabulary. This factor might account for some of the coolness which certain teachers have shown the audio-lingual materials. Many teachers find themselves indirectly judged by their students' performance on such reading comprehension tests. Eager to have their second and third-year students do well on the College Boards, some teachers have been supplementing the new audio-lingual materials with outside reading in an effort to increase their students' vocabulary. The teachers also realize that most present standardized listening examinations have written options and that consequently unless the student knows how to read he paradoxically won't pass a listening comprehension test.

---

4. For sample copies and a brief discussion of the Advanced Placement Test, please consult: *The French Review,* XXXIX, Dec. 1965, pp. 439-456; *German Quarterly,* XXXVIII, Sept. 1965, pp. 415-528.

The gravest misuse of standardized examinations is the overt practice of teaching for the test. Students are coached to do poorly the first time so as to show significant improvement on the second administration. Where limited forms exist, such as the case for the MLA Cooperative Tests, a few teachers have gone so far as to drill items from the test in class and even give out answer keys to be memorized. Such practices are ruinous. The measurement of student achievement is a legitimate factor in language teaching, but the ultimate aim must always remain the development of student proficiency in the target language.

Bibliography

Cooperative Test Division. "Modern Languages: Teaching and Testing". (Princeton, N. J.: Educational Testing Service, n.d.) This work kit, designed to accompany a filmstrip program, contains sample items from the MLA Cooperative Tests and a useful article by Nelson Brooks entitled "Making Your Own Language Tests".

Lado, Robert. *Language Testing. The Construction and Use of Foreign Language Tests.* (New York: McGraw-Hill Book Company, 1964).

Valette, Rebecca M. *Foreign Language Tests.* (New York: Harcourt, Brace & World, 1967).

CHAPTER FIVE

Audio-Lingual Materials

by

Glen D. Willbern

Director of Statistical Research

Modern Language Association of America

Most introductory textbooks produced before 1960 gave a more prominent role to reading and writing in the early learning stages than the advocates of the audio-lingual approach are now willing to accept. In the transition period between the traditional textbooks and the completely new materials developed with audio-lingual orientation, many publishers issued revisions of older books, in which the changes consisted chiefly of new exercises grafted onto the original text, and of tapes on which many of the drills were recorded.

Since 1960, however, several completely new series with audio-lingual orientation have been produced. Typically, these consist not merely of a textbook but of a whole package of "integrated" materials: textbook, student's manual and workbook, teacher's manual, discs, filmstrips, and tapes. Other series are in preparation.

Representative samples of integrated materials which have appeared since 1961 are cited below. The titles are taken from a bulletin entitled "Source Materials for Secondary School Teachers of Foreign

Language," prepared by Esther M. Eaton and Mary E. Hayes and published by the U.S. Office of Education. Mention of these titles does not imply endorsement or evaluation, nor should any significance be attached to the omission of any title.

Holt, Rinehart and Winston has produced series in French, German, and Spanish. Presented in the audio-lingual approach, they are designed for beginning study in the 7th, 8th, or 9th grade and continuing through the 12th grade. Each series is composed of a student's book and a teacher's edition, workbook, tests and grading charts, and cue cards. Disc recordings and tapes are available for home, classroom, or laboratory work.

A series called *Audio-Lingual Materials* has been produced by Harcourt, Brace & World for secondary school courses in French, German, Italian, Russian, and Spanish. Included in each series are student's text, teacher's manual, practice record set, student text answer forms, record and tape sets for classroom or laboratory practice and testing, dialogue posters, and cue cards.

McGraw-Hill's *Learning French (Spanish) the Modern Way* is a two-year series consisting of tapes, films, filmstrips, student practice discs, student text, teacher's manual, and student tests.

Spanish for Secondary Schools, published by D. C. Heath, is designed for beginning study in the 7th, 8th, or 9th grade and continuing through the 12th grade. The set is composed of a student's text, teacher's manual, student practice records, teacher's laboratory records and tapes, wall charts, and cue pictures.

Two courses have been produced by Encyclopaedia Britannica Films: *El Español por el Mundo, La Familia Fernández,* which is listed as the first level of a three-year integrated course, including 54 sound-color films and filmstrips, drill and test tapes, student's text, and teacher's manual; and *Je Parle Français,* described as a "film-tape-text" two- or three-year course.

Proponents of a new approach to language learning have not confined their attention to the modern languages. The University of Michigan Press has published a two-year series for secondary schools entitled *Elementary Latin: The Basic Structures.* This course is based upon modern linguistic analysis rather than the traditional semantically-based grammar, though it has kept the traditional terminology. Filmstrips are available, and the use of tapes is recommended.

A Spanish series, intended primarily for college use, has been published as a project of the Modern Language Association. It consists of an elementary text, *Modern Spanish* (second edition), which is accompanied by a teacher's manual, discs, and tapes, and a follow-up course, *Continuing Spanish* (I, II), with teacher's manual and student workbooks. The elementary course is designed to develop some proficiency in the audio-lingual skills; the second course is intended to give some skill in reading and writing while maintaining and reinforcing the audio-lingual skills.

Since this series was developed from the first step to the last as not merely a new book but a new kind of book incorporating the principles of the audio-lingual approach, it may be instructive to examine its organization in some detail on the theory that an example will do more to illuminate the theory than a set of generalizations.

The same principles are applicable at all levels, so that the implementation devised for one level may be adapted to another. The course concentrates at the beginning on the learner's hearing and speaking the language, whatever his level or his objective. Pronunciation, therefore, receives an unusually full treatment. In *Modern Spanish,* pronunciation exercises continue through a full third of the course, with extensive drills on intonation patterns as well as on the sounds.

The heart of each lesson is a dialogue which the student is required to memorize. The dialogues reflect natural and authentic speech patterns in the foreign language. Since they present full utterances in a meaningful context, they provide the student from the beginning with vocabulary and structures whose usefulness is not confined to the classroom.

Grammar is presented inductively, with summary statements after drill. The object is to use drills that will give the student enough practice in the basic patterns of the language to develop his ability to use and respond to these patterns automatically. The drills are designed to give the learner the feel of the language as soon as possible. Having memorized a frame sentence from the basic dialogue, he expands it through whatever range of vocabulary he controls, gradually building up a store of complete utterances that he can use as occasion requires.

To perform their basic function of providing a means for the student to use the speech patterns in new and meaningful combinations, the drills must be planned with extreme care. First of all, they should evolve in a logical planned sequence from the dialogues. At the beginning, when major attention must be devoted to development of good pronunciation and natural intonation, simple repetition drills may be used, but even at this stage it is desirable to use complete utterances and authentic speech.

As skill is built up, the utterances become longer. To aid the student in building up skill in memorizing, the teacher may want to break longer utterances into segments and practice each separately until the entire unit can be spoken fluently. It is often possible to build up the sentence from the end rather than from the beginning, a technique that makes it easier to preserve natural intonation. As an example, the Spanish sentence ¿ No dijiste que querias ir al cine? might be developed in three parts: ir al cine? / querias ir al cine? / No dijiste que querias ir al cine?

How the student is to work outside of class becomes an important question in the audio-lingual approach, since it is obviously desirable that he work with an oral model. It is here that the language laboratory can perform an invaluable function, provided always that the lab work is an integral part of the course and that the drills are as carefully planned and as tightly controlled as those used in the classroom. Since many of the tapes used in the lab carry the voices of native speakers, they can add another dimension to the teaching and provide practice in listening comprehension, the skill that is perhaps most often slighted in many courses. If a good share of the memorization, pronunciation, and intonation drills can be done in the lab, valuable time is freed for the teacher in the class hour. In the audio-lingual approach to language learning, the class hour should be spent as fully as possible in hearing and speaking the language. The teacher must also prepare the student for new points, check his progress, and review previous work.

The teacher should examine some of the types of drills commonly found in textbooks with audio-lingual orientation. The study of examples may be instructive for the teacher who wishes to try his hand at developing pattern drills to supplement his present textbook. Whatever form the pattern drill takes, it will generally be built upon a single point and developed in such a way that it will elicit only slight variations of the model or pattern sentence. The utterances used in the drills should be as natural and plausible as possible. Drills are designed to give the student practice in saying the right thing in the foreign language without going through English.

So far as the student is concerned, the goal is complete mastery. His preparation is not complete until he can give answers without hestitation in oral recitation with books closed.

A teacher who wishes to learn more about pattern drills will find much useful information in *Pattern Drills in Language Teaching,* by James Etmekjian, New York University Press. The author's purpose was to present a step-by-step development of the techniques for creating and using pattern drills effectively in the teaching of French, regardless of the text being used. At the same time, teachers of other languages should find the book helpful, for the basic principles of pattern drill construction are much the same for all the commonly taught languages.

The audio-lingual approach to language learning lays heavy demands on both the teacher and the student, but if the method succeeds, the rewards are worth the extra effort. The teacher's manuals which are standard equipment with almost all such courses contain much advice on what to do and not to do for maximum benefit from the textbooks. Most of this advice is sound, since it is based on the experience of the authors, at least, and in many cases on the experiences of other users. A good example of a manual of this type is the one that accompanies *Modern Spanish, Second Edition.* It was prepared by a committee of teachers, and, since it is for a second edition, these authors have had the benefit of reactions to the original text. Though based on Spanish, the method itself is valid for other modern languages. The difficulties that may arise in teaching a text of this kind are identified and practical suggestions are made for dealing with them.

The authors emphasize that the teacher's role is central, as it must be, of course, with any method or any textbook. His role may be considered even more crucial in the audio-lingual approach, however, since so much of the learning activity must take place in the classroom. Every minute must be made to count so that the students get maximum exposure to the language, which means that the teacher must always be in firm control as he decides at what point the drills have achieved their purpose, when to review, when to move on to a new point.

Pattern drills based on a dialogue are generally the core of any audio-lingual course, and concrete suggestions for making effective use of them are of particular utility to a teacher who is interested in the approach.

In assigning drills, the teacher may introduce the first utterance by explaining its meaning in the foreign language or by setting up a context in which it might be used. The exercise, then, becomes a practice in saying something to someone. It might be introduced with a few simple questions about the students themselves or about some situation they recognize, employing the drill structures in a real context. Obviously, such groundwork furnishes motivation by showing the need and utility of the structures.

It is vitally important, says the manual, that the students be conscious of what the drill sentences mean. One device for achieving this purpose is to use gestures whenever possible, pointing at "this" or "that," or "him" or "her," and so on, and encouraging the students to do the same in their responses. Another device is to throw in an occasional question in the foreign language that will force the student to think of the meaning.

Clearly, all such steps must be planned, so that the flow of class activity will be smooth.

The authors take care to point out, however, that even though the class schedule must be rather detailed, it must allow for some flexibility, and that provision must always be made for variety. Performing a long set of drills can become very boring. When the teacher senses that boredom is setting in, he should shift to a different type of exercise and resume the first type only after it can be approached with new vigor. At times a breather will be needed, not merely a slight shift in direction. Nothing is to be gained by pushing ahead and leaving the class behind. At such times, the class might review earlier dialogues, which will now seem simple and thus give a sense of achievement; or the teacher might talk slowly and informally on a topic suggested by a cultural note in the text, thus giving the students the pleasure of following a lecture in the foreign language. When the class is far enough along, the teacher might start a short conversation based on one of the dialogues. The point to be made is that the teacher must adapt the material to the situation in his class and that it is his prerogative to guide his students toward a mastery of each successive point at a pace that is suitable for them.

Tests play a key role in the development of a course based on the new materials. Teachers know that students study when they are going to be tested. It would do very little good to tell students to concentrate on understanding and speaking if they knew they would be tested on reading and writing. Obviously, tests must be carefully planned and integrated with the teaching. Some of the student's most effective study efforts come when he is preparing for a quiz or a test. Tests of understanding and speaking are more difficult to administer than those over reading and writing, but it is necessary to reinforce the aims of the course by giving prime attention to those skills. Short, frequent tests, concentrating on one or two skills at a time are deemed to have the greatest effectiveness. The student should know precisely what each test will cover and the portions of the text that will be emphasized. But he should realize that his knowledge of the language is cumulative and that points studied earlier will be involved, in addition to the new points stressed on this test. In short, an effective testing program must be comprehensive in its coverage and must employ a variety of techniques so that the student will be enabled to demonstrate the full range of his skills and the degree of his mastery. A thorough discussion of testing in the foreign language class is found in Chapter Four.

Elementary textbooks with the audio-lingual approach are now in good supply and new ones are in preparation. Attention is being increasingly directed toward the teaching of reading to students who have devoted a year or two in acquiring some skill understanding and speaking the foreign language without excessive reliance on books. The problem is not merely how to teach reading but how to teach it while maintaining and strengthening the audio-lingual skills that have been so laboriously built up in the earlier stages of learning.

A measure of the concern with effective approaches to the teaching of reading is seen in the fact that the Northeast Conference on the Teaching of Foreign Languages devoted a large part of its 1967 meeting to a discussion of the problem. The Conference published a list of a dozen "key propositions" which represent both a clear statement of the goals and a recognition of the distance yet to be traveled in meeting them. The basic premise is that reading, understanding, and speaking the language must be integrated into a single learning process. It follows that the transition to reading must be gradual and that the audio-lingual skills should be used in the development of direct comprehension of the printed page and away from translation in the narrow sense of "decoding."

Some textbooks are based on the integrated approach to the teaching of reading, one of them being *Programmed French Readers, Books 1–3*, by Hugh Campbell and Camille Bauer (Boston: Houghton Mifflin Co.). Two books for German are *Intermediate Course in German: A Linguistic Bridge to Literature*, by Albert M. Reh and Carol W. Reh (New York: McGraw-Hill), and *Der Weg zum Lesen* (New York: Harcourt, Brace & World). For Spanish, a book (already cited in this chapter) prepared under the aegis of the Modern Language Association has been published. This is *Continuing Spanish* I, II (New York: American Book Co.). All of these books use a great variety of devices and procedures designed to achieve an integrated approach to reading. The Northeast Conference report on reading points out that an adequate supply of new textbooks will not be available at an early date, in view of the vast field of literature that remains to be explored. Until more books are produced with the full battery of exercises that seem to be required, the individual teacher may want to produce his own integrated approach by supplementing existing materials. Many teachers have their favorite stories which they would like to continue reading with their classes. It is possible to adapt such texts to the integrated approach, and the published report of the Northeast Conference gave an example for Spanish, which is quoted later in this account. Let us turn first, however, to a brief mention of some of these devices.

The first lesson in *Continuing Spanish* is prefaced by a brief statement on the art of reading without knowing all the words. This is an introduction to the art of "sensible guessing," which the report of the Northeast Conference advocates, though it admits that it is a topic which badly needs further study. Perhaps a description of the exercises used in this sample text to further this skill will be helpful to the teacher who wishes to increase his own stock of techniques. The first exercise consists of a list of 18 sentences, each with one word in bold face, which is probably new to the student. Following the sentence are three choices, one of which is a close equivalent of the word whose meaning is to be inferred. The key word in the first sentence is *surgido* ("... han *surgido* tantos problemas..."), and the word which is given to suggest the proper inference is *aparecido,* which appears with *desaparecido* and *solucionado* as one of three possible choices.

In a subsequent lesson, the text introduces an elaborate exercise in six parts to give further practice in "sensible guessing." Part 1 gives a brief passage with six words replaced by dashes, and the student is asked to try to understand the meaning, solely from the context. In Part 2, he is asked to choose which of three summaries expresses what he has just read. This exercise is designed to demonstrate that it is possible to get the gist of a passage without knowing every word in it. Part 3 repeats the original passage, now with three possibilities replacing each of the blanks, so that the student may choose the most probable meaning of the omitted words. In Part 4 there is a continuation of the first passage, with words, probably unfamiliar, which are numbered; the student is asked to try to understand their meaning without looking them up. This exercise is followed by three summaries, with instructions to choose the one that best expresses what has been read. Finally, the new words are repeated in new sentences, with three choices from which the student selects the most probable meaning.

The purpose of the preceding exercises is explained by the authors as development of the student's skill in reading around unknown or partially known lexical items and guessing intelligently at their meaning, thus discouraging the needless looking up of words. To complement these exercises, there are explanations of the false cognates that are found in the lesson, lest the student be led into traps by the technique of inference that he is learning to use.

The "pre-passage" exercises lead into the new reading passage itself. Additional guidance is given here by means of glosses; presumably unfamiliar words are defined in simple terms, or supplemented by synonyms that the student probably knows.

Following the reading text, there is a wealth of exercises designed to extend the student's skill in understanding and speaking the language at the same time that he is learning new grammar and new vocabulary. One exercise, based directly on the reading passage, consists of a list of questions that cover the entire passage and which are phrased in the form of alternatives: Did a character do this or that? Did he then say this or the other? In answering, the student must make the correct choice, to demonstrate comprehension of the text, but he is not yet asked to invent or supply novel utterances. A second

exercise may furnish a drill on the past tense through a summary of
the reading passage expressed in a series of short sentences, all in
the present tense. The teacher may read the first sentence, ask the student to repeat it exactly as he hears it; the teacher then repeats it
and asks that the student reply with the verb changed to the past.
The types of drills cited above may be among the numerous varieties
that are introduced in the first year or two of audio-lingual teaching.
The only difference is that they are integrated with the teaching of
reading and that they are closely tied to the structures of the reading
passage.

The example below, from the 1967 report of the Northeast Conference, is cited as one way of adapting an existing text to the purposes of the integrated approach.

Writing in the foreign language is the last of the fundamental skills
to receive concentrated attention in the typical audio-lingual course,
but some practice in writing may be introduced quite early in the
course. The procedures recommended for teaching writing will provide no surprises for anyone who has pondered the means employed
in teaching the other skills. The goal is to write directly in the authentic patterns of the foreign language, without the intervention of
English. Writing is not approached as an independent area of study
but rather as an extension of work already done. This means, in practice, that the student will begin by writing only what is already familiar to him—material that he has heard and said many times. It is
possible to introduce dictation exercises for early writing practice,
using lines from a dialogue that the student has already memorized.
Because the passage is familiar, complete utterances can be taken
down, rather than single words or short phrases. To correct errors,
the student can be asked to copy the original passage from his text.
The writing exercises become more varied, of course, as the student's
other skills develop. The kind of drills used for gaining fluency in
speaking are equally useful for writing practice. In a well integrated
course, practice in writing will also reinforce the other skills.

Much useful information on the audio-lingual approach to the
teaching of writing in any of the foreign languages can be found
in a student manual entitled *Writing Modern Spanish,* published by
Harcourt, Brace & World, 1966. The drills in this manual are designed to be written outside class *after* the student has mastered the
corresponding oral drills. They then serve to confirm the student's

understanding of particular structures while giving him practice in the writing of correct Spanish. In addition to the kinds of drills mentioned and illustrated briefly in the descriptions given above of procedures used in teaching speaking and reading, the manual makes much use of progressive substitution drills, particularly for review purposes.

In closing this chapter, we reiterate that we have not attempted the obviously impossible task of providing in these few pages a complete listing of all the audio-lingually oriented teaching materials that have been published in recent years, much less a detailed analysis of these materials. Our aim has been to provide a representative list and to point out some of the ways in which the material is organized and some of the teaching procedures recommended. It has not been our purpose to argue for or against the audio-lingual approach to language learning but only to present as objectively as possible the point of view of the advocates of that approach.

CHAPTER SIX

New Developments in
the Foreign Language Classroom

by

Violet E. Bergquist

University of Illinois, Chicago Circle

The Classroom as a Cultural Island. There are many factors which help to determine a successful foreign language program. One of these factors is the total atmosphere or climate of the school and classroom. The physical environment in which the language is to be learned may furnish the student several important clues regarding the subject and the teacher with whom he will spend 130-180 hours during the ensuing school year.

To create a classroom permeated by an atmosphere related to the foreign culture requires initiative, imagination and creativity on the part of the enthusiastic teacher. A wise teacher will involve his students in the planning and establishment of an attractive and stimulating place for learning. According to Maria Montessori, the secret of success in the education of our youth lies in the imaginative ability to stimulate interest and motivation through the use of attractive literary and pictorial material all correlated to a principal, central idea.

The *prepared environment* will lead us more quickly to an understanding of the people whose language we are studying, for we must perceive deeply, and quickly, and we must acquire an absorbing insight into their culture.

Let us consider a few ideas which may help bring about a greater degree of total classroom immersion into the culture of a foreign country. The selection of the objects and displays within a room should indicate something about the behavior of people; these objects should be vitally related to the culture of the country represented and thus help increase the basis for communication. It may be advisable to secure the aid of the art department, library, city art museum, and individuals who are interested in contributing to such a worthwhile project.

A collection of representative, colorful textiles artistically mounted or displayed can improve the acoustics and enhance the aesthetic quality of the classroom. A few well-chosen water colors, ceramics, examples of sculpture, typical musical instruments, some manufactured products, and various other artifacts with captions should be well-displayed and neatly mounted.

There is much value in the students becoming involved in the process of developing a classroom museum. They should be given the opportunity to examine objects closely, to handle them and possibly even take some home on a circulatory loan basis. One large midwestern high school has a Spanish classroom in which the upper walls are painted with murals depicting outstanding scenes from the life of Don Quixote. At one time the furniture, draperies, etchings, copper plates, wood carvings, Spanish tiles, a collection of beautifully illustrated copies of the literary masterpiece, even the desk set and bookends all bore the dominant theme. Collecting art objects pertaining to Don Quixote is a lifetime hobby of the teacher.

In one area of the room a bulletin board dedicated to current events and seasonal activities may be presented in an organic relation to the rest of the environment. Responsibility for this section can be assigned to selected students or student teachers under the guidance of the classroom teacher.

It is not always possible that a foreign language teacher have a classroom exclusively for his own classes. Crowded conditions exist in most of our schools and it is often necessary for two or more teachers to share a classroom throughout the day. Whenever possible, however, certain rooms should be shared only by foreign language classes because of the uniqueness of the materials required. Unless a division of responsibilities is worked out by the teachers involved, personal pride in the appearance of the classroom may be lessened when it is used by several different teachers.

Even when a foreign language teacher must share a classroom with teachers of other subjects, a *part* of the room should be set aside to give at least some foreign cultural emphasis. Often teachers of other courses are willing to relinquish their share of the room if the imaginative language teacher assumes the responsibility for making the classroom more attractive for all.

Also in many FLES programs, where the foreign language specialist circulates from school to school and enters the classroom for a few minutes for each lesson, much can be done by the innovative teacher to introduce something of refreshing cultural interest to his class each day. This cultural interest can be enhanced through the cooperation of the regular classroom teacher. There can be excellent coordination of foreign language activities and projects relating them to programs in language arts, social studies, home economics, art, music, and also, through games and folk dances, in physical education. Thus the influence of foreign language instruction can permeate an entire scholastic community.

Immersion in the Foreign Language. In order to exploit fully the potentials for creating a foreign language atmosphere, there must be a variety of encounters with the language and the culture on the part of the student. The primary emphasis must be placed on the need to use the language, not only in the foreign language classroom, but at every possible opportunity *outside* the classroom. Some of the foreign language club activities should include the use of native speakers, discussion groups, conversation groups at lunchroom tables, and other means of communication and interaction in the foreign language. Many colleges and some high schools have established foreign student exchange programs. Hundreds of high schools, colleges, and universities have organized travel and study groups, with or without academic credit, to Mexico, Europe, and other places at fairly modest cost during spring and summer vacation periods.

Several years ago the outstanding educator Alfred North Whitehead pointed out the need for educational goals emphasizing culture and receptivenesses to humane feeling, as well as specialized, expert knowledge. He was one of the first to advocate exploring the relationships between different areas of subject matter, particularly between the study of foreign language and history. Bilingual programs in which some or all academic subjects are taught in the foreign language are being developed to an extensive degree in a growing number of schools and colleges in the United States.

In the Evanston, Illinois Public Schools there have been special summer school programs, one in French and the other in Spanish, open to all pupils in grades 1-5. The languages have been taught by well-qualified, bilingual teachers. Intensive language study is supplemented by a well-integrated cultural program in art, music, creative dramatics and physical education, all taught by specialists in their respective fields. The entire program has been enriched by language films, assemblies, plays, field trips, etc. The total *school* atmosphere is aimed at approaching that of the countries in which French or Spanish are spoken. This program is continued on a weekly basis throughout the school year until the sixth grade when all students begin to study a foreign language as part of the regular daily program.

Electronic Classrooms. The use of coordinated colors of walls, chalkboards, furniture, floors, even lockers, greatly increases the attractiveness of a school. In addition to adequate board space, the ideal classroom is provided with work areas, counter space and storage cabinets. Many of the new language series include motion pictures, filmstrips, tapes and records for the reinforcement of language learning. Thus it has become necessary to assign such equipment as projectors, tape recorders and phonographs for permanent use in the foreign language classroom. Either Polaroid windows or opaque window shades are helpful in eliminating as much daylight as possible. Much glare from daylight is reduced by using special projection screens such as the lenticular type. Mobile carts for the A-V equipment and three or four well-placed electrical outlets are needed. Adequate lighting and acoustical treatment of ceilings, floors and walls enhance every learning situation.

In addition to a language laboratory, many foreign language classrooms are electronically equipped with rather moderately-priced consoles and individual headsets. The sound from the motion picture projector can be connected into the console thereby assuring improved hearing of the foreign language by each pupil regardless of his location in the room. Thus the teacher is able to monitor and correct the students individually.

Electronic Centers. A more recent trend in our newer schools is to have an electronic central area as part of the library or the A-V department. All the materials such as audio-tapes, video-tapes, motion pictures, and film-strips or slides are stored on reels or in cartridges on electronic racks in this center. Then, from any classroom or booth in a study area which is wired to the program source, one can dial the proper number or signal and get the desired program automatically on the receiver and headset. Instead of individual receivers, a classroom may be equipped with large TV receivers and a loudspeaker system. At the end of the program, the material at the program source is automatically re-wound at a very rapid rate and ready for use at any time.

Nova High School in Fort Lauderdale, Florida, is using much of the equipment described above. Evanston Township High School in Evanston, Illinois, and many other progressive schools and colleges are using the first phase of this system which is limited to dialing into the center for programs recorded on audio tape. The number of tape-recorded lessons available can vary depending upon the need of the individual school as well as the financial investment.

In the more versatile lecture rooms it is now possible to control multi-media from the teacher's podium which contains a master switching panel. From this position the teacher is able to control the lighting in the auditorium and on the stage, the curtains on the stage, the rear-view motion picture projector, the rear-view slide projector, the tape-recorder, the TV receiver, etc. At Illinois Teachers College, Chicago North, such equipment is supplemented by a testing unit in which each student has a series of six buttons on the armrest of his chair. It is possible to give a response of true or false, yes or no, or multiple-choice answers A, B, C, D, or E. The student response is immediately available to the teacher at the podium or console.

New School Designs. From the time of the little red school house to the present large urban high school of 100 to 200 classrooms, the main pattern until recently had been to divide the school into box-like classrooms, each one like the next, with the teacher's desk facing 30, 40 or more pupils' desks fixed to the floor. In a few schools the pupils' desks were movable but, for the most part, they too were placed in the same pattern in front of the teacher.

However, because of changes brought about in education by electronic aids and changing methods of instruction, the new key in building planning today is to provide maximum flexibility incorporating multi-purpose facilities. New school designs are based on the concept that students must be taught to accept greater responsibility for their own learning. Educational resource centers ideally bring together faculty, students, library facilities, curriculum materials and laboratory equipment. The student needs special guidance as a school goes through the transition period in which it changes from a teacher-dominated center to one of greater flexibility.

The inadequate supply of well-qualified foreign language teachers, the increase in enrollments, and the instructional revolution have resulted in several worthwhile experiments, one of which has been large group instruction.

Team teaching or large group instruction is a process which involves two or more teachers in cooperative planning. It combines the best talents of the teachers, provides a greater flexibility of instruction, and sharply focuses attention on the material being presented. For the past few years at a large suburban high school in Illinois, different levels of foreign language classes have been taught in large groups of 75 to 100 pupils by a team composed of one or two master teachers, one or two beginning or less-experienced teachers, and one or two student teachers. This team cooperatively plans the long-range and immediate goals and procedures of the course. The master teachers devote their time to the planning and development of policy and the content of the course. They also determine the procedures for evaluating the effectiveness of large group instruction, the language laboratory drill program, as well as small group drill sessions, dialogue practice and review periods. The other members of the team assist in operating equipment in the team room, preparing materials and conducting small group sessions.

It should be emphasized that the various combinations of large group instruction and small seminar grouping require very specific planning long enough in advance to adjust adequately to meet the needs of the students. It is imperative to eliminate the confusion which would result from inadequate planning.

To be most effective, team teaching, flexible scheduling, and small discussion group techniques require a variety of architectural changes in the school building. Varied-size classes require the addition of partitions or the removal of walls. There is a need for certain areas for highly specialized activities, such as lecture centers, conference rooms, individual study carrels, and teacher workrooms where teams can confer and materials can be prepared. Movable, reasonably sound-proof walls which can be opened or closed eletcrically may be used to divide a large space into small areas for discussion or drill groups.

Careful thought must go into the planning of these combinations of rooms in order to assure an atmosphere conducive to maintaining the attention and interest of the students. The acoustical treatment of the ceilings and walls, and draperies over the windows helps substantially to eliminate excessive noise. When the floors are covered by a very sturdy, neutral-color carpeting, not only is there a muffling of the noise of moving feet, but there is often an improvement in conduct on the part of the students. Another important factor to be considered in the construction of these large classrooms is that of an adequate line of vision. This may be achieved by elevating the middle and back rows of seats in tiers, and by placing the teacher's lectern on an elevated platform.

In addition to the equipment already mentioned, one should consider using an overhead projector, with its several advantages over the blackboard, in large group instruction. Information prepared on a transparency is projected on a raised screen and enlarged sufficiently to provide adequate viewing for all students. With careful planning prior to the class meeting, these transparencies, especially when used with overlays, can be most effective in developing presentations, providing frequent, quick drills, drawing out generalizations from the students, and in furnishing rapid, systematic review sessions. Much time is required to develop a good series of transparencies, but the great advantage is that they can be used thereafter. Any teacher who prepares transparencies for large group instruction will want to use these same transparencies in the small classroom as well. Hence we have need for additional overhead projectors in the individual classroom.

Flexible Scheduling of Classes. Flexibility is an increasingly important ingredient in the scheduling of classes in the modern school. Instead of the standard 45- to 55-minute classes meeting five days a week, the unit of time or *module* usually is reduced to 15, 20, or 30 minutes. Some classes may meet for one module of time, others may meet for various combinations of two or three modules. Also the number of modules for a specific class may change from day to day. The length of the class period and the size of the group should be determined by the nature of the learning experience. Content presentation, supplemented by audio-visual devices, can be prepared for large groups, whereas division of the large group into smaller groups based upon the ability or specific needs of the students, offers direct focus on the individual's understanding and participation. The single module may be a very convenient unit of time for language laboratory drill. Some schools are successfully using the following time allotments: 20% of a week's schedule in large group sessions; 50% in small group drill sessions; and 30% in language laboratory drill.

Recent Innovations and Developments. As further advances are made in the areas of programmed learning, in electronic equipment, and above all in our knowledge about language learning, the next ten years should bring even greater changes in methodology.

At the University of Illinois, for example, foreign language students are now using the telephones in their residences to dial directly into the communications learning center for a regular language laboratory drill at any time of the day or night, seven days a week. As these facilities are being used more extensively, some of the language laboratories are being converted into a student-record tutoring service for individual students who are having difficulties with the listening-speaking portion of their language studies.

The use of television may bring a museum or laboratory directly into the classroom or home. The potential of this medium, using satellites to relay live programs instantaneously from any place in the world, was well demonstrated by a television network showing the masterpieces of Pablo Picasso in eleven cities in Europe and North America. This event was climaxed by an art auction conducted simultaneously in London, Paris, New York and Dallas-Fort Worth.

At present it is possible to direct broadcasts from Russian and Japanese stations into classrooms in the United States. In the January-February 1967 issue of the *DFL Notes* (Department of Foreign Languages of the NEA) there is a report of a "live" interview with Dr. Erich Mende, West Germany's Vice Chancellor, conducted by students of German in San Diego. This opportunity was arranged as an experiment via the transatlantic telephone cable, and the voices were amplified by use of speaker-phone equipment.

In the foreseeable future, television receptors will provide us with permanent printouts or copies of an international newspaper or business report. Dialogues are held between the computer and typewriters. Through teleprocessing, a typewritten message is converted into a spoken message using the audio-response unit. Machines now picture the voice, and typewriters are being developed which write, in simplified phonetic script, any information given to them orally.

With all the technological improvements and inventions, it is difficult to envision the foreign language classroom of the future. However, surely more effective language learning will result from these multisensory experiences which can serve as prods to develop, not only the basic language skills, but to develop a spirit of inquiry as motivation for independent study and exploration.

CHAPTER SEVEN

The Language Laboratory: Valuable Instructional Aid

by

Robert W. Cannaday, Jr.
University of Hawaii

Planning for the Language Laboratory

The installation and successful use of a language laboratory is, of necessity, complex. Technical, pedagogical, linguistic, financial, and administrative questions abound. A great deal of hard work, much of it in areas unfamiliar to those who have to perform the work, is involved. Language laboratory planning, therefore, should be careful, systematic, thorough, and well-coordinated. One or two years is not too much to devote to the planning, if it results in a well-equipped laboratory, provided with suitable and sufficient materials, staffed and administered by a competent faculty, and with its use closely correlated with the procedures and philosophy of the total audio-lingual program.

Some Basic Considerations. In addition to the principles governing the relationship of the language laboratory to the total modern foreign language program, and preliminary to a listing and discussion of the elements and sequence of planning, these considerations must be emphasized:

1. The language laboratory is a *laboratory*—it is *not* a classroom. It is a place for controlled experiment and correction. It is not designed for the teaching of shorthand or of one's native language, or for expository classroom instruction in any subject. (And, in fact, if proper planning and use of the laboratory are made, it will never be free for such instruction.)

2. Language laboratory equipment is *machinery*. Since it is machinery, it cannot teach; since it is machinery, its effectiveness depends entirely upon the quality of materials and methods used with it. This quality, in turn, depends entirely upon the human beings who determine it. Since it is machinery, those who control and use it—teachers and students—require orientation, training, and practice in that use; and its successful use demands close correlation of materials and methods with those of the classroom. Those responsible for that correlation—the teachers—require training and time for the work involved.

3. The language laboratory cannot replace the teacher. It cannot plan, program, select, guide, interpret, analogize, define, relate, react, or (in the human sense) communicate. It cannot evaluate. Used properly, it is an extremely valuable aid to the teacher, making his work much more efficient than ever before, but requiring, in turn, much more work of him than ever before.

Responsibilities of the Modern Foreign Language Faculty. Primary responsibility for the choice, installation, and use of language laboratory equipment and materials rests with the modern foreign language teachers of a school. It is a responsibility which cannot be relinquished to school administrators, audio-visual specialists, outside consultants, equipment suppliers, or publishers. All of these persons should be consulted regularly at every stage of the planning process, but none of them will be faced—once equipment and materials are adopted—with the day-to-day problems of using them successfully.

The planning responsibility of the teaching faculty breaks down as follows:

1. Study of professional and commercial sources of information on equipment and materials and their use.

2. Professional preparation for use of the laboratory (reading; attendance at workshops and conferences; enrollment in university courses on language laboratory operation).

3. Consultation on and observation of successful laboratory operation in other schools.

4. Work with the school administration in preparing schedules and in the formulation of administrative procedures for the proposed laboratory.

5. Preparation of definitive recommendations on selection of laboratory equipment and its mode and place of installation; selection and use of all laboratory materials; administrative and curricular integration of the laboratory into the total audio-lingual modern foreign language program.

Responsibilities of the School Administration. The school administration shares with the modern foreign language teachers the responsibility for planning and operating the language laboratory. Its role, however, is a secondary one, and the chief school administrator is ill-advised not to involve the teachers intimately at every stage of the planning process, making them in every sense responsible for the selection and use of the laboratory equipment and materials. Not to do so is to court indifference, apathetic acceptance and use, poor correlation of the laboratory with classroom instruction, and errors in selection, installation, utilization, and administrative procedure. The administrator's chief responsibilities in laboratory planning are:

1. Arranging for the financing of equipment and materials of a laboratory suitable to the present and predictable needs of his school.

2. Coordination of the laboratory planning effort (or delegation of that responsibility): appointment of study and observation committees; arrangements for faculty consultation with state, regional, or local audio-visual and language laboratory specialists, and with laboratory equipment and materials suppliers; administrative arrangement for faculty orientation and training in the use of the language laboratory.

3. Work with the modern language faculty in preparing laboratory schedules and in the formulation of administrative procedures.

4. The most careful consideration (and acceptance, whenever feasible) of joint faculty recommendations on: selection and use of all laboratory equipment and its mode and place of installation; selection and use of all laboratory materials; administrative and curricular integration of the laboratory into the total audio-lingual modern foreign language program.

Sources of Information and Assistance. Teachers and administrators of schools with existing *successful* laboratories are the best single source of information and assistance available to those planning a language laboratory. Often such schools are nearby; but, even if they are not, the expense of frequent and regular visits, particularly during the planning stage, represents the soundest of investments. (Information as to the location of schools with successful laboratory use is usually available from the modern foreign language supervisor in a state department of education.)

Valuable information and, usually, active assistance can be obtained through the state department of education by requesting it of the modern foreign language coordinator and/or the audio-visual specialist. The U. S. Office of Education and the Modern Language Association (62 Fifth Avenue, New York, N. Y. 10011) are other good sources of information.

Published materials available are listed in the bibliography for this chapter. Key items, however, are: (General) Hocking, Holton et. al., Hutchinson, and Stack; (Equipment) Hayes; (Materials) Ollman (ed.), *MLA Selective List of Materials;* (Teacher preparation) Cannaday and Gamba.

The Sequence of Language Laboratory Planning. The four basic elements of a language laboratory plan are: (1) Aims and objectives; (2) Studies, visits, and consultations of teachers and administrators; (3) Specifications, contracts, and warranties; and (4) Installation of the laboratory. A summary discussion of each of these elements follows.

(1) *Aims and Objectives.* Possibly the most common cause for failure in existing language laboratory usage is that teachers and administrators, in planning for the laboratory, neglect to relate its use to (a) the basic objectives of improved understanding and speaking ability and (b) the methods and materials of the total modern foreign language program of the school involved. As is often the case with other innovations, language laboratory equipment is purchased and installed *first;* then materials, programming, teacher preparation, and integration of the laboratory work with that of the total program are considered. This cart-before-the-horse procedure results, inevitably, in confusion, disillusionment, and ineffective use or abandonment of the laboratory. At best, months are spent in the training of teachers, the selection of appropriate materials, and the formulation of ad-

ministrative policy—all in an effort to "make the program fit the lab."

A more logical procedure, and one that has proved effective in use, is the following:

The modern foreign language faculty sets language proficiency objectives, working back from Grade 12 (so that continuity of instruction between high school and college will not be interrupted), for each level of the program. These objectives are spelled out in the greatest practicable detail for the four basic language skills (understanding, speaking, reading, and writing) and for cultural knowledge and understanding, including appreciation of literature.

Methods, materials, and evaluation procedures leading to the attainment of the above objectives, appropriate to each level and coordinating closely with those of the surrounding levels, are decided upon.

If the school's program, methods, and materials are of the audio-lingual nature, planning for the language laboratory, as a vital element at all levels of instruction, proceeds. And, if the above procedures are conscientiously followed under a sound administrative plan, students can be expected, at the end of the program, to perform significantly better in the understanding and speaking areas than they would have without laboratory training.[1] If, on the other hand, traditional goals of proficiency in reading, translation, and formal grammatical knowledge are chosen as the principal ones; if there is disagreement among the faculty, and lack of coordination as to aims, methods, and materials for the program; then proposed use of the language laboratory, an audio-lingual instrument, should be abandoned until such time as the total program is made audio-lingual, sequential, and coordinated.

(2) *Studies, Visits, and Consultations of Teachers and Administrators.* Once audio-lingual objectives, methods, and materials are decided upon for the total modern foreign language program, language laboratory planning can and should begin in earnest. The

---

1. Karl S. Pond, ("Setting Realistic Goals" in: Holton, et. al., *Sound Language Teaching,* pp. 186-191), provides high school and college modern foreign language teachers with concrete suggestions as to the formulation of program goals. See also Remunda Cadoux (editor), *French for Secondary Schools: Content and Organization for 4- and 6-Year Sequences; Spanish for Secondary Schools: Content and Organization for 4- and 6-Year Sequences;* and *German for Secondary Schools.*

bulk of the planning period is given over to: a careful and systematic examination of successful laboratory operation in other schools and available laboratory equipment and materials; preliminary teacher training; a survey of scheduling and other administrative factors; and a study of laboratory cost, location, and maintenance considerations. Let us examine these planning steps in more detail.

Successful Laboratory Operation in Other Schools. Aside from the negative value of learning what *not* to do, there is little point in visiting, indiscriminately, language laboratory installations. The primary interest of a school planning for the language laboratory is in learning how and why an existing installation is successful. Visits to successful laboratories are usually inexpensive and easily arranged.

Language Laboratory Equipment. Expert help is needed here. Working within the requirements of the total modern foreign language program, and bearing in mind cost and space limitations, teachers and administrators of the planning school make a thorough survey of the professional literature on the subject with a view to eliminating those types of equipment which would not meet their needs. Then technical specifications are drawn up by qualified audio-visual and electronics specialists, who establish the specifications with reference to standard guides. To arrive at a final choice, visits to other schools are again in order, and demonstrations and consultation with commercial suppliers can be arranged.

Language Laboratory Materials. The initial selection and order of tapes and discs will be determined almost exclusively by the materials and methods used in the audio-lingual instruction of the classroom. To insure correlation of method and content, the basic laboratory tapes should constitute one component of the course materials used there. Supplementary tapes and discs must be chosen with this same correlation factor in mind. This means that a most detailed examination of materials must be made before money is invested.

Cost, of course, is again a factor. But the guiding principle is always that laboratory materials *must* (1) correlate with the classroom materials and methods and (2) be of a quality and quantity sufficient to the needs of the modern foreign language program and of the students following that program.

Preliminary Teacher Training. Teachers cannot learn the basic techniques of programming and control once the laboratory is in use. Certainly students should not be made the guinea pigs for this sort of "in-service" education. While the commercial supplier is held responsible for an orientation of teachers in the use of the mechanical equipment, the school must see to it that every teacher is thoroughly familiar with the materials to be used, the techniques of programming, methods of control, and testing techniques. Provision must be made, too, for similar training of teachers joining the faculty *after* use of the laboratory has begun. During the planning period, professional reading on the subject is required, and attendance at workshops, institutes, and special courses is strongly encouraged. (Of particular value are NDEA Institute and university courses stressing audio-lingual methodology and the application of linguistics to the teaching of modern foreign languages.)

Scheduling. Tentative laboratory use schedules should be drawn up during the planning period. A number of factors are involved: (a) the laboratory is most effectively used in frequent, regular, short time periods; (b) the laboratory must be made available to teachers for the preparation of tapes and for the evaluation of student tapes; (c) more time is given to first- and second-level classes than to advanced classes; (d) advanced classes can perform a considerable amount of work on an individual, or "library" basis.

Ideally, five laboratory periods (10-15 minutes each) would be scheduled each week for first- and second-level classes. In most cases, of course, the realities of time, space, and distance make such a schedule impractical. What is important is that teachers and administrators bear in mind the ideal, as it represents the application of the principle of *regular, frequent, short* laboratory periods.

Well-programmed work in the language laboratory is intensive and demands concentration. Experience shows that 20 minutes or so of such work in one session is about the limit for a highly motivated adolescent or adult. Thus, the apparently simple "solution" of scheduling each modern foreign language class section into the laboratory for one class period per week defeats its own purpose. The regular and frequent individual practice required in audio-lingual language instruction is missing, and the length of the laboratory session is such that half the period is, in effect, wasted.

Equally undesirable is a "free" schedule, where teachers use the laboratory at their own discretion. What practice students have becomes irregular, and teachers who tend to be afraid of the equipment use it so seldom that they never become confident in that use. Those

SPLIT-PERIOD SCHEDULE
LANGUAGE LABORATORY

	MON. Teacher Time	TUES. Teacher Time	WED. Teacher Time	THURS. Teacher Time	FRI. Teacher Time
Before School	Span. I-A German II-B	Span. II-A Span. I-A	German II-B German IV	Span. II-A Span. I-A	German IV Span. II-A
First Period	French II-A Span. II-B	German I-A Span. I-B	Span. II-B Span. I-B	German I-A French II-A	Span. I-B German I-A
Second Period	German I-B German III	German III French II-B	Span. II-C German I-B	German I-B TEACHER	Span. II-C French II-B
Third Period	French I-A German I-C	German I-C French III	German I-C French I-A	French I-A TEACHER	German I-C French III
Fourth Period	TEACHER	French I-B LIBRARY	TEACHER TEACHER	LIBRARY French I-B	TEACHER French I-B
Fifth Period	LIBRARY French IV	TEACHER	French IV TEACHER	TEACHER LIBRARY	LIBRARY TEACHER
Sixth Period	Span. III German II-A	French I-C Span. I-C	German II-A Span. III	Span. I-C French I-C	French I-C Span. I-C
Seventh Period					

Level I—3 sections each section 3 times a week
Level II—2 sections each section 2 times a week
Level III—1 section each section 2 times a week
Level IV—1 section each section 2 times a week

Figure 7-1

teachers who *do* wish to use the laboratory often have scheduling conflicts.

One solution to the problems of laboratory scheduling is split-period, or *modular scheduling*. Each class period is divided into two laboratory periods, each about 25 minutes long. If language classrooms are near the laboratory, as they should be, the extra five minutes or so each hour is enough to move classes to and from the laboratory and to set up and put away laboratory materials. (Such a schedule also permits extra laboratory time for teachers, who need it to prepare and evaluate materials.) Two such periods per week, while not ideal, are arranged relatively easily; and if good programming and control are provided, and every minute of each period is made to count, they can constitute an effective laboratory schedule. See **Figure 7–1.**

As noted above, beginning classes—because of the fact that they must spend so much time on listening and speaking practice (as opposed to reading and writing)—need more laboratory time than advanced classes. This does *not* mean (colleges take note!) that advanced classes should not use the laboratory regularly and frequently. The most important consideration here is that the beginning student has difficulty in recognizing his own errors of oral production[2] and that the teacher can monitor only one student at a time. This means that the playback-compare facility provided by a tape recorder becomes completely effective only when a student has advanced to the point of being able to take full advantage of it. This may occur only after two or three years of language study.

Cost, Location, and Maintenance Factors. The cost of a language laboratory installation is affected, of course, by many factors: the number and type of student stations, the number of tape recorders provided, console facilities offered, and so forth. Some basic considerations, however, obtain:

The aims of the total program are dominant. If it is decided that regular and frequent laboratory instruction is important at all levels to the attainment of those objectives, the number of laboratory positions made available will have to be sufficient to provide each modern foreign language class section with at least two ½ hour laboratory sessions per week.

---

2. See the report by Bernard and Lorge (chapter bibliography) for a contrary research finding.

The number of student positions must exceed the number of students in the largest modern foreign language class by about 10%. This is a safety factor which allows for repairs being made at individual stations and for students doing make-up work.

As long as laboratory equipment meets the precise technical specifications set by the school, and as long as the meeting of those specifications and satisfactory maintenance service are guaranteed by written contract, the school is usually justified in accepting the lowest bid among suppliers for the purchase and installation of equipment.[3]

A school must maintain a 10%–20% spare parts inventory for the laboratory. The cost of such a stock is usually equal to 3%–5% of the school's initial budget outlay for the entire laboratory installation.

The number of program sources at the teacher console will vary according to need, but in the average secondary school modern foreign language class, at least three tape decks, plus a record player, are needed to provide for individualization of instruction (through multiple programming) and testing.

Modern foreign language enrollments continue to rise steadily each year, and expansion of facilities must be a constant factor in the planning of the initial installation.

Location. The chief consideration here is proximity to modern foreign language classrooms. Ideally, the laboratory would be at the center of a modern language area, surrounded by the classrooms. In any case, it must be close enough to the classrooms to permit all class sections to meet efficiently the laboratory schedule (minimum two ½-hours weekly) described earlier.

Maintenance. In addition to the spare parts inventory (which, coupled with the 10% safety factor in the number of student positions, will protect the school in the case of temporary, "normal" breakdowns), money must be set aside for maintenance service not covered by the supplier's warranty. For a flat annual fee, the school can negotiate a "continuous-service" contract with the equipment supplier

---

3. Stack (see chapter bibliography) offers a well-taken warning on this point: ". . . the bid system encourages manufacturers to reduce costs (and thereby quality) in order to meet low bid requirements. The lowest priced items are not necessarily the most economical. *Au contraire.* Although high quality, desirable laboratories cost more to manufacture . . . they are economical over a long period because of low maintenance and long life. . . ." *The Language Laboratory and Modern Language Teaching,* p. 22.

or with a local firm. This contract should be so worded, however, that the school is protected against total or partial shut-downs of the laboratory, and it should require *immediate* service for serious trouble and for service within two or three days for minor repairs.

Another planning consideration here is personnel. Provision should be made for the appointment of a language laboratory director and for the training and use of student assistants.

(3) *Specifications, Contracts, and Warranties.* The establishment of technical specifications for language laboratory equipment and its installation has been discussed earlier. However, even when these specifications are accepted and guaranteed by the school's purchase contract with the commercial supplier, let the buyer beware! Delivery of equipment should never be accepted as complete until a qualified specialist (who is not an employee of the supplier) has certified to the school that its specifications have indeed been met by the supplier. Suppliers have been known to install "standard-line" equipment not meeting specifications, knowing that, once the equipment has been installed, schools are reluctant to demand that it be dismantled and replaced. (Similar caution is justified in regard to the purchase contract and to the supplier's warranty: both are legal documents, and the school's attorney, as well as a qualified specialist, should check them thoroughly prior to their signing by the school administration.)

The purchase contract must be spelled out in the greatest detail. Particularly important are: delivery and installation dates; a guarantee that the equipment to be installed is precisely that which is ordered in accordance with the school's specifications (which would be embodied in or appended to the contract); and the provision by the supplier of free equipment orientation for the school's teachers and laboratory assistants.

The supplier's warranty normally guarantees that, during a period of one year from the date of accepted installation, he will replace any defective equipment and repair all malfunctions free of charge. The school should negotiate a contract (as described above) for service beyond this one-year period.

(4) *Installation of the Laboratory.* Technical and legal factors are treated above. The most important consideration remaining is that planning must provide for thorough orientation of teachers and student assistants in the use of the equipment *before* classes begin to use

it. Many schools arrange for installation so that suitable workshops can be held just prior to the fall term. Others devote an entire spring term to teacher training with the new equipment.

Successful Use of the Language Laboratory Materials

We stated earlier that, since language laboratory equipment is *machinery,* its effectiveness in the modern foreign language instruction program depends entirely upon the quality of the methods and materials used with it, and that quality, in turn, depends entirely upon the human beings who determine it. It is obvious that a school which invests all its available money in equipment, to the detriment of methods training for teachers and language laboratory materials, is practicing false economy.

The most important consideration in the selection and use of language laboratory materials is that of their relevance to the school's total modern foreign language program and to the classroom instruction given to the students using them. Since the laboratory is basically a place for practice (as opposed to learning) and since laboratory time is usually limited, it goes without saying that this time must be used for efficient reinforcement of what has already been presented in the classroom. When basic program tapes do not constitute a component of the course materials; when supplementary drill tapes are not revised to eliminate unknown vocabulary and structural items; when unfamiliar taped directions and procedures are used in the laboratory; or when too great a period of time (more than a few days) separates the work done in the laboratory from that done previously in the classroom, confusion and apathy result, and the time spent in the laboratory is wasted time.

Planning for Materials Acquisition. Planning for the acquisition of laboratory materials, like laboratory planning in general, should be unhurried and systematic. Aside from the prime consideration of correlation with classroom materials and procedures, the following factors have to be taken into account:

The Plethora of Recorded Materials Available. Each year brings a flood of new materials claimed to be suitable for use in the language laboratory, and the person responsible for acquisitions is soon overwhelmed with commercial brochures, catalogs, and advertisements. This is essentially healthy, since some of the materials are excellent and constitute real improvement over existing ones. Others, of course, represent nothing more than attempts to capitalize on the growing interest in audio-lingual instruction. One must be particulary wary of (a) recorded materials, seemingly sound and attractive, which bear no specific relationship to materials used in the classroom [4] and (b) recorded materials to accompany printed texts which are not audio-lingual in context and method. The use of "traditional" tapes is a contradiction in terms; indeed, as noted earlier, the use of the laboratory itself with traditional methods and materials in the classroom is a contradiction in terms. Yet a considerable number of publishers have re-issued grammar-translation-reading texts, complete with "audio-lingual" tapes. The danger is in acquirng "Pattern Drills," "Audio-Lingual Exercises," "French Stories," and so forth, without first knowing their exact linguistic and teaching content.

Some of the most reliable criteria for materials selection are: (a) the recommendations of the MLA's *Selective List of Materials* (see Bibliography) and those of the materials review sections of the reputable professional journals; (b) recommendations of present users; and (c) the degree of correlation with classroom materials as determined by personal examination of the materials prior to purchase. These criteria apply to *visual* laboratory materials as well as to recorded items.

Basic Program Tapes. Basic materials for the laboratory consist of the tape component of the integrated audio-lingual course materials used in the classroom. (The term "integrated audio-lingual course materials" refers to those sequential sets of course materials in which each component—teacher manual, student test, tape, disc, film, filmstrip, wall chart, flash card, test—relates to the other components at every point to form a coordinated system of audio-lingual instructon.) These tapes reproduce the basic content of the classroom components in forms suitable for use in the laboratory: repetition drill, listening comprehension drill, pattern practice, and so forth.

Supplementary Tapes. Taped components of integrated audio-lingual course materials, while adequate as basic laboratory material, do not meet all the needs of a well rounded audio-lingual program.

---

4. An exception may be made here in the case of listening comprehension and other supplementary tapes for advanced classes. In all cases, however, prospective buyers, prior to purchase, should request publishers to provide transcripts of tape and disc content.

Supplementary materials will be needed in the following areas: speech production drill, structural drill, cultural enrichment, advanced listening comprehension exercises, and testing.

Listening Comprehension Tapes for Advanced Classes. Existing sets of audio-lingual materials are somewhat lacking in varied listening comprehension tapes. This is particularly true for advanced classes. These students should be using the laboratory frequently on an individual or small-group basis, working with carefully graded material. Some of the material should be unfamiliar to them to provide a challenge to their more highly developed skills and to appeal to their specialized interests.

There is available a vast amount of recorded material, much of it on discs—stories, plays, narratives, poems, and songs—suitable for use with advanced classes. These materials are disparate, however, and they are not specifically related to any set of course materials. To make the material suitable for use by advanced classes in the laboratory is an exacting task, and it requires a considerable amount of time and hard work by the teachers; but the results can be highly rewarding. The following check-points should be observed in preparing this type of material for the laboratory:

1. The content of selections used must be appropriate to the general background and foreign language proficiency of the students.
2. Students should be orientated, by teacher direction, to the general content of the tape before they hear it. At this point, key words or expressions with which they are not familiar should be explained.
3. Care must be taken to see that literary selections used contain material that by nature might normally be *heard* rather than *read*—dialogue, informal narrative, plays, etc. The tapes are designed to develop understanding of the *spoken* language; they are not exercises in reading comprehension.
4. To insure students' active participation in the listening comprehension exercise, they should be told what to listen *for*. This is done in the form of taped introductions, explanations, and directions. The students' attention can be directed to very specific points: factual information (as opposed to minute detail), or to a point of interpretation, such as the attitude of a speaker on a tape.
5. Finally, after being told what to listen for, students should be

informed as to how they will be expected to use the information gained from the listening practice. To provide the student with a basis for self-evaluation, and to provide himself with a check on the student's grasp of the material, the teacher records, at appropriate points, objective-type questions for the student to answer; or, at the end of the selection, he has the student perform a specific task requiring mastery of its content.

Thus, a good listening comprehension tape provides for: (1) a selection of suitable length and content; (2) student orientation to content; (3) material that reflects spoken, not written, language forms; (4) selective listening; (5) specific directions as to the use to be made of information gained, and (6) suitable follow-up activities. Of these six elements, commercial tapes and discs usually provide only the first. The other elements must be supplied by the teacher.

Testing Tapes. Despite the unique capacity of the language laboratory for listening comprehension and oral production testing, only general proficiency tests for the modern foreign language are currently available commercially on tape. Other test tapes for the laboratory will have to be prepared by teachers. (See "Testing in the Language Laboratory" below.)

Visual Materials. The use of films, television, slides, and filmstrips in the language laboratory will undoubtedly increase as suitable materials become readily available. Even at present, some of the film and filmstrip elements of the integrated audio-lingual course materials can be used effectively there. And, if carefully coordinated with appropriate teacher-prepared tapes, any number of the existing films and filmstrips available, particularly those of a cultural nature, are highly suitable for laboratory use. Successful use of these visual aids in classroom foreign language instruction demonstrates clearly their value as a powerful reinforcement of the audial element. That same use, however, indicates once again the necessity of the close correlation of materials with the other instructional components.

PROGRAMMING; INDIVIDUALIZATION OF INSTRUCTION

The capacity of the language laboratory for the provision of programs suitable to individual and small-group needs is one that is often neglected or overlooked entirely. The consideration of individual capacities and requirements is just as important in the laboratory as it is in the classroom, where the teacher often gives remedial work to slow pupils, special projects to the advanced, and average work to the majority of each class. Indeed, such individualization of instruction is much simpler to effect in the laboratory than in the classroom because of the separate-channel facility and multiple tape decks.

The principle of *multiple programming* is similar to that of the split-period, or modular laboratory schedule. Here, however, subject modules, not time modules, are in question. Basically, this type of programming is a matter of deciding which sequences of taped material are best suited to the needs of specific groups of students within a given laboratory session, then selecting and recording on a single tape the entire program for each group. Again, the preparation of these individualized programs requires time, care, and extra work by the teacher, who must correlate the programs at all times with the progress of his students in the classroom and in the laboratory. He selects taped exercises for each laboratory group only after checking method and content thoroughly. He usually selects only one portion of a given tape for any one program, and he draws from several tape sources those sections which provide variety, progression, and thoroughness for the program of each ability group. Finally, he re-records on one tape the content of each complete program, thus eliminating the necessity of changing tapes during the laboratory session.

Multiple programming does not mean that a school must buy two or three times as many tapes as it would need otherwise. It affects only the playing order of material on the tapes already owned. Since the number of individualized programs needed for a given laboratory session is usually small—two or three—re-recording of the original material will require only that same number of extra blank tapes.

A description of the development of a typical multiple program [5] follows: The teacher starts from the central subject-procedure theme of the laboratory session and adapts this to the various groups. (Here, the base experience is with the Spanish verbs *ser* and *estar*.) He begins with Group 2—the "average" group:

To get the students "back into Spanish," he uses first a taped "warm-up" drill, perhaps a dialogue review; he follows the "warm-up" with a recording of the current dialogue (for listening comprehension and speaking practice), or with narrative material, according to the content

---

5. I am indebted to Professor Terry Gamba, Purdue University, for this description.

of the current classroom lesson. The third portion of the program consists of patten practice with sentences using *ser* and *estar*. He can be more flexible in his choice of materials for the fourth—and last—module, since the "average" group has completed the most essential parts of the material. It could now listen to an anecdote, do a directed-response drill, or hear a musical selection or poem.

Students work, during the 20-minute period, not from entire tapes but from pertinent sections of tapes. Each of the four modules could be approximately five minutes long—normally quite enough time to spend on a single activity during a given laboratory period.

The teacher now plans the program for Group 1—the "slow" group. His guiding thought is that this group will need more time to review and practice than the other groups. The first module is, again, a "warm-up"; and, since the "average" group is using a review tape, the same one could be used for Group 1. The second module is the current pattern practice on *ser* and *estar*. It is probable that one practice session with the pattern drill material will not be sufficient for these students, and they will have to repeat it (third module). The fourth module is used for rerinforcement and review of an earlier pattern drill with *ser* and *estar* or with other structural items.

The program for Group 3—the advanced group—is as follows: The first module consists of a "warm-up" drill—the same as used for Groups 1 and 2. A listening comprehension tape could be used for module 2, but, to challenge this group, it should contain some unfamiliar material. The third module is used for the current pattern drill on *ser* and *estar*. However, since this group is probably quite proficient in drill use (through earlier practice in the classroom), the problem is, again, to give its members extra challenge. The teacher assigns the group to the booths with tape recorders for self-evaluation of the work on the *ser* and *estar* pattern drill. This playback-compare-correct activity constitutes the fourth module. See Figure 7–2.

TESTING IN THE LANGUAGE LABORATORY

The testing process is of particular importance in modern foreign language instruction, where students must master a whole new set of communication habits and where learning involves trial, error, and correction at every stage. With the emphasis placed upon listening comprehension and oral production skills in the audio-lingual program, the language laboratory—an audio-lingual instrument—has

PLAN OF WORK *Spanish I → 5th period,*

Language Lab - 2/16

Ser - Estar

Group 1	*Group 2*	*Group 3*
Warm-up *dialogue review* *(SP-I-032)*	*Warm up* *dialogue review* *(SP I-032)*	*Warm-up* *dialogue review* *(SP I-032)*
Pattern Practice *ser-estar* *(SP I-121)*	*Listen / Speak* *current dialogue* *(SP I-034)*	*Listening Comp* *(SP I-341* *[Toledo]*
Pattern Practice *ser-estar* *(SP I-121)* *(Repeat)*	*Pattern Practice* *ser-estar* *(SP I-121)*	*Pattern Practice* *ser-estar* *(SP I-121)*
Review *(SP I-118)* *exp of time*	*Anecdote* *(oral follow-up)* *SP I-485*	*self-evaluation* *record/playback*

Figure 7-2

unique capacities for the testing of these skills, capacities which are often overlooked.

Language is basically speech, and the development of understanding and speaking skills takes first place in the audio-lingual instruction program. We teach speech; so we must *test* speech. The testing and grading of the speech skills must be in proportion to the primary emphasis they receive.

Learning problems occur when the units and patterns of the language being studied, their grammatical distribution and meaning, or the ways they are used, have no close counterparts in the student's native language. In such instances, his natural tendency is to think in terms of the forms and patterns of his own language, in the ways they are used in his language, and to express himself accordingly. Each of these differences, then, constitutes an obstacle for him to overcome; or, looking at it another way, a new habit which he must learn. The extent to which a student solves these problems, or to which he establishes the new habits, is the extent of his control of the foreign language. This is precisely what we want to test in the classroom and in the language laboratory. Thus, to test control of the foreign language we test control of the *problems* offered the student of that language, as they occur in authentic linguistic and cultural situations. Testing time is precious time, and it cannot be wasted on items that offer no real difficulty for students. To determine systematically what specific problems exist for the student in the target language, the teacher should have access to a detailed contrastive linguistic analysis of English and that language. This type of analysis provides an exact description of each difference in the sound, grammar, and vocabulary systems of the two languages.[6]

Objective testing of understanding and speaking ability requires good acoustic conditions, precise directions and timing of pauses, and objective-type answer formats. These conditions are much more easily met in the laboratory than in the classroom; moreover, group testing of *oral production* is possible in the laboratory but virtually impossible in the classroom, where students must respond individually to test items different from those given other students.

Informal Laboratory Testing. As in the classroom, the teacher may use any format he desires for informal testing, but it should be simple, and so should the ratings given. In the two major areas of listening comprehension and oral production, students should be rated on performance in the following: sound system (phonemes, intonation, stress, rhythm, and juncture), grammar (control of the structural item, or items, being rated), and vocabulary. However the teacher grades *only one specific problem in the work being done by each group in the laboratory at a given time.* The rating key should contain no more than three digits: "1" for superior, "2" for average, and "3" for unsatisfactory performance.[7]

Formal Laboratory Testing. Formal testing in the laboratory is just an extension of the informal. Rating areas are the same, although equipment used, and test formats and methods, will be different. One of the main differences is that formal laboratory testing must be as objective and precise as it can be made. As noted earlier, periodic and

6. See chapter bibliography for a listing of contrastive analyses now available for English: German, Spanish, and Italian. Similar studies for English: French and Russian will be forthcoming from the same publisher.

7. See Karl S. Pond, "Objectives, Tests, and Motivation," NEWSLETTER of the National Association of Language Laboratory Directors, II, No. 1 (December, 1967), pp. 11-15, for a concise statement on the interrelationship of daily laboratory work, testing, and program aims.

end-of-year tests suitable for use in the language laboratory are not now available. Teachers usually have to devise their own. Construction of a good test for speech skills takes time and the most careful planning for objectivity, reliability, and validity.[8] A good test for the laboratory, like laboratory work in general, always relates closely to the work and methods of the classroom. If it does not, it is not a valid test.

Listening Comprehension Testing. The things that distinguish listening comprehension testing from testing of oral production are the equipment used (a tape recorder is required for the latter) and the fact that, for listening comprehension tests, the student is not required to speak. Procedures and the construction of test items differ accordingly.

Basically, listening comprehension test items are designed to force the student to choose between or among minimally different units of sound, structure, or meaning. A test tape, playing from a program source at the console, gives the student a test item, followed by a pause during which he responds by marking his answer sheet, which has an objective-type format and which is very easy to grade.

Oral Production Testing. This type of test is no more difficult to administer in the laboratory than a test of listening comprehension; on the other hand, it is more difficult to grade objectively. All students taking the test *hear* the test items at the same time; but answers to the test are *spoken* answers, and they have to be recorded. Some schools arrive at a partial solution of the problem by providing half the student booths with tape recorders. This permits testing half of each class at one time, and arranging two relays of students within a class period is not too difficult.

The teacher should have students record *only the answers* of oral production tests; otherwise the grader wastes a great deal of time listening over and over again to the recorded test items. Students should record their names (for tape identification) at the beginning and at the end of their test tapes. At the end of the test, the teacher may have each student re-wind his tape and leave it on the machine. Later, tapes may all be re-recorded on one or two tapes by a student

---

8. Excellent testing guides for the modern foreign language teacher are: Robert Lado, *Language Testing*, and Rebecca Valette. *Modern Language Testing* (see chapter bibliography). Particularly valuable are the numerous examples of test items provided.

assistant. The teacher thus avoids the necessity, during the grading process of having to place *each* test tape on a recorder and remove it before proceeding to the next.

Formal oral production tests cannot be graded by monitoring or by recording student responses at the console. Since the teacher can listen to only one student at a time, he would be grading everyone on a different section of the test; and he can record simultaneously only the performances of a number of students equal to the number of tape decks at the console.

The basic *subjectivity* of oral production test grading constitutes a real problem. One is obliged, nevertheless, to make grades just as objective as they can be made. There are several ways of doing this:

A grading committee, composed of the teacher and one or two other members (teachers or native speakers of the language) can rate students' performances. Each committee member assigns a rating on a given point, and the ratings are averaged. With considerable practice, committees often arrive at very good correlations of scores.

A very restricted rating scale—one with just a few digits or letters—should be used. This eliminates the need for fine judgments, saying, for example, only that a student's production of one specific linguistic element is *superior* (like that of a native speaker), *satisfactory* (not as good, but clearly understandable to a native), or *unsatisfactory* (not clearly understandable to a native speaker.)

A grade should be given a student on *only one specific point of one specific skill at any one time.*

Laboratory Testing Pointers. There are several reasons for not attempting to administer "live" laboratory tests. First, a test should be as objective as possible; and, if the teacher makes a few human mistakes in delivery, it will not be. Next, if pauses for student responses are not of the uniformly right length, that will also distort objectivity. What is needed is *a good recording made from a good script.*

The use of foreign language in the test directions may pose a problem. Although the teacher's use of English in the classroom may be minimal, it is difficult to avoid all English in giving procedural directions, since the vocabulary is somewhat specialized. The best solution seems to lie in common sense. If the directions will be clear and simple in the foreign language, use it—if not, use English.

Paper-and-pencil techniques are suitable for use with both listening comprehension and oral production tests, but their use with the latter may require construction of rather intricate test items. A good tip is to put listening comprehension test items in multiples of five, or ten, for easy grading.

As a guide for test preparation, the teacher does well to list specific problems, in all the linguistic categories, on file cards. Model items for testing these could also be entered on the card, together with the specific elements from his own course materials that he wishes to test.

Following administration and grading of the tests, the teacher should re-play the listening comprehension test for the whole class (with each student checking the items against his corrected answer sheet). If possible the teacher should review the recorded speaking test with each student individually; at least, a graded sheet for the speaking test, giving the content of test items, the correct responses, and all errors made, should be returned to each student.

Language Laboratory Equipment and Its Use

Types and Arrangements of Equipment. The term "language laboratory" encompasses a very wide range of equipment and arrangement of that equipment. Language laboratory use may involve a single student, listening to a recording under controlled conditions, or many hundreds of college students, in dormitory and fraternity rooms far from the central laboratory station, dialing their choice of programs from as many as a thousand recordings available to them.

There are three basic combinations of equipment found in the conventional installation: audio-passive, audio-active, and audio-active-record.

Audio-passive. An audio-passive arrangement of equipment consists of a program source (a tape recorder or a record player) connected to earphones worn by a student. With good equipment, the fidelity of sound can be high, but the student's rôle is essentially "passive"—he listens. If he does respond or repeat the material, much of his voice will be dispersed into the air, and the rest will be blocked by his earphones and distorted by the bone structure of his head. He cannot compare his performance accurately with the models of the program source; nor can the teacher monitor his performance. See Figure 7—3.

Audio-active. This combination is a type commonly used in the language laboratory today. Like audio-passive equipment, it consists of earphones connected to a program source, but a student microphone and amplifier, connected to his earphones and to the teacher console

AUDIO-PASSIVE

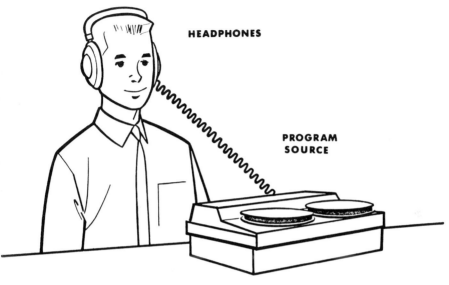

Figure 7-3

(for monitoring and two-way communication) are added. With audio-active equipment, the student can receive sound with good fidelity both from the program source (usually a tape deck at the teacher console) and from his own microphone. Hearing his voice in this way enables him to compare his performance with that of the program models. He participates actively—hence, audio-active. See Figure 7–4.

Audio-active-record. This installation is the same as the audio-active, but the record-playback-compare facility (provided by a tape recorder) has been added. It has all the advantages of the audio-active arrangement, plus the playback-compare feature. If enough positions are of this type, group oral testing in the laboratory becomes feasible. See Figure 7–5.

The Conventional Language Laboratory. A typical language laboratory today is located in a room used exclusively for foreign language study. The room holds fifteen or more student booths, each separated from the other visually and acoustically and each equipped with earphones, a microphone, and an amplifying apparatus. The typical laboratory will have as many as twenty percent of the student positions

AUDIO-ACTIVE

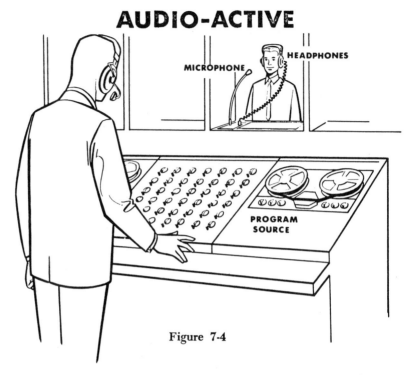

Figure 7-4

Figure 7-5

AUDIO-ACTIVE-RECORD

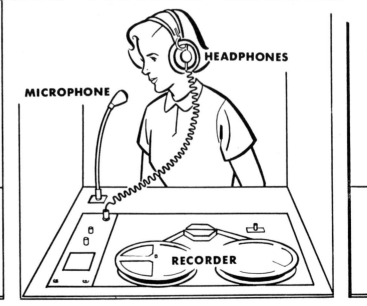

equipped with audio-active-record equipment. Each student position is connected by covered wiring to the control center of the laboratory—the teacher console. From this console, the teacher provides the students with one or more programs, listens in on student performance, and corrects the students individually, by rows, or as a group. The console will have as many as four program sources, three tape decks and a record player, but with add-on capacity. See Figure 7-6.

Remote-control and Random-access Laboratories. The remote-control type of laboratory is essentially the same as the conventional one, except that all student tape recorders—and sometimes the program sources—are located on racks in the laboratory or even in an adjoining room. The advantages of this arrangement are that students do not have to thread tapes on booth recorders; the disadvantages are that, in some installations, the fixed-length tapes (loaded in cartridges) replay only when they have reached their end; the student cannot control them, and thus he cannot work at his own speed. Further, it is difficult to match program length with the running time of these tapes.

A random-access installation can be equipped with a library of as

Figure 7-6

A "TYPICAL" LANGUAGE LABORATORY

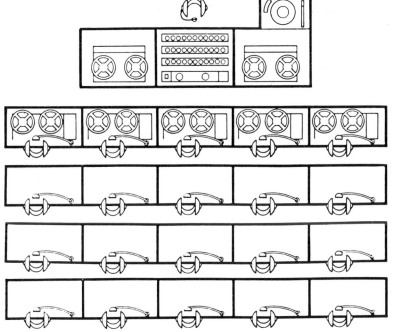

many as a thousand different programs and, using telephone switching procedures, it can be used by hundreds of students at one time. A student obtains the desired program by consulting a directory listing the content of each program and then dialing its number. The number of students listening simultaneously is restricted only by the number of sets of receiving equipment. The advantages of this complex arrangement are that the variety of programs that can be offered at one time is practically unlimited, and so is the number of students who have access to them. Disadvantages are the high cost of equipment, installation, and operation, plus the non-feasibility of monitoring, intercommunication, and use of record-playback facilities.

The "Electronic Classroom"; the "Wireless" Laboratory; the "Portable Laboratory"; "Public Distribution Systems." The first three equipment combinations have a common characteristic: They represent an attempt to save money and space. Equipment components are relatively inexpensive, and they can be installed and used in an ordinary classroom. After use, the "wireless" and "portable" laboratory equipment can be completely removed, if desired.

The "Electronic Classroom." This is simply a classroom in which student desks have been equipped with audio-active laboratory components connected to a program source at the front of the room. Advantages: When the laboratory equipment is not in use, the room may be used as a regular classroom; equipment and its installation are relatively inexpensive; monitoring and intercom facilities are used. Disadvantages: Wiring and student desk equipment may be bothersome and in danger of damage, in ordinary classroom activity; only one program source is usually available; recording facilities are not readily available; each language classroom has to be equipped as an "electronic classroom"; there is no privacy for students; sound conditioning is impossible.

The "Wireless" Laboratory. This installation provides for a broadcast of a program by radio from the front of the classroom to the students' receiving equipment by way of an antenna wired around the walls of the classroom. The student equipment permits audioactive functions, but monitoring and intercom facilities are absent. The record-playback facility is optional. Advantages: Low cost, absence of wiring (except for the antenna); ease of moving transmitter and receiving equipment from room to room. Disadvantages: There is no privacy for students; sound conditioning is impossible; there is no monitoring or intercom facility; the audio signal may vary in strength and quality.

The "Portable" Laboratory. This combination consists of audio-active equipment which can be carried by hand or is moved from room to room on a cart. Student headsets are connected by wiring to the console on the cart (or in carrying case) or to jacks installed with permanent wiring around the walls of the classroom. The cart (or carrying cases) contain the program sources, together with monitoring and intercom equipment. Advantages: Low cost; mobility; monitoring and intercom facilities. Disadvantages: No recording facilities; no privacy for students; sound conditioning is impossible; setting up and putting away student equipment cay be clumsy and time-consuming.

A number of factors, many of them peculiar to a given locality, will influence the decision of a school in its selection of language laboratory equipment and arrangement. The decision is often a most difficult one to make.[9] In the final analysis, the school must key its decision to this question: Which equipment and which arrangement best meet he needs of *our* foreign language program?

A few schools have installed, in addition to conventional or non-conventional laboratory equipment, so-called public distribution systems (consisting of high fidelity loudspeakers connected to a broadcast source in the language laboratory) in all modern foreign language classrooms. Such systems permit classroom work with listening comprehension exercises and tests, news and other radio broadcasts, and special recordings.[10]

Components of Language Laboratory Equipment. No attempt will be made here to discuss these components from a technical point of view. Hayes, Stack, and Crossman (New York State Education Depart-

---

9. Edward Stack (see chapter bibliography) has a sound comment on this: "The primary pedagogical consideration must be whether the proposed equipment will perform all the functions desired. Salesmen may quote impressive frequency-response figures for their microphones, headsets, amplifiers, tape decks, etc., but the real question is how good the *system* is, once all these components are connected together." (*loc. cit.*) Stack's work also contains an excellent set of systems specifications as a guide to schools purchasing laboratory equipment (Appendix A, pp. 209-211). See also New York State Educational Department, Hayes, and Regenstreif listings in chapter bibliography. Regenstreif's article provides an excellent summary of the advantages and disadvantages of non-conventional laboratory arrangements.

10. Information on "public distribution" systems may be obtained from Professor Charles P. Richardson, Director of the Language Laboratory, Ohio University, Athens, Ohio 45701.

ment) are good sources of this type of information, and Hayes gives specifications which all components should meet. It is rather our intent simply to list the chief components of teacher and student equipment, describing briefly the function of each, and to indicate important points related to their actual use.

Teacher Equipment (Teacher Console)

1. *Earphones.* These should be sturdy and cover the whole ear. An extra set should always be available at the console—as a spare set in case of trouble with the other, and for monitoring by visitors.

2. *Microphones.* Sturdiness and ease of handling are required. Teacher and student microphones are generally of three types: hand, gooseneck, or boom-type. All are capable of giving satisfactory service, but the hand microphone requires constant attention as to where it is held, and it can easily be dropped, damaged, or broken; the gooseneck microphone can be twisted and damaged, and again the teacher must take care that he speaks at the proper distance from it; the boom-type (which may be a part of the headset) usually requires only one adjustment for distances from mouth, it cannot easily be dropped or damaged, and it is probably the most satisfactory of the three.

3. *Tape Decks.* A tape deck is a tape recorder, installed in the teacher console, which provides a program source for the student stations. The teacher must know how to thread tapes on these machines, and he must be thoroughly familiar with their mechanical operation.

4. *Record Player.* It is recommended that the teacher console be equipped with one high-quality record player, needed for disc recordings (in use, it constitutes an additional program source).

5. *Transmission Mechanism.* In order to channel a program to an individual or to a group of students in the laboratory, the teacher uses selector switches, arranged in rows on a panel before him. Typically, each switch has a position number which corresponds to the number of a specific student station. The switch may take the form of a numbered dial, with the numbers corresponding to the numbers of the program sources available (Tape Deck No. 1, Tape Deck No. 2, Record Player, etc.). Working from his laboratory plan for the day, the teacher transmits specific programs to specific booths by setting the selector switches for those booths to the number of the program desired. For example, students in Booths 1–6 are to get program No. 1;

so he sets the switches for those Booths at "1". Booths 7–18 get program No. 2; he sets those switches at "2", etc.

Just beneath the booth selector switches is a lever which controls normal transmission and the monitoring and intercom functions. Before starting transmission of programs to the student booth, the teacher sets all levers at the "normal" position. This enables the students to receive the program assigned to their booths.

6. *Monitor and Intercom.* These functions are carried out through use of the control lever described above. As noted, when this lever is in "normal" position, the student receives the program assigned to his booth. When the teacher wishes to monitor student performance, he pushes the lever to the "monitor" position, which allows him to listen to a particular student without the student knowing it. To speak to the student, or to make corrections, the teacher pushes the lever to the "intercom" or "communicate" position, which action cuts out the student's reception of the program and permits two-way communication.

7. *"All-call" Switch.* The teacher uses this switch, which is located on the control panel or on top of the console, to speak to all of the students at the same time. Since use of the switch cuts out students' reception of all programs, teachers should use it sparingly, generally only at the beginning and at the end of the laboratory period.

8. *Test Control Switch.* Some consoles are equipped with a switch that allows the teacher to start and stop all booth recorders. Such a facility is especially useful for group oral production testing, where uniform pauses for spoken responses are required.

STUDENT EQUIPMENT

1. *The Student Booth.* Each student position is normally enclosed on at least two sides by partitions which are partly soundproof. The front of the booth may be of glass, which helps to isolate sound while still permitting the teacher (if the console is located at the front of the laboratory) to observe all students. Since the laboratory as a whole is sound conditioned, these booths provide for adequate, though not perfect, acoustics. The booths also provide privacy and freedom from distraction, which are important in the successful accomplishment of the exacting work done in the laboratory, all of which requires a high degree of concentration on the part of the student. Within each booth

is located a table or desk in which is installed audio-passive, audio-active, or audio-active-record components. On one inside wall of the booth is a hook for storing headphones when the booth is not in use.

2. *Earphones and Microphone.* (See the description and discussion of these components under "Teacher Equipment" above.)

3. *Tape Recorder.* This machine provides the basic element of the record-playback facility referred to earlier. The recorder permits the student to record both the program models and his own responses and to play them back for comparison and correction. By starting his recording equipment, the student automatically records the program model, as well as his own responses. To play back and compare, he rewinds the tape, which brings him back to the beginning of the exercise, and then starts the tape forward again. To correct a response, he may re-record over his first version during the pause provided. This erases the original version and leaves the second one, which is used in another comparison.

SPECIAL EQUIPMENT

1. *Visual Equipment.* Where visual aids are used in the language laboratory, teachers must be able to operate the basic items of equipment: an 8 or 16 mm film projector and a filmstrip/slide projector. (Overhead transparency and opaque projectors may also be used effectively in the laboratory.) The use of this equipment, which requires projection tables and a viewing screen, raises a point as to installation. Care must be taken that booth walls do not obstruct the students' vision from any angle, and correct placement of all visual equipment must be a strong consideration in initial and subsequent planning for the language laboratory. If film projectors are to be permanently installed, they should be placed in an enclosed booth or room at the rear of the laboratory where noise will be isolated.[11]

2. *Special Recording Equipment.* A recording studio, separate from but contiguous to the laboratory, may be installed. Its purpose is to provide facilities for teachers and laboratory personnel to: record master tapes; re-record taped material on individual program tapes; review and grade student tapes; and to copy, edit, and repair tapes.

---

11. See Pond, "A Language Teaching Tool: The Overhead Projector" (chapter bibliography) for an exposition of factors to be considered in the choice and use of visual equipment in the classroom and in the language laboratory.

Since the equipment used in the recording studio is similar to that of the laboratory itself, no special problems for teachers arise if they are skilled in the operation of the latter.

Language Laboratory Administration

Teacher Orientation and Training. It has been demonstrated that thorough familiarity with the capabilities, equipment, materials, and procedures of the language laboratory is a *sine qua non* of its successful use; most of the ways and means have already been discussed in some detail. It is a point, however, that bears reinforcement here, since the responsibility for training is shared by the school administration and by the teachers themselves: *Unless modern foreign language teachers understand what the laboratory can, and cannot do; unless they are deeply involved in the planning and operation of the laboratory; unless they can operate laboratory equipment with ease; unless they can select, program, and control the use of materials intelligently and in logical relation to the total modern foreign language program; then the capacities and advantages of the laboratory will be largely lost.*[12]

Two considerations, however, remain: first, *teacher training must be on-going,* and—very important—teachers entering service in the school after use of the language laboratory has begun must receive the same systematic and careful training as that given the other teachers. Second, *time must be provided for teachers* if their work with the language laboratory is to be effective: time for planning, time for examination and evaluation of materials; time for programming, time for recording, and time for correction of student tapes. It is not reasonable to expect a secondary school teacher in charge of five classes each day to prepare classroom instruction for each of those classes, plus accomplish the numerous tasks required in the laboratory, without some reduction in his total work-load. Administrators must ponder this, and they must face the fact that, unless such a reduction is made, the laboratory cannot fully perform the functions expected of it.

Scheduling. Also treated above, this topic, like teacher training, bears reinforcement here. Provision must be made for all modern

---

12. See the author's "Teacher Training and the Language Laboratory" (chapter bibliography) for a detailed discussion of the importance of teacher preparation in successful operation of the language laboratory.

foreign language classes to have laboratory practice as regularly and as frequently as possible—the minimum provision is two ½-hour periods per week. Advanced audio-lingual classes need the laboratory as much as do lower-level classes, and, if record-playback facilities are available, *they* will be the ones to draw full benefit. Laboratory periods must be relatively brief—20 minutes or so. This implies the adoption of split-period, or modular scheduling, which, in turn, implies classrooms located near the laboratory.

There is nothing sacrosanct about the conventional, hour-by-hour schedules used by most schools. A schedule is simply a device to meet best the learning needs of the students: *It has to be changed if it does not do that.*

Tape Storage and Cataloging. Failure to store and catalog taped and disc material with care results in chaos in the laboratory. Shelf categories and codes are decided upon, and stored materials are marked accordingly. Then a card, with identical coding, is made for each stored item. Shelf items (boxes, reels, discs, and disc covers) and their cards are also color-coded by language for ready identification: blue for French, green for German, etc.

The materials card catalog, usually a 3″ × 5″ file, is established and kept up to date. Here is a sample card:

```
                                                 SpI-01

                    Basic  Course  Tapes  #1

        Test: pp. 1-13
        Content: form of address
                 verb agreement
                 verm forms w/o subject pronoun
        Running time: 20 minutes

```

(*Explanation:* The catalog number is entered in the upper right hand corner. The "Sp" indicates that this is a Spanish tape, the Roman numeral I indicating Level One. "01" means that this is the first tape in the basic course material series. The numbers to the right of the dash can be used to distinguish among types of materials: 01-199 for basic course materials; 200-299 for supplementary structure drills; 300-399 for listening comprehension tapes; 400-499 for cultural, musical, literary materials; 500-599 for tests and examinations; and so forth. In the center of the card are listed the title, the textbook correlation, and the structural items treated. The running time of the tape is given in the lower left hand corner. All of this information is recorded on the tape box, and the catalog number is marked on the tape reel.)

A catalog of subject cards, cross-referenced to the materials, is also maintained. A sample card:

Verbs:	
Conjugated with *sein*	
GI-020	Text, p. 103
GI-024	Text, p. 131
GI-225	Quick Change Drills
GI-226	" " "
GI-227	" " "

(*Explanation:* Of the five tapes listed, the first two—020 and 024— are part of the basic program tapes; the remaining three are supplementary structure tapes. Planning a pre-test review of these verbs will be simple: The teacher knows which tapes are pertinent and where they are located.[13])

The Language Laboratory Director. Schools usually find it advisable to appoint, from among the members of the modern foreign language faculty, a full- or part-time language laboratory director. His basic duties are to coordinate and supervise all activities involving the laboratory; to schedule laboratory use; to train and supervise student assistants; to conduct in-service training for teachers; and, in general, to handle all laboratory administration.[14] A reduction in his teaching load is required, to allow time for the accomplishment of these duties.

Language Laboratory Assistant. Personnel are needed to assist

---

13. See Stack (*op. cit.*, pp. 48-82) for other routine forms useful in language laboratory operation.

14. Stack (*op. cit.*, pp. 66-68) provides an extensive checklist of the language laboratory director's duties.

the language laboratory director in the performance of his duties and to perform routine maintenance of laboratory equipment. They also may erase, copy, repair, and record tapes, and serve as assistants to teachers during the regular laboratory sessions. All of these duties can be performed effectively by students trained by the laboratory director. They should be volunteers but should be paid at standard student rates. Good sources of supply in college are foreign language and physics majors (or electrical engineering students) and, at the high school level, interested students from the electronics shop. Careful training is the key to successful use of these assistants, whose work can be invaluable in the smooth operation of the laboratory.

Student Orientation. All students, like teachers, need training in the use of the language laboratory. The purposes of laboratory work, and its specific relationship to classroom work, should be carefully outlined to them before they enter the laboratory for the first time, and "ground rules" of behavior should be explained. It should be made clear whether they will be financially responsible for damage or destruction of equipment and materials caused through their willful negligence. The teacher should also explain laboratory booth assignment, storage of books and materials not needed in the laboratory, care of headsets, procedure for drawing tapes, and so forth.

The use of an *orientation tape* is recommended for the first laboratory session. Such a tape, prepared by the teacher, contains directions for the use of equipment in the student booth, as well as samples of directions and exercises of the type to which students will be exposed regularly. This orientation tape can be used over and over again with new classes, and it furnishes a chance for students to get used to laboratory equipment and procedures at the same time as they receive necessary information. The tape should be carefully scripted and made as specific as possible in its direction and examples. The playing of the tape may be accompanied by projected photographs or drawings and, afterwards, mimeographed instructions, a class seating diagram, and laboratory regulations may be distributed to the students.

SUMMARY

The language laboratory is a collection of machinery which cannot teach but which, when used by a trained teacher in an audio-lingual program, with materials and methods correlating closely with those of the classroom, under a schedule of frequent, regular, and brief practice periods, will produce significant gains in the understanding and speaking skills of modern foreign language students.

Use of a well-planned laboratory, operated under these principles, offers three major advantages in the form of capabilities impossible to duplicate in the average classroom:

1. Opportunity for the vast amount of *individual* student practice essential to mastery of a spoken language;
2. Opportunity for individualization of instruction through multiple programming;
3. Opportunity for objective listening comprehension and group oral production testing.

Modern foreign language teachers play the decisive role in successful laboratory planning and operation. They should be given primary responsibility in both areas, and they must be trained, on a systematic and on-going basis, to perform the specialized tasks required of them. Some arrangement must be made to provide teachers with time during the school day for selection, programming, evaluation, and correction of student tapes.

The needs of advanced classes must not be neglected. The fact that they have attained substantial levels of language proficiency enables them to take full advantage of the record-playback facility of the audio-active-record equipment, and their need for continuous individual comprehension and structure practice is no less great than that of lower level groups.

Successful use of the language laboratory, like successful teaching in general, requires a great deal of study, ingenuity, and hard work of both teachers and administrators—a significant investment of time and effort. But hard-earned experience proves that such effort is a sound investment, one that pays off in the knowledge that students have received the best foreign language instruction that can be given them. See Figure 7–7.

Bibliography

Agard, G. B. *The Sounds of English and Italian,* (Contrastive Structures Series). (Chicago: University of Chicago Press, 1965). 76 pp.

Bernard, Edward G., and Sarah W. Lorge. *The Relative Effectiveness of Four Types of Language Laboratory Experience.* Unpublished

Figure 7-7

California State College, Hayward, uses video carrels (*below*). At the far left of the TV receiver is the control plate (*left*); right of receiver is the digital program selector (*right*). (*Laboratory equipment by Robert C. Merchant*)

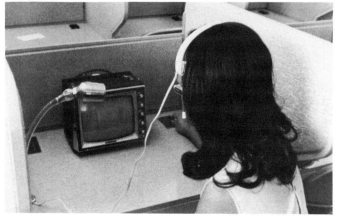

Fifty-five students can choose any of 24 different programs simply by dialing a number. (*Providence College; equipment by RCA*)

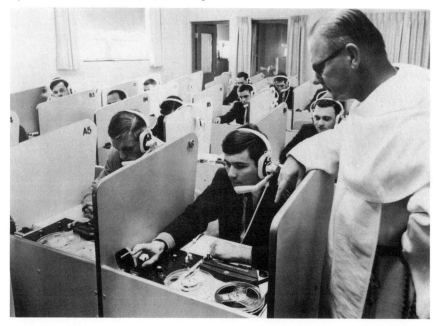

At North Carolina State University, the instructor controls all functions: (*before him*) program distribution and monitoring; (*at right*) various projectors; (*at left*) console for automated programmed instruction and testing. The latter tabulates and analyzes students' responses to multiple-choice problems presented by tape or projections on the screen (*upper left*); booths contain a push-button response device. (*Designed by Prof. Edward M. Stack; laboratory equipment by DuKane; programming and testing equipment by Edex*)

Figure 7-7 (*cont.*)

research subventioned by New York State Education Department, 1962-1963.

Brooks, Nelson. *Language and Language Learning, Theory and Practice.* (New York: Harcourt, Brace and World, 2nd Edition, 1964). 238 pp.

Belasco, Simon and Alfred Valdman. *Applied Linguistics: French,* (Boston: D.C. Heath and Company, 1961). 116 pp.

Belasco, Simon and J. W. Marchand. *Applied Linguistics: German.* (Boston: D.C. Heath and Company, 1961). 47 pp.

Belasco, Simon and Daniel Cárdenas. *Applied Linguistics: Spanish.* (Boston: D.C. Heath and Company, 1961). 62 pp.

Belasco, Simon and Thomas F. Magner. *Applied Linguistics: Russian.* (Boston: D.C. Heath and Company, 1961). 88 pp.

Bolinger, Dwight. *Aspects of Language.* (New York: Harcourt, Brace and World, 1968). 326 pp.

Cannaday, Robert W., Jr. and Terry Gamba. *Successful Use of the Language Laboratory,* Pennsylvania Department of Public Instruction, 1965. (Eight 15-minute films, 16 mm., with accompanying workshop guide, for teachers.)

Cannaday, Robert W., Jr. "Teacher Training and the Language Laboratory," *International Journal of American Linguistics,* Part II, XXXII, No. 1. (January, 1966), pp. 197-202.

DiPietro, R. J. *The Grammatical Structures of English and Italian,* Contrastive Structures Series. (Chicago: University of Chicago Press, 1965). 76 pp.

Hayes, Alfred S. *Step-by-Step Procedures for Language Laboratory Planning: Some Suggestions for Schools and Colleges,* Tacoma Park (Md.), The Author, 1960. (Available from Modern Language Association). 16 pp.

———. *Language Laboratory Facilities: Technical Guide for the Selection, Purchase, Use and Maintenance* (U.S. Office of Education Bulletin 1963, No. 37, DE-21024). (Washington, D.C.: Government Printing Office, 1963). 119 pp.

Hocking, Elton. *Language Laboratory and Language Learning.* (Washington, D.C.: National Education Association (Department of Audio-Visual Instruction), 1964). 210 pp.

Holton, James L. and P. E. King, G. Mathieu, K. S. Pond. *Sound Language Teaching: The State of the Art Today.* (New York: University Publishers, 1961).

Hughes, John P. *Linguistics and Language Teaching.* (New York: Random House, 1968).

Hutchinson, Joseph. *Modern Foreign Languages in the High School:*

The Language Laboratory (U.S. Office of Education Bulletin No. 23). Washington, D.C., 1961. 85 pp.

Kufner, H. L. *The Grammatical Structures of English and German* (Contrastive Structures Series). (Chicago: University of Chicago Press, 1962). 95 pp.

Lado, Robert. *Language Teaching: A Scientific Approach.* (New York: McGraw-Hill Book Company, 1964). 239 pp.

———. *Language Testing.* (London: Longmans, Green, 1961). 389 pp.

Léon, Pierre R. *Laboratoire de langues et correction phonétique.* (Paris: Didier, 1962). (Available from Chilton Books, Philadelphia). 275 pp.

Marty, Fernand. *Language Laboratory Learning.* (Roanoke, Va.: Audio-Visual Publications, 1960). Available from the author at Hollins College, Hollins, Va. 256 pp.

———. *Linguistics Applied to the Beginning French Course.* (Roanoke, Va.: Audio-Visual Publications, 1963). 271 pp.

Moulton, William G. *The Sounds of English and German* (Contrastive Structures Series). (Chicago: University of Chicago Press, 1962). 145 pp.

Modern Language Association, *Planning and Operating a Language Laboratory or an Electronic Classroom in a High School: A Dozen Do's and Dont's.* (New York: Modern Language Association, 1961). 4 pp.

———. *Selective List of Materials for Use by Teachers of Modern Foreign Languages in Elementary and Secondary Schools.* Edited by Mary J. Ollman. (New York: Modern Language Association, 1962). Supplement, 1964. 162 pp.

New York State Education Department, *French for Secondary Schools: Content and Organization for 4- and 6-Year Sequences.* Edited by Remunda Cudoux. (Albany: New York State Education Department, 1961).

German for Secondary Schools. (Albany: New York State Education Department, 1961.)

———. *Spanish for Secondary Schools: Content and Organization for 4- and 6-Year Sequences* (edited by Remunda Cadoux). (Albany: New York State Education Dept., 1961).

———. *The Electronic Classroom: A Guide for Planning* (prepared by David Crossman). (Albany: New York State Education Department, 1964).

Norstrand, Howard L., D. W. Foster, and C. J. Christensen. *Research on Language Teaching: An Annotated International Bibliography, 1945-1964.* (Seattle: University of Washington Press, 1965).

Politzer, Robert. *Foreign Language Learning: A Linguistic Intro-duction,* preliminary edition. (Englewood Cliffs, N.J.: Prentice-Hall, 1965). 155 pp.

———. *Teaching French: An Introduction to Applied Linguistics,* 2nd edition. (New York: Blaisdell, 1965). 140 pp.

———. and Charles N. Staubach. *Teaching Spanish: An Introduction to Applied Linguistics,* 2nd edition. (New York: Blaisdell, 1965). 198 pp.

Pond, Karl S. "A Language Teaching Tool: The Overhead Projector." *Modern Language Journal,* XLVII (January, 1963), pp. 30-33.

———. "Objectives, Tests, and Motivation," *Newsletter* of the National Association of Language Laboratory Directors, II, No. 1 (December, 1967), pp. 11-15.

Regenstreif, Harry. "The Language Laboratory vs. the Electronic Classroom." *Newsletter* of the National Association of Language Laboratory Directors, II, No. 2 (March, 1968), pp. 14-17.

Stack, Edward M. *The Language Laboratory and Modern Language Teaching,* 2nd edition. (New York: Oxford University Press, 1965). 234 pp.

Stockwell, R. P., J. D. Bowen, and J. W. Martin. *The Grammatical Structures of English and Spanish* (Contrastive Structures Series). (Chicago: University of Chicago Press, 1965). 328 pp.

——— and J. D. Bowen. *The Sounds of Spanish* (Contrastive Structures Series). (Chicago: University of Chicago Press, 1965). 168 pp.

"Taking the Mystery out of the Language Laboratory," St. Paul (Minn.), Minnesota Mining and Manufacturing Company, 1963. (Three filmstrips, three tapes, and study guides. An orientation kit for modern foreign language teachers.)

Valette, Rebecca M. *Modern Language Testing* (New York: Harcourt, Brace and World, 1967) 200 pp.

CHAPTER EIGHT

Audio-Visual Learning
and Foreign Languages

by

Elton Hocking

Purdue University

The unique power of the audio-visual presentation is that its total impact is greater than the sum of its parts. For better or worse, it multiplies the qualities—or the weaknesses—of its subject.

This mysterious new power has brought various reactions. Some persons are alarmed; they predict that TV will produce some great actor-demagogue—a kind of electronic Pied Piper who will lead us all like rats to our destruction. Others reply that improved education will prevent such evil use of audio-visual communication. But evidently, in order to do so, education itself must learn to use it well.

So far, it has not. Our schools and colleges have been slow to accept the audio-visual devices, and the humanities in particular have been reluctant, probably because of what has been called "the humanist's distrust of the machine." [1] Although it has long been customary for science teachers (most of them, men) to work with equipment in the laboratory, the humanists (mostly women) handle only books and perhaps a piece of chalk. Accordingly, the lion's share of NDEA funds

---

1. W. R. Parker, *The National Interest and Foreign Languages.* Third edition. (Government Printing Office, Washington, D. C. 20202, 1962), p. 63.

for equipment and materials has been requested and obtained by our colleagues in science; a mere fraction—in some states as little as 1½%—has gone to foreign languages. Only a minority of the high schools have a language laboratory; of these, perhaps 10% are equipped to use visual materials.

Why this extreme lag? Misinformation or distrust, first of all. The humanist is prone to associate "movies" with mere entertainment; the average language teacher, moreover, thinks of instructional films as travelogs, frequently with the sound track in English. Only since 1961 have we had *integrated* visuals: sequences of films, filmstrips or slides which present the content and use the linguistic forms and constructions of the tape and the textbook. Also, since most teachers belong to no FL society, they have heard little or nothing about the new integrated courses. Even the professional journals have generally failed to report them adequately. Textbook reviewers are unpaid volunteers who are interested in books; often they simply discuss "the book" and not the accompanying visual materials or even the tape recordings.

Cost has been another hindrance. Unlike the teaching of science or physical education, for which it is customary to spend considerable sums for equipment and supplies, foreign language instruction is generally considered "book learning" and therefore cheap learning. The average school board is shocked when asked for thousands or even only hundreds of dollars for a French or Spanish film series. Nevertheless, a fair number of school systems have purchased the most costly integrated courses because the teachers had made a convincing case for them—sometimes it was the PTA, more enlightened or more vigorous than the teachers. But in every case, a clear understanding was essential, first to get money, and then to get good results in the classroom.

"Audio-Visual Aids" vs. the Integrated Audio-Visual Course

It is generally agreed that, since most people are "eye-minded," a pictorial follow-up adds interest, and therefore motivation, to learning through sound or through silent reading. Conversely, the presentation of the subject matter may be made first of all by pictures, in which case the sound track or the printed text serves merely as reinforcement. In either case the multisensory presentation is more generally appealing and memorable than the monosensory. Market research in advertising has established that, despite the enormous cost, the most profitable "commercial" is the one which uses the utmost variety of sensory devices: picture, voice, text, color, motion, rhythm, music— separately and in combinations. Such a multisensory presentation is sometimes known as the "systems approach," meaning a systematic combination of mutually reinforcing stimuli which act upon the various senses.

Systematic, multisensory materials for language learning are much more sophisticated than the traditional, unrelated "audio-visual aids." Frequently mere pictures of "realia," the latter usually serve to arouse interest in a subject which is only peripheral to the course. While actual or pictured menus, tickets, programs, coins, etc., can be lively curiosities, the vocabulary is strange to the class and of dubious value if learned in isolation. Show-and-tell is on a higher plane when it involves imported slides of the teacher's 8 millimeter movies and if they provide some artistry and sequence; at worst it degenerates into fun-and-games.

No doubt an occasional diversion is needed to break monotony or relieve tension; "singing along" with an imported disc can lift spirits while it teaches good diction; a professional travelog or documentary film, if it avoids the merely picturesque and the posh, can convey some understanding of the foreign country and its people. Such occasional activities can be valuable in an incidental way, but they are not to be confused with the organized learning of language and culture.

Midway between these "one-shot" materials and the complete course is the sub-course: a short sequence of films or filmstrips with closely related tapes or discs, flash cards or workbooks which reproduce pictures from the films, a manual for the teacher, and—unless the materials are intended for FLES—a printed exercise book. The best of these sub-courses achieve true integration, that is, a multisensory attack upon identical aspects of the language. The great weakness of such a short course is inherent in its very shortness. After completing it, the class must turn to a different course, with the usual problems of duplication or omission of content.

A more valuable "middle way" is the use of a complete sound-film series (Encyclopaedia Britannica Films, McGraw-Hill, etc.), as audio-visual supplements to the intermediate and advanced courses. At these levels there is a general tendency to stress reading at the expense of audio-lingual practice. This tendency can be overcome by the systematic use of the various film series: intended primarily for use at the first level, their vocabulary and constructions are the high-frequency items which students most need to review and practice actively. Integration of the linguistic content is thus achieved by the very nature of these film series, although (and because) they were devised as parts of an elementary course using basic language materials.

Complete A-V courses are recent, scarce, and—in the U.S.A.—restricted almost entirely to French and Spanish. Among the first were those produced in Sweden and France for the teaching of English.[2] The latter employs principles, materials and techniques which have been widely followed:

> The spoken language must be taught. . . . It must be authentic. . . .
>
> The materials include disc recordings, cartoon-type color filmstrips, tests of the dialogs (with indications of the melodic patterns), and, facing them, the filmstrip pictures again. This combination must not be fragmented. The A-V aids are no mere bonus or diversion. They are an integral part of the method—the basis of the system. . . .
>
> The filmstrips provide the meaning, so that there is no need to analyze or explain. . . . At this early stage, we consider grammatical or phonetic theory to be unnecessary or even dangerous. Reading, writing and spelling will be introduced after the first 30 or 40 hours of class. . . .
>
> Grammar will be studied, but only at the end of the second year. . . .
>
> The use of A-V materials is no mere supplement to "be modern" or arouse interest; they save time and effort for the teacher and enable him to present a living language.[3]

Notable in this course is the use of the picture as a specific cue. The synchronized recording provides a certain question or statement for each cartoon of the filmstrip. Each cartoon reappears in the book, with the previously-heard question or statement printed alongside but covered by a cardboard mask. The picture serves to evoke the related

---

2. "English Without a Book" (for FLES) by Max Gorosch, was developed progressively and used experimentally from 1957 to 1961. It uses filmstrips and tapes. Similarly "Passport to English" (for secondary schools), by G. Capelle and D. Girard (see footnote 3).

3. G. Capelle and D. Girard, *Principes méthodologiques de "Passport to English"* (Paris: Didier, 1962), pp. 9-10, 12, 16-18 *passim*.

sentence, and vice versa. This use of the picture-cue exemplifies the principle of associative learning and recall.

Similar techniques and principles first became familiar in America chiefly through "Voix et images de France," produced in France for use throughout the world.[4] The content of this course derives from a unique tabulation of the most frequently-used expressions in *spoken* French. The course uses cartoon-style filmstrips, and synchronized tape recordings, largely in dialogue form. The use of English is banned completely, and there is a long pre-reading period. The course occasionally uses sound films for the teaching of culture rather than language. For the teacher there is a manual, and the American distributor provides shared-cost workshops for special training.

Another elaborate and entertaining A-V course is "En France comme si vous y étiez," [5] first broadcast by NBC in 1963–1964. Now a revised version for school use reduces the 26 half-hour films to 39 thirteen-minute segments, and replaces the actress-interlocutor by language analysis, largely in the form of graphics and cartoons.

Deceptively entertaining at first glance, this course combines innovation with scholarship: vocabulary and structures from *Le français fondamental,* with frequent "re-entries" disguised by the different contexts but made memorable by subtle camera work. Each film stresses one aspect of phonology and a few grammatical structures; also it introduces some 30–40 new words. All these linguistic elements are developed through skits and songs and sometimes by "gags" such as comparing the negative *ne . . . pas* to a sandwich. Unorthodox, no doubt, but surely memorable.

In addition to the 39 films the course includes: (1) three series of tapes which include all the dialogues and songs, the exercises on grammatical structures as printed in the texts, and the various phonetic exercises; (2) a manual for the students; (3) for the teacher, (a) a detailed manual, lesson by lesson and skit by skit, (b) a printed "Introduction to French Phonetics" and "Phonetics Lessons for the Teacher," accompanied by a series of phonetics exercises on tape; (c) a book of phonetics exercises, using examples from the skits, frequently reinforced by IPA symbols or graphic indications of intona-

---

4. Distributed by Chilton Books, Chestnut at 56th Street, Philadelphia, Pennsylvania.

5. Produced in France by Hachette; distributed in America by Hachette, Inc., 301 Madison Avenue, New York, New York.

tion, liaison, stress, etc. This school edition of "En France comme si vous y étiez" is perhaps the most detailed and elaborate French course to be found.

American-produced A-V courses are also based on films or filmstrips, and sometimes both. The first one of considerable scope was "Je Parle Français." [6] There are 120 films (about ten minutes each, made in France) which serve as the very core of study—hence the producer's term "a film-and-text course." There are also 120 tapes, a detailed exercise book for the student, and a manual for the teacher.

By the same producer is the more recent "La Familia Fernández," with 54 short (three-minute) films and an equal number of filmstrips, laboratory tapes and test tapes, a manual for the teacher, and two books for the student: (1) for homework, picture or cartoon cues to recall the projected visuals and the language associated with them; (2) for reading and writing, a textbook composed of the filmed conversations, narratives of each lesson, and review narratives. "Emilio en España," the second level of this course, has 27 longer (6–9 minutes) films, an equal number of filmstrips and tapes, two textbooks for the student, and a manual for the teacher.

Less elaborate and costly, using narrated film instead of lip-synchronized dialogue, are the three film courses produced by the Webster Division of the McGraw-Hill Company.[7] Using filmstrips, tapes and student study books, these courses provide a more systematic form of pattern practice than the others mentioned so far.

More recent than any of the above, and the only course intended for the intermediate and advanced levels (high school or college) is "Images de la France contemporaine." [8] Thirty-two color filmstrips are synchronized with tape-recorded narration (followed by oral exercises); both are duplicated and amplified in the book. The cost of this course is moderate, for filmstrip is much cheaper than narrated movie film, which in turn is less costly than film with lip-synchronization.

All these courses are based on one essential premise: that the A-V components are not mere "aids;" the book is the "aid," while pictures

---

6. Produced by Encyclopaedia Britannica Films, Inc., Wilmette, Illinois, in 1961. (In color or B&W).

7. 1154 Reco Avenue, St. Loius, Missouri 63126. The three courses are (1) "Learning French the Modern Way"; (2) "Learning Spanish the Modern Way"; (3) "Beginning German with Films." (The last-named is primarily for college use).

8. International Film Bureau, Inc., 332 S. Michigan Avenue, Chicago, Illinois 60604.

and sound are the primary materials. In our traditionally bookish profession, this assumption is revolutionary and deserves special consideration.

Rationale of Audio-Visual Language Learning

Beginning with the so-called "Army Method" of World War II, the structural linguists gradually established the basic premise that language is *sound,* or "organized noise," rather than printed material. Generally accepted today, this premise has resulted in the so-called audio-lingual approach, exemplified by the sequence of hearing, speaking, reading and writing. In its extreme application, the behavioristic or "mechanistic" doctrine considers language only as organized noise, without regard to meaning. Accordingly, some linguists and programmers devised beginning language courses from which meaning was banished for a considerable length of time.

Although mature and highly motivated students succeeded in such courses, there was a heavy percentage of dropouts. The less radical audio-lingual course-writers, in response to student objections, found it advisable to provide meaning at an early stage, usually by English translation. Apparently the linguists' theory of language as mere sound, though perhaps valid as a definition, was scarcely applicable to the classroom or the language laboratory.

> Obsessed with structure, the linguist never pondered over the process that takes place in the FL classroom—language *learning.* . . .
>
> The most serious shortcoming of these materials is that they constitute a closed system. The student learns a finite stock of basic sentences which he can parrot if the proper circumstances present themselves. . . .
>
> At the syntactic level New Key textbooks had to revert to traditional techniques, primarily translation drills. . . .
>
> The attempt to dissociate the expression level of language from its content runs counter to an experienced teacher's intuition, and furthermore the Skinnerian view of verbal behavior on which this attempt rests is challenged by current theories of language and of verbal behavior, notably those of Chomsky and Miller respectively.[9]

9. Albert Valdman, *The Implementation and Evaluation of a Multiple-Credit Self-Instructional Elementary French Course* (Indiana University, 1965), pp. 13-15, 79.

This testimony of a linguist is confirmed by that of a psychologist, who concludes that the audio-lingual theory has become unacceptable as learning theory: "It was perhaps, fifteen years ago, in step with the state of phychological thinking at that time, but it is no longer abreast of recent developments. It is ripe for major revision. . . ." [10]

A distinguished European linguist concurs, specifying the essential oversight of the audio-lingualists:

> There is another element in language learning which the habit-formation theory overlooked . . . *meaning* . . . Meaning has to be taught . . . Of course the traditional way of giving but perhaps not teaching meaning . . . was by translation . . . *Translation is unmemorable* and therefore a highly inefficient way . . . Studies of learning have shown that we remember best that which is related in various ways to what we already know. Translation of an item does not reveal these relationships. These latter are acquired only by experiencing the item in a large number of different linguistic and situational contexts. . . .
>
> The way we learn our mother tongue is by observing the linguistic items as they occur in the real-life situations in which we hear language spoken. It is a slow way . . . Nevertheless it is the best and ultimately the surest way. [11]

The same author warns that pattern practice is "unrelated to the circumstances in which it occurs, and to some degree therefore meaningless." [12] Conversely, he finds that a presentation in context teaches meaning and is also motivating, because the learner finds it to be a meaningful activity. "This is where film and television come in.

---

10. John B. Carroll, "The Contributions of Psychological Theory and Educational Research to the Teaching of Foreign Languages," *Moderner Fremdsprachenunterricht*, (Berlin: Pädagogisches Zentrum, Franz Cornelsen Verlag KG, 1965), p. 380. Cf. also Carroll, "Research on Teaching Foreign Languages," in *Handbook of Research on Teaching*, edited by N. L. Gage (Chicago: Educational Research Association, Rand McNally & Company, 1963), pp. 1076, 1077, 1089-1090.

11. S. Pit Corder, "Films and TV in Modern Language Teaching." [Address to the ninth triennial Congress of the Fédération Internationale des Professeurs de Langues Vivantes.] Mimeographed, 1965, pp. 8, 9-10. The emphasis is Corder's.

12. Corder, *op. cit.*, p. 11. The tendency of pattern drill to become meaningless and mechanical has frequently been satirized. To counteract this tendency, a few resourceful teachers are developing line drawings (on filmstrips) to serve as cues for pattern practice. Accompanied by the oral stimulus, the drawings serve to keep the meaning always in mind.

Through them we have, for the first time, the means to present the language in fully contextualized form." [13]

In brief: Language is, for our purposes, a vehicle of meaning, and meaning is, in turn, a function of the context—visual as well as auditory, the situation as well as the sound. Until recently, such context has been available only to those persons who could go abroad and live there. But now, thanks to films and television, the complete situation can be brought into our classrooms and laboratories. Indeed, the filmed version can provide a better vehicle for learning than the original context. With artful selection, camera work and final editing, the film can eliminate distracting details and, like the seasoned traveler, concentrate on the truly significant.

The implications of all this are considerable, not only for language learning but also for the appreciation of literature and culture.

Audio-Visual and "Deep Reading"

Some thirty years ago, Robert M. Hutchins, then President of the University of Chicago, remarked that any professional translation was superior to the efforts of most of our foreign language students. His statement is still worth consideration. How many of our students, even those in advanced classes, derive a literary experience superior to what a professional translation would afford them?

On the other hand, it has been stated that:

> ... although students, even at the graduate level, do not know how to read a literary text ... and have little feeling for style or the power of words ... it is up to the teacher of literature to bring to their awareness the existence of those different realms of knowledge and perception . . . A literary masterpiece is meant not only to be read and reread, but to be conquered or conquered by ... Ideally, the meeting between masterpiece and reader should be a violent, emotional encounter. . . .[14]

Since this total experience of the literary work is not achieved by all readers to whom the language is native, it is doubtless even more

---

13. Corder, *ibid.*

14. Editorial by Leon S. Roudiez, *French Review*, xxxvi, 3 (January 1963), pp. 307-308.

difficult for our students to whom the language is still more or less foreign. First of all, there is the problem of language as such:

> Surely, for literature to convey any other value whatever, it must first give pleasure. And to enjoy it, one has to handle the language with a measure of ease. For the benefit of literary studies, the student must have the ability to handle the ordinary non-literary language comfortably... And yet, knowing this, we still introduce extensive literary texts long before they can be read with pleasure....[15]

Second, the student's difficulty with the distinction between the two *kinds* of language is too often forgotten, and it seems to cause concern especially to the linguists:

> We want to construct . . . a springboard of common but correct language, a basis of current good usage, from which we can later depart to explore other varieties of English, other kinds, other levels of language. Then it will be posssible to appreciate . . . the peculiar qualities which constitute originality and esthetic value. How can anyone appreciate Racine or Shakespeare if he meets their language too soon, along with the language of conversation, and if he is unaware of the gulf that separates the two?[16]

The distinction between "kinds . . . varieties . . . levels of language" is frequently a matter of sound:

> We insist that appreciation of a work of art can be complete only when the appreciator has the faculties needed to achieve communication with the artist. The color blind can never fully understand a painting, nor the tone deaf a musical composition. And one who has only a distorted impression of the sound of a language can never sense the effect that words and phrases made upon the author's ear as he wrote them down.[17]

This testimony is confirmed by that of a distinguished French phonetician:

> We must recall the oral origins of our literature, the poems which were to be sung before being spoken. We must repeat

15. Robert P. Stockwell, "Literature, Language Teaching, Linguistics," ACLS *Newsletter*, xiii, no. 8 (December, 1962), pp. 1-7.

16. Capelle and Girard, *op. cit.*, p. 12.

17. Donald D. Walsh, *PMLA*, LXXVI, 2 (May, 1961), pp. 18-19.

that a language is spoken before it is written. Our greatest stylists . . . are "musicians" of the language rather than "writers." How can we appreciate them, and our drama, too, if we remain unaware of spoken "style"? . . . To appreciate the sonorities, the rhythms, the melodic syntax of a language, there is no better way than to experience them oneself, first of all.[18]

The musical qualities of artistic language are heard inwardly by the perceptive reader of his native language, for he heard and spoke it before he learned to read it; therefore the literal symbols evoke the sounds. Indeed, silent reading always involves some sub-vocal articulation. But for the foreigner to appreciate the stylistics of sound requires a long apprenticeship of hearing and speaking. Without it he will read Racine or Shakespeare without awareness of poetic qualities.

"Deep reading," if we may call it that, involves not only the stylistics of sound but also awareness of the cultural heritage of the country and its people. The author and his compatriots share from the beginning a national patrimony of fact and fiction, ideals and prejudices, attitudes and taboos and underlying assumptions which skew the "meaning" of a situation, even though the reader may be quite unaware of them. An author's reference to any of these may be explicit or merely implied, but their presence is generally assumed by the creative artist who is writing primarily for his fellow countrymen. "The spirit of '76" has historical and emotional overtones only to Americans; *les trois glorieuses* only to Frenchmen. A reference to 1812 means one thing to an American, another to an Englishman, still another to a Russian. And so it goes.

Superficial reading is inevitable for the non-native reader until he acquires a fair degree of acculturation, which involves, as Howard Nostrand has demonstrated, two kinds of awareness: *knowledge about* the foreign culture, and *experience of* it. The former can be acquired by considerable reading of expository materials—history, geography, sociology, etc.—and fortunately the denotative language of exposition is generally meaningful to the intermediate student.[19]

Experience of the foreign culture is not such a simple matter. The

---

18. P. R. Leon, *Laboratoire de langues et correction phonetique* (Paris: Didier, 1962), p. 231.

19. Professor Laurence Wylie recommends the reading of children's literature in order to learn the early influences on impressionable minds.

obvious solution is to go and live abroad for an extended period, to "go native" and gradually become a native. For students who cannot do this, the most authentic and rewarding substitute is foreign films and television. Because of their explicit and multisensory nature they are apprehended more easily and fully than the literary forms, and their content is generally more representative. Not all films, of course, are equally useful for this purpose, and expert guidance must provide the choice. But a well chosen repertory of films and TV programs can provide an extensive and revealing experience of foreign life and culture.

A vigorous case for the cultural value of commercial films is presented by Ronald Hilton: "If one is concerned with creative forms, the movies tell us more about a country than do its poetry, its plays, and its novels. The movie seems to me the only genuine literary form in the modern world . . . Our courses on modern Spanish literature should concern themselves primarily with Spanish-speaking movies." Mr. Hilton adds in a footnote: "It is significant that in June 1962 the French Academy broke a precedent by electing movie director René Clair. In his inaugural address, the new 'immortal' said that his election represented formal recognition of new art forms such as the movie, radio and television." [20] The point, though perhaps exaggerated, is nevertheless well taken: films have, for the most people, a superior power to present contemporary foreign life. This may well be why, for many years, M. Paul Féraud has been bringing thousands of secondary school students to the Gaumont Theatre in Paris for his Thursday showings of British and American feature films. Back in school the next day, the children write a film review or essay and hand it to their English teacher. The writers of the best essays are called up on the stage of the Gaumont on the next Thursday and are presented with prize books—in English, of course.

Unlike the experimental and "art" films, commercial feature films tend to present the "regularities" of a culture more frequently than do the masterpieces of the novel or the drama, whose heroes are, by definition, extraordinary persons. Such characters are less commonly found in films, where, moreover, the "background" is clearly there for

20. Ronald Hilton, "The Teaching of the Cultural Context of a Foreign Language," in *Seminar in Language and Language Learning*, (Seattle: University of Washington, 1962), p. 56.

all to see, regardless of linguistic ability. Frequently it is this background which the foreigner most needs to learn and which the film—even the old silent film—has usually presented with clarity and impact. While verbal descriptions, like those of Balzac, tend to be tedious and to lose focus, the artful camera encompasses detail as well as over-all effect, without effort and frequently without words.

Like the drama itself, film and TV can communicate the dramatic illusion by which the spectator is caught up, carried away, robbed of all awareness of himself. This almost hypnotic power of involvement is probably the ideal inducement to learning, for the spectator becomes a part of the action. No doubt a powerful novel can exert the same effect upon the reader, provided that he can read as effortlessly and as "deeply" as he experiences the dramatic action of the film or play. But until he can do so, "the play's the thing"—whether on stage, film or TV screen—which will give him a vicarious "experience of" foreign life and culture, as well as "knowledge about" it, thus gradually preparing him to appreciate it in its most difficult form: the work of art.

Parenthetically it should be added here that ordinary commercial TV can and does teach American English to immigrants—and doubtless also it teaches a peculiar version of our way of life. There are authentic examples of war brides, for example, who learned to understand and *to speak* our language, primarily by dint of constant attention to the TV set. This is one more demonstration of contextual learning by TV, despite the heterogeneous nature of the entertainment programs. It is also an example of what has been called "massive listening," about which we need to learn more, as Alfred S. Hayes has suggested.[21] Finally, it recalls the warning of Simon Belasco about the present state of audio-lingual learning:

> In its present stage of development, the audio-lingual approach is far more lingual than it is audio. The most underestimated and least understood aspect of foreign language learning today is audio comprehension.[22]

To return to the subject of films: not only can they present the

---

21. Alfred S. Hayes, "New Directions in Foreign Language Teaching," *Moderner Fremdsprachenunterricht*, (Berlin: Pädagogisches Zentrum, Franz Cornelsen Verlag KG, 1965). Cf. especially pp. 192-196.
22. Simon Belasco, *Modern Language Journal*, XLIX, 8 (December, 1965), p. 491.

performing arts as we commonly know them [23] but also the art of poetic recitation, which has almost disappeared from the American scene. We tend to forget the recitative and even musical origin of most poetry, but in Europe one still finds the *diseur,* inheritor of an ancient and noble art.

At the University of Washington, Howard Nostrand recently brought off a novel and rewarding project: the filming of a poetry recital by the talented French actor Pierre Viala.[24] The film was divided into four short reels, one for each educational level, and then experimental viewings were held in various parts of the country. The purpose was to determine whether such a film would serve:

1. To teach the language, with its rhythms, intonations and facial expressions;
2. To arouse a favorable attitude toward poetry and contribute to love of literature;
3. To give insight into the cultural and social context of a foreign language and literature.

The responses to these three questions were positive and very encouraging. There was general agreement that the A-V presentation was more effective than a recording of sound alone—that the association of auditory, visual and kinetic stimuli elicited complementary responses.

Mr. Nostrand concludes that there is a need for additional filmed materials of various types and for several purposes:

1. Situational dialogues, to teach language.
2. Recitations by contemporary authors.
3. Interviews with authors.
4. Interviews with representative social types.
5. Talks by political and other leaders.
6. Tests of auditory and oral skills (by requiring the student to react to filmed excerpts).
7. The motion picture as an art form and social document.

---

23. For example, the filmed performances by the Comedie Française, and various of the "Ici la France" films marketed by the McGraw-Hill Company.

24. "Film Recitations," 41 minutes, color. After experimental use of the film, the comments of the users, plus bibliographies, vocabulary helps, etc., were edited and compiled in *Film-Recital of French Poems: Cultural Commentary,* by H. L. Nostrand et al., (University of Washington, 1964), p. 183.

A further publication from which quotations are made above, is *Filmed Recitations of French Literature: Evaluation of the Film and Cultural Commentary,* Final Report by H. L. Nostrand and M. G. Steisel, (University of Washington, 1964), p. 29.

It seems clear that films offer great possibilities for the learning of language and for providing the "knowledge about" and "experience of" a foreign literature and culture.

Apparently, in the case of Mr. Nostrand's experiment, the "experience" was an interpersonal one between Mr. Viala and each student. Perhaps this is just another proof that, in teaching, nothing can equal the combination of empathy and fine performance.

Noteworthy among the comments sent to Mr. Nostrand were the frequent references to the effectiveness of gesture, facial expression, and body movement or posture. The various aspects of the foreign paralanguage and kinesics are commonly neglected in our language classes, largely because they are unfamiliar to the American teacher. But the "silent language" [25] can be eloquent in itself, and as an accompaniment to speech it can profoundly modify or even negate the spoken word. If you "smile when you say that," you may not really mean what you say. But the smile must be seen; the message must be audio-visual.

If a single gesture can be eloquent, an organized sequence of kinesics, as in pantomime, can achieve complete communication. Such a sequence may be an artistic solo performance as demonstrated by Marcel Marceau, or a simple dialogue such as one can see every day in the streets of Naples.[26] But the "silent language," normally interacting with the oral, produces a richness and "depth of field" which neither can achieve unaided.

Lacking this richness and depth, printed material often fails to achieve full communication even in the native language, where "poor reading habits" plague the majority of students, especially with abstract material. Authors are accordingly urged to "illustrate" their meaning by giving concrete examples for word pictures. Since Comenius, we have had "illustrated" books; today the sound film and TV are developments of the same principle. Language regains its full dimensions when the speaker is both seen and heard. And those full dimensions are especially needed by the learner of a foreign language.

All this is not, of course, to argue that our students should be

---

25. Edward T. Hall, *The Silent Language*, (New York: Doubleday, 1959).

26. In a letter to the author, Howard Nostrand comments: "Mime films cannot generally be used to show the kinesic patterns natural to a given language, since the mime uses an international tradition of effective motions."

illiterate in the foreign language, but merely to put first things first, now that A-V materials make it possible to do so. The very first thing is to hear language used and to see the circumstances in which it is used. This contextual learning provides the multisensory imagery to serve as referents for the literal symbols learned later. Without those referents, the symbols must be referred, via the dictionary, to symbols in the native language. In this way the student learns to read, after a fashion, but at best he is competing with the professional translators. As Mr. Hutchins implied, that is unfair competition. Instead of reading in depth, the student finds himself beyond his depth.

The general principle was well expressed by Donald D. Walsh when speaking to the General Session of the MLA meeting in 1960:

> We have felt obliged to dispute the contention that an interest in language as communication, language as sound signifying something, is opposed to the written language, and therefore opposed to literature, civilization, culture, decency, and motherhood . . . But we insist that appreciation of a work of art can be complete only when the appreciator has the faculties needed to achieve communication with the artist . . . This is no time to bicker about language *versus* literature. It must be language *and* literature, hand in hand. . . .[27]

By Television or Film

This is no place to discuss FLES as such, or instructional TV as such; books have been written on each subject. But FLES via TV has inspired no book, although there have been many articles on the subject, ranging from ecstatic praise to fiery denunciation. Probably the wisest and best-informed account, although now several years old, is found in J. Richard Reid's survey report,[28] from which the following lines are quoted:

> (1) The use of TV in language instruction is growing rapidly and seems clearly here to stay. (2) It is neither the answer to all our problems nor a fiendish invention that will

---

27. Donald D. Walsh, *PMLA*, LXXVI, 2 (May, 1961), pp. 18-19.
28. Richard J. Reid, "An Exploratory Survey of Foreign Language Teaching by TV in the United States," in *Reports of Surveys and Studies in the Teaching of Modern Foreign Languages*, (New York: Modern Language Association, 1961), p. 197 *et seq.*

destroy us . . . (3) The average of TV teaching is probably better than the average of classroom teaching, though this clearly can not be proved. (4) There is some poor TV teaching, and a considerable amount of good TV teaching inadequately followed up in the classroom . . . There is also great promise in the medium, which it behooves us to realize.

The "great promise in the medium" is largely a matter of how well it is exploited in the classroom. Especially in FLES there is no such thing as "total teaching" by TV; the finest broadcast becomes a waste of time unless it is reinforced by daily follow-up practice directed by a classroom teacher with intelligence and enthusiasm—qualities which, according to the research, are more important than her linguistic skill. As one member of the teaching team, her role is to reinforce the work of the other member—the TV teacher.

The great promise of TV depends not only on the local teacher but also on the TV teacher, who may be ineffectual for various reasons—linguistic, pedagogical, temperamental, etc. Even the good TV teacher's efforts may be hampered by poor materials, clumsy camera work, primitive studio facilities and an inadequate budget. There are indeed so many obstacles and pitfalls that one wonders how foreign language programs by TV can succeed. The answer is that most of them don't. Of the scores of programs throughout the country, most serve only to bring discredit upon the TV medium and the subject it purports to teach. Yet the promise remains bright because of the potential of the medium.

Television vs. Motion Pictures

An instructional broadcast is subject to certain classroom handicaps: the screen is small and, unless shielded, it may reflect a glare of light; the loudspeaker is frequently a tiny "tin horn" whose distorted sound is made worse by turning up the volume; reception may be poor, for various reasons; the instrument itself may fail. Although these local problems can be corrected or prevented by careful management, frequently they are not, for many teachers think of TV as a public utility that one merely "turns on," like an electric light.

These problems disappear when the TV films are projected directly in the classroom. The projection screen provides a large picture, and the colors of the film add interest and realism. No longer dependent on the TV station, the showing can be scheduled at any convenient time and repeated at will. Best of all, it is a school activity for which the teacher feels responsible, and she can impart this feeling to the children by delegating certain tasks: Arranging the chairs, darkening the room, operating the projector. This sense of involvement stimulates interest and encourages active participation in the follow-up activities.

The use of films in the classroom also has its disadvantages: the noise of the projector, the relatively poor quality of the optical sound track, the need to darken the room, and—unless there is air-conditioning—impairment of ventilation. The greatest problem, however, is doubtless the high cost of films. Nevertheless, promising solutions are at hand. Increasing sales will surely lower progressively the price of the standard 16 millimeter films, and meanwhile a dramatic change seems possible with the recently-developed 8 millimeter equipment. At about half the former cost, excellent visual and sound quality is provided on an endless film loop enclosed in a cartridge which is simply inserted into the projector, like a coin into a vending machine. With no threading or handling, "untouched by dust or human hands," the film can be used hundreds of times, and thus its cost is further minimized.

The projector, in turn, is a self-contained box which resembles a TV receiver, with a picture screen of similar size and even greater brilliance. No darkening of the room is needed, and no projection screen. The motor makes almost no sound, and its operation is extremely simple.

One drawback is the relatively small screen which, like a TV receiver, restricts the viewing distance and is hard for a large class to see. Moreover, there are three different types of 8 mm projectors, and the films are not compatible with all three. Finally and most important, not many schools have bought 8 mm projectors because there are still few films for them; in turn, not many such films are being made because the "market"—the schools with the new projectors—is too small. Until this vicious circle is broken, the prospect of a general change-over to 8 mm films will remain a tantalizing mirage.[29]

---

29. Of the various foreign language courses on film, only "Parlons Français" is available in either 16 mm or 8 mm. The small size film in color sells for the same price as the large size in B&W.

The Future of Audio-Visual Learning

In general, there is a good prospect that instruction through A-V methods and materials will accelerate, for several reasons:

1. There is a trend toward starting FL study in school (rather than college), where there is greater faculty acceptance of A-V instruction.

2. Even at the college level, where faculty resistance is greatest, leadership in pedagogy is gradually being assumed by the more progressive members of the faculty: supervisors of lower-division courses, "clinical professors," structural linguists.

3. The "alumni" of FLES-by-TV (or film) will increasingly demand such instruction.

4. Appropriate materials are increasing in number and quality, especially in French and Spanish.[30]

5. The language laboratory is steadily evolving into a facility for individual programed instruction, which in turn promises to become A-V instruction, perhaps with a TV screen in each booth or carrel.[31]

6. Teacher shortages and mounting budgets cause pressure to seek relief through technology.

7. Federal funds for A-V purchases will continue, and probably increase.

8. Because of their acknowledged value in the teaching of the undreprivileged, the new media will doubtless be used in the federal government's teaching of English as a second language in the "Poverty Program."

9. Research and experimentation, both in America and in Europe, reveal increasing confidence in the value of A-V methods and materials. Valdman states:

. . . There is no doubt that the use of slides, film strips, motion picture films, and well executed line drawings would have made the materials more interesting and would have

---

30. Teachers of French have a unique resource in FACSEA, which provides a wealth of materials at nominal cost. Address: 972 Fifth Avenue, New York, New York 10021.

31. Such an installation is technically feasible but costly; moreover the A-V "programs" are not yet available. However, such instruction is definitely planned by a few institutions.

aided display session instructors in transporting the students to France, thus permitting a smoother and more natural transfer of linguistic habits acquired by auto-didactic practice to real communication situations. We also suspect that the use of imaginative visuals would facilitate and accelerate the acquisition of grammar and vocabulary and would reduce the need to match French utterances with their English equivalents.[32]

10. Rejuvenation of the FL teaching personnel in the public schools.

This last is a matter of vital statistics, primarily, and the statistics are not available. Yet it is obvious that although the average age of language teachers increased during the long period (1920-1955) of declining FL enrollments, the trend has now been reversed. The profession is being strengthened by an annual increment of hundreds of young graduates who were born after World War II, brought up in the era of TV, and attuned to the spirit and pace of contemporary life. A rejuvenated profession will inevitably be more hospitable to the methods, materials and devices of their own day.

A similar but belated development is now evident in practice teaching and the observation of teaching. Because of the multiplying number of teacher-candidates and the consequent impossibility of placing them physically in appropriate school classrooms for doing their observing, various colleges are beginning to make and use films or videotapes as a partial substitute. The advantages are obvious: saving of time, greater selectivity of the teachers and the techniques observed, and—during film projection—the possibility of repeated viewings, or of stopping at any point for discussion. Most of these advantages accrue also to A-V recordings of the candidates' practice teaching. For the first time it is now possible for our neophyte teachers to see (and hear) themselves as others see (and hear) them. Such an experience, repeated at will and elucidated by the critic-teacher's comments, should be uniquely valuable.

The filming of the individual candidate's practice teaching must of course remain a home-made operation, and it can be simplified by using an 8 mm camera and a tape recorder. Demonstration films, however, should be made by professionals and distributed widely.

---

32. Valdman, *op. cit.* p. 242.

We already have a few excellent films,[33] but many more are needed: (1) to illustrate the use of the several methods, materials and techniques of teaching at the various levels of student proficiency; (2) to illustrate the special requirements of the several academic levels, from FLES up to college. Since dozens of films will be needed for each language, the financial cost alone will be great, not to mention the expenditure of professional time and effort.

It would therefore be unwise, and probably disastrous, for each institution to make its own films or videotapes. (As someone has commented: "Why should everyone have to invent the telephone?") Yet that is precisely what is happening, with each institution starting from scratch, proceeding by trial and error, and duplicating each other's amateurish product. Recent experience with TV production should have taught us the folly of such procedure. We need only a few producing centers, each with expert direction and an adequate budget.

In addition to full-scale demonstration films there should also be short "single-concept" films or loops, each showing a single technique or practice. Most suitable is the 8 mm film cartridge, which uses an endless loop of almost any short length. Placed at the disposal of an individual or a group, it drives home any "concept" by dint of identical brief repetitions. This inexpensive device holds great promise for teacher education.

Much more costly and versatile is the videotape recorder-reproducer, which already is used for almost all network TV programs. As with the familiar tape recorder, the recording can be used repeatedly or erased at the flick of a switch. A film is still better for permanent use, but the videotape is far cheaper, simpler to make, and its magnetic sound track is superior. For relatively short-term

---

33. Notably: (A) "Principles and Methods of Teaching a Second Language," sponsored and produced by Modern Language Association, Center for Applied Linguistics, Teaching Film Custodians, Inc. Five films (B&W), available from Teaching Film Custodians, 25 West 43rd Street, New York 36, New York; (B) "New Techniques for Teaching FLs," by Pierre Capretz. Two films, 30 minutes, 16 mm, sound, B&W, in each of four languages (French, German, Spanish, Russian), 1963. (For rental information write to AV Center, Indiana University, Bloomington, Indiana; for purchase information write to Norwood Films, 926 New Jersey Avenue, N.W., Washington, D.C.) (C) "Parlons Français"; 160 instructional films, 15 demonstration films, and many A-V supplementary materials, some for pupils, some for the teacher. Available from Heath de Rochemont Corporation, 285 Columbus Avenue, Boston Massachusetts 02116.

use, the videotape will doubtless enjoy great popularity in the "Methods" course as the price is progressively reduced. Already there are small models which cost only one-fourth as much as the first ones, and it is expected that eventually prices will range in the hundreds, rather than the thousands, of dollars. When that day comes, teachers will record (through their home TV set) a foreign broadcast relayed by satellite and on the next day play it back on the classroom TV set.

Other electronic marvels are doubtless in store for the teacher of tomorrow—for example, a computer-based instrument which shows visually whether the imitation of a given sound is accurate (surely a boon to the tone-deaf!). For the moment, however, the problem is to enable the teacher to use the devices already at hand: the tape recorder, the various projectors,[34] and the language laboratory.

The United States is a rich country and it will surely provide the excellent new equipment and materials to the schools, secondary and elementary, where the teaching of language will more and more be concentrated. Less sure, however, is the future role of the institutions which prepare teachers. In this connection, the late William C. DeVane, dean of the college at Yale, quoted a statement by Robert M. Hutchins: "It is hardly an exaggeration to say that university departments exist to train people to teach in university departments." Dean DeVane commented:

> Old or young, such teachers are obsessed by one idea—insofar as they think of teaching—and that idea is to push their students as far as possible along the road towards a doctor's degree in their own field.[35]

Such a practice is harmful when it does not distinguish between prospective research scholars and future school teachers—and many departments, including some of the most prestigious ones, do not make the distinction. Unless this practice is modified, the public interest will demand that some other agency, perhaps a new one, shall provide appropriate training for our teacher-candidates. The education of

---

34. See Karl Pond's article on the uses of the overhead projector, in *Modern Language Journal*, XLVII, 1 (January, 1963), pp. 30-33.
35. *Liberal Education*, L, 2 (May, 1964), p. 205.

teachers is a public trust, and it must not be subverted by selfish interests.

Public education is doubtless the most important enterprise of our democracy. It will be served by our profession to the degree that we make enlightened use of all resources, including A-V devices and materials.

CHAPTER NINE

Planning for
Community Involvement

by

Lester W. Mckim

Foreign Language Coordinator

Bellevue, Washington Public Schools

This chapter suggests ways to stimulate community interest in the development of successful foreign language programs. Secondary objectives are to justify an emphasis on foreign language learning, to describe activities involving community participation, to suggest criteria for the choice and number of languages for a community, and to outline a realistic policy for student enrollment.

During recent years there have been many publications in support of foreign language study. One that describes vocational opportunities is the Indiana Language Program booklet entitled *Translating Foreign Language into Careers.* Another practical publication is *A Handbook for Guiding Students in Modern Foreign Languages.* Both include selective bibliographies for those interested in further reading.

Despite recent emphasis on foreign language learning, there is still widespread apathy. This apathy has frequently been overcome by a dedicated group of educators and lay people. Relevant statistics and information are at the crux of any educational program to develop community support.

Most people are aware that the already large number of travelers to and from the United States increases every year. National statistics are impressive, but local application makes the figures more meaningful at the community level. For example, without counting Mexicans and Canadians, there are over 750,000 foreigners who visit the United States annually. This number exceeds the total population of eleven different states: Alaska, Delaware, Hawaii, Idaho, Montana, Nevada, New Hampshire, North Dakota, South Dakota, Vermont, and Wyoming. Once again excluding Mexico and Canada, there are over two million Americans who travel abroad each year. This number exceeds the population of an additional ten states, for a total of 21 states and the District of Columbia. These additional states are Arizona, Arkansas, Colorado, Maine, Nebraska, New Mexico, Oregon, Rhode Island, Utah, and West Virginia.

The major causes for this extensive travel to and from the United States are tourism, education, business, and government service. Few communities of any size are exempt from some involvement in this activity. Even a cursory canvassing of the community can usually result in the identification of individuals, institutions, or corporations with vital interests in foreign affairs. An alert foreign language teacher will capitalize on this foreign interest.

In addition to the practical reasons for foreign language learning, a community should not be allowed to overlook cultural enrichment benefits. Communication facilities have been improved and greatly extended. The number of "ham" radio operators and families with shortwave radio receiver sets continues to increase dramatically making foreign radio programs readily available. Television programs emanating from other parts of the world are also becoming more available as a system of satellites is developed. Improved transportation facilitates cheaper and speedier world travel for important individuals, theatrical groups, art collections, etc. An introduction to another culture gained through effective foreign language training increases one's ability to benefit from such cultural opportunities.

Parents and school administrators tend to justify foreign language training in terms of educational requirements. Most state departments of education can provide statistics showing the importance of secondary school foreign language training for all students planning to attend college, especially those who may wish to become foreign language majors.

A clear understanding of vocational, cultural, and educational justifications for foreign language instruction is essential to those involved in developing a strong foreign language program. Community interest can be gained without an excessive expenditure of teacher energy. Naturally, highly effective teaching attracts attention and support; it is the essential element of any successful program. A combination of effective teaching and an informed community accelerates program development.

Plans Involving Local Organizations

A forum which is frequently used for informing the community about an academic program is the local Parent-Teachers' Association. It should not be forgotten that the elementary school PTA is just as vital to long-range plans as is the secondary school organization. The following sample programs are a few which the writer has either observed or in which he has participated.

A few years ago a commercial television station in a small western city offered time to the local schools to be used for some form of educational television. A popular series of films for elementary school instruction in French was purchased, as well as the necessary TV sets and teaching materials for all sixth grade classes. Other towns in the TV reception area were invited to participate. The city school district purchased the first-level films; participating schools from other towns assumed the responsibility for the second level. All schools cooperated in planning and holding workshops. The State Supervisor of Foreign Languages coordinated the efforts.

A neighboring town had ten teachers involved the first year. In March, a district-wide PTA program was planned in order to gain community support for an expansion of the program the second year, entailing a sizable expenditure for films, additional TV sets, and second-level teaching materials.

The State FL Supervisor opened the PTA program with a few remarks concerning FLES programs in general and the program which was being used in particular. Then a demonstration "follow-up" class was taught by one of the teachers, using students from her regular class. Finally the State Supervisor joined a school administrator for a discussion of costs, long-range program objectives, and other questions of interest to the audience. Variations of this program were presented in other participating towns. With public approval, the districts were able to expand the program the second year. In the town referred to above, a high school French teacher was employed by the district to hold after-school language classes for the elementary school teachers and to help coordinate the program.

Foreign language classes have been conducted at the junior high school level in the United States for many years. Nevertheless, there is a strong tradition of starting the instruction at grade nine. Daily language instruction beginning at grade seven has been strongly advocated and frequently implemented since well before "Sputnik." A lack of appropriate teaching materials, a shortage of teachers, inflexible schedules in many departmentalized junior high schools, and crowded curricula have combined to hamper growth of foreign language programs in grades seven and eight. There is still a great deal of experimentation going on at that level, and there is a basic lack of comprehension of related problems. Consequently, schools developing strong junior high school programs have a special need to gain community support.

The PTA program described here was given in the late 1950's. Spanish had been taught in grades seven and eight for several years. The previous year French had been added, and in the year of this program German was also being offered. The foreign language staff assumed the responsibility for planning one of the spring PTA programs. Student skits illustrated the differences in approach used for seventh and ninth grade beginning students. Second-year French students and third-year Spanish students were used to show the progress made possible by the three-year sequence. Ninth-grade Latin students presented a skit showing clearly that they did not consider Latin to be "dead." One teacher from each language made a short presentation, then all four were available as a panel to answer questions from the audience. School administrators and guidance personnel also helped to answer questions. The number of students involved in the program assured a large audience of interested parents.

The Parent-Teacher Association is generally less effective at the high school level than it is on the elementary and junior high school levels. As a consequence, high school PTA does not offer an effective forum in many communities. In communities where there is a strong high school PTA, there is an opportunity for a much greater variety of programs than is possible at the other two levels. It is just as important to keep the parents informed. The types of programs discussed below can be used for PTA meetings as well as for civic organizations.

In an effort to retain student interest, there is often a well-planned observance of National Foreign Language Week. School assemblies and special school programs with the public invited provide an opportunity for the alert teacher to gain recognition for his foreign language program. Materials are available from national professional organizations to help the teacher with the details of program planning. In some cities a series of programs is planned including speakers from foreign countries, foreign language entertainment groups from local schools, radio or television interviews with foreign language teachers and advanced students, and special exhibits.

In most communities, civic organizations are vitally interested in education. As a first step in gaining their support for foreign languages, leaders can be informed of teacher willingness to meet with the club and discuss the school FL program. There are several films which are effective in stimulating such a general discussion. Among these are "To Speak with Friends," "The Alphabet Conspiracy," "The Nature of Language," and selected films from the Henry Lee Smith series. (See Bibliography.)

An offering of services to civic organizations may encourage their leaders to participate in foreign language student activities. A well-organized student foreign language club has educational as well as social value. Leaders of civic organizations can often enhance the value of a foreign language club by providing speakers for special programs. As these leaders become involved in foreign language activities, they become better informed and more enthusiastic in their support.

Most civic organizations are interested in fostering worthwhile projects. A teacher who has demonstrated a willingness to work closely and intelligently with civic leaders will find a more receptive public audience when he asks for financial support for such worthy undertakings as student or teacher exchange programs, special language summer camps, foreign study programs, or local visits by foreign speakers, touring groups, films, and exhibits.

It should not be overlooked that the local news media are interested in items related to student and teacher activity. There are often special aspects of the foreign language program that can be featured on radio or television or in a series of newspaper articles. A sixty-minute television program in one city made possible a very thorough discussion of foreign language instruction in the local elementary schools, junior high schools, and high schools. The elementary program was just being developed, so a basic informational program was presented with demonstrations by different groups of students and their teachers.

Featured was a junior high school which cooperated with the American Friends Service Organization in carrying on an exchange program with a school in Germany. Although the students were too young to be involved in a personnel exchange program, letters, tape recordings, photographs, and materials of special local interest were exchanged. This program was discussed by the sponsoring teacher and a few of his students. Examples of materials sent and received were shown.

American and foreign secondary school students and teachers who were current or past participants in various exchange programs were featured for the secondary school part of the TV presentation. There was enough singing and dancing to provide entertainment and enough information to give the public an idea of the values derived from the exchange programs as a part of the FL instruction.

There are literally dozens of possibilities for making the public aware of the importance of foreign language study. A foreign theme can be used to draw together an otherwise American Christmas program. Foreign language entertainment groups have been featured in one town as half-time entertainment during basketball games. Community leaders may be invited to examine a new language laboratory and to try it out with a foreign language lesson specially prepared for them. Local foreign language conversation groups are often willing to sponsor programs honoring outstanding foreign language students. Recognition programs for secondary school foreign language students who win special honors help develop community pride in local foreign language instruction.

It would seem appropriate to add a word of caution at this point. Effective instruction is the primary concern of the teacher and the necessary element in the program. If teacher involvement in community affairs becomes so great that it jeopardizes his effectiveness in the classroom, then the point of diminishing returns has been reached. A carefully planned instructional program can include activities that lend themselves to public demonstrations and increase student language acquisition through motivation of interest at the same time that it increases public support. Interested parents and civic leaders can help shoulder the responsibility for planning programs such as those discussed above. For example, without the help of one civic leader, the TV program described above might not have been possible and certainly would not have been as successful. Naturally, all these projects cannot be included in a crash program for one year. The development of community support for a strong language program often requires several years of effective work both inside and outside the classroom. Effective teaching leads to teacher and student pride in the program. The degree to which this pride can be transferred to the school administration and the lay public determines the degree to which community support can be gained.

Which Language for Your Community

In communities that are planning new foreign language programs, the question of which language to teach inevitably arises. Today, most communities offer foreign language instruction in their secondary schools. For them the question concerns the choice of the language for expansion, perhaps building toward long-sequence instruction starting at the elementary school level. There are various factors to be considered; A few of them are described here.

The availability of teachers for initiating the program and for later expansion or replacement is frequently an important factor. The popularity of French and Spanish at the college level has led to a steady increase in high school enrollment in those two languages. As German teachers have become more available, high school enrollments have risen dramatically. On the other hand, the lack of well-trained Latin teachers has been a major cause for decreasing enrollments in that language.

With languages that are less traditional, language enrollment has not reflected teacher availability to the same extent. Other factors have served as a counter-balance. For example, high school Russian enrollment has increased steadily since 1958, but not in proportion to teacher availability. The same is true for Italian, Portuguese, Hebrew, Arabic, and Chinese. Even communities without a vital interest in foreign language instruction find courses in French, German, or Spanish acceptable. Latin retains a special (or "affectation") appeal that has largely protected it from any extreme encroachment by the modern languages. Schools that introduce one of the more uncommon languages, however, may find opposition rather than mere apathy. If effective teaching and a careful job of public education are not implemented, the new program may fail. When commmunity leaders are included in the planning stages for the new language, the odds in favor of success are increased.

A second consideration is the availability of college programs for post-high school study. Although most reputable colleges and universities offer basic training in the *commonly* taught modern languages, including Russian, students interested in the less commonly taught languages often have difficulty finding a college where they can continue their studies without traveling to another part of the United States. A reasonable solution might be the development of national or regional centers for such languages. For example, universities with strong programs in Chinese might take a leading role in developing community interest, providing teaching materials, and supplying qualified teachers. Universities in other parts of the nation could do the same for other important languages. There are at least fourteen languages with over fifty million native speakers each, and many others such as Cantonese, Korean, Vietnamese, Hindustani, and Swahili that are of vital importance in world affairs. It is doubtful that many of them will be taught successfully below the college level without some deliberate planning. Indeed it would seem foolish to encourage a random offering of these languages. There would be little chance to gain community support at the beginning, and opposition to foreign language teaching in general might be the final result.

Desirable teaching materials are still not available for all important foreign languages, especially those that are not commonly offered at the secondary school level. Foreign language programs that include six or more years of instruction require highly sophisticated teaching materials. Integrative features should include adequate emphasis on speaking and understanding at the beginning, with a logical progression to a careful teaching of reading, writing, grammatical analysis, and culture. New textbooks plus necessary audio-visual teaching aids require an expenditure that has only been related to foreign language teaching since the National Defense Education Act. After several years of the NDEA, there are still frequent criticisms that expensive gadgetry is purchased for show purposes and is poorly used. Once again, an effective program designed to keep the community informed can avoid much of this criticism.

A consideration of local ethnic groups sometimes determines the language to be emphasized. It is natural that Spanish should receive special attention in the Southwest and that French should be emphasized in New England. Cities such as Seattle and San Francisco would have an easier time gaining community enthusiasm for Chinese or Japanese than would midwestern cities of comparable size. On the other hand, the local ethnic group may provide a negative factor to be considered. For example, the experiences of two world wars have left their marks on many communities with a strong German heritage. In these communities, there appears to be a complex that has discouraged the teaching of the language that is most natural for the students. Imaginative German teachers who manage to develop community pride in its cultural heritage find that their language program benefits.

There are still many citizens of the United States for whom English is a second language. In communities where there are large numbers of these people, teachers have special problems. Some students are ashamed of the language spoken by their parents and of the culture it represents. There is a need for a special instructional program to overcome these negative feelings and to help students improve their ability to use their mother tongue. Foreign language programs designed for English speaking students simply do not meet the needs of these communities. Parental support is gained by teachers who are sincere in their efforts to tailor a program for the students involved.

In the final analysis, the choice of the language is not so important as effective teaching. There is no way to predict the language a student may need later in life. It can be predicted, however, that a student who gains real fluency in one foreign language will learn a second foreign language with greater ease.

Much has been said in this chapter about the importance of gaining community support. However, there is danger of an "oversell." When this happens, more language instruction becomes equated with a better language program. It is not unusual to hear an enthusiastic school administrator of a small high school, with a new four-year offering in one or two foreign languages, outline plans for adding other languages in the near future. Such attitudes are often caused by pressure groups from the community—partisans of a language that is not being offered.

Language Program Organization

It does not take much imagination to see that the number of successful programs that can be developed in any school is at least partially dependent upon the size of the school. A realistic recommendation would be that a four-year sequence be established in existing languages before adding others. Considering the normal attrition, as students pass from one level to another, at least 100 students are needed in a given language at the freshman level to be reasonably sure of enough seniors still studying that language to form a fourth year class. In schools where there is an established foreign language program, there is an established policy concerning student enrollment which determines the proportion of students to be included. School potential can be quickly estimated on the basis of total enrollment and school policy.

For example, School A is a four-year high school with 1,000 students. Three hundred of them are freshmen. About 75% are encouraged to enroll in foreign language classes. If the students are divided equally between two languages in this hypothetical school (highly unlikely), there will be four classes with 25 to 30 students in each class for each language. If normal attrition takes place over the years, the second year there will be three somewhat smaller classes, the third year one large class or two small ones—probably not more than thirty students total—and the fourth year class will be large enough to be approved without administrative reservations. Adding a third language to this school will either mean that the new language cannot be offered for four years or that one of the existing languages will suffer.

It should be pointed out that this situation, even though it is superior to the typical high school program, could be ameliorated through a change of policy. Let us suppose that School A has a group of very effective teachers who are able to get the support of the school administrators, guidance and counseling personnel, and the community for the following policy:

1. All public school students should be exposed to foreign

language instruction for a period of not less than one high school year.

2. All students capable of completing an academic curriculum should gain a mastery to the "courtesy level" of understanding and speaking, and should be introduced to reading. This presupposes two years of training.

3. All college-bound students should gain a "practical" mastery of understanding, speaking, and reading skills plus an introduction to writing—a minimum of three years instruction.

4. All students in the upper 20% of the graduating class, plus college-bound students with special language aptitude, should complete a four-year sequence.

Such a policy is not a usual one, but it is realistic if the justifications for foreign language study which are given at the beginning of this chapter are valid. Now let us see what such a policy does to the picture at School A.

There are either three or four freshman classes in each of three languages (rather than two), with the enrollment varying from 80 to 120 students for each language. Recognizing that students learn at different rates, there is one group in each language that moves more slowly than the others. Many of these students drop out after the first year, but this special section is filled with students who are not able to maintain the pace set by the other classes. During the second year, about 75% of the students are continuing, and there are still three sections of varying sizes for each language. By the third year, the top students have been identified and sectioned by themselves to make it possible for them to move at a faster pace. There is also a slower group in each language where a great deal of reading is done, but where the emphasis is on fundamentals of understanding and speaking. Some of the students from the slower third-year group will continue their foreign language study at the college level, but they are not capable of maintaining the pace set by the top group. During the fourth year there is still a good sized group in each language, totaling between sixty and seventy-five students in any single year. Many of these students have also studied a second foreign language for two or three years.

A combination of teacher effectiveness and overall support would probably lead to other program changes. Language instruction might be started at grade seven or earlier, making it possible to offer a fifth level of instruction to the better students. However, it is doubtful that School A will be able to add a four-year sequence of a fourth language without jeopardizing one of the existing languages unless there is a sharp increase in school enrollment.

Summary

Community planning is not the panecea that will end all problems related to foreign language program development. It has an importance, however, that is too often overlooked. An informed community can cause a school embarrassment if the professional staff is not interested in quality education. On the other hand, the support of an informed community is vital to the development of a system which will provide quality education. This chapter has attempted to show how a community can become involved in foreign language activities and to provide guidelines for those interested in developing an outstanding foreign language program.

Bibliography

Indiana Language Program. *Translating Foreign Language into Careers.* Available from I.L.P., 101 Lindley Hall, Indiana University, Bloomington, Indiana 47401.

Remer, Ilo. *Handbook for Guiding Students in Modern Languages.* Bulletin 1963, No. 26, OE27018 U.S. Department of Health, Education, and Welfare. (Washington, D.C.: U.S. Government Printing Office, 1963).

CHAPTER TEN

Local Administration of
the Foreign Language Program

by

Donald K. Davidson

Harvard Graduate School of Education

In trying to meet the ever-changing demands of our rapidly expanding, technological, egalitarian society the comprehensive secondary school has done very well. Its principal limitations have been occasioned, in a sense, by its virtues. Local autonomy has led to a wide variance in the quality of academic offerings, and the restrictions of size in the smaller communities have prevented both the wide range of offerings and the ability groupings within these offerings which probably are necessary in providing for individual differences in a truly comprehensive school.

In response to these needs, the current trend is to consolidate smaller school districts into larger schools and to establish more precise state-wide standards. For a limited, but increasingly large portion of college-bound students, the CEEB, the ACT, and similar examinations provide some degree of nationally standardized measurement of achievement.

The *specialized* public secondary school has existed principally in the larger cities. These cities often provide, in addition to comprehensive schools, highly specialized schools for selected pupils with liberal arts, scientific, commercial, secretarial, and a host of technical-vocational and artistic aspirations.

The homogeneity of interests and abilities in this type of school tends to avoid some of the educational problems inherent in a comprehensive school (especially in the smaller ones), but at the same time to lose some of the philosophical and educational advantages of the latter.

In addition to the public specialized school, a number of independent and parochial schools operate on a specialized basis, usually in the college preparatory field.

The foreign language program in the various kinds of high schools must approach in different ways the problem of providing for individual differences. Since the academically-oriented school avoids many of the problems of individual differences by serving a rather homogeneous clientele we shall concentrate principally upon the problems of the comprehensive school.

School Size, Heterogeneity, and Provision for Individual Differences

The size of the school and the aspirations of its population will determine, in large measure, the extent of the foreign language offerings. A comprehensive secondary school should be large enough to provide a reasonable variety of curriculum offerings with adequate physical facilities and yet small enough to allow for close personal communication and relationships among the students, parents, faculty and administration. This figure might be 900–1,200 pupils in a three-year comprehensive high school.

In considering a full program, including at least three (preferably four) years study in each language offered, built firmly upon the junior high program (if any), the number of potential students becomes a primary factor. The inclusion of several offerings such as Latin, French, Spanish, German, Russian, Italian, and the so-called exotic languages, will be largely dependent upon the size of the school population that supports them.

As the breadth and intensity of subject matter moves downward from the college level to the secondary school, a further matter for consideration is the question of the appropriate division of responsibilities between the secondary school and the college or university.

Based upon a sound background in a commonly taught foreign language or two, introduction into the more exotic languages for the linguistically able student might better be the responsibility of the college level.

In all subjects at the secondary level there is a tendency for teachers to place primary emphasis in providing for individual differences upon a system of ability grouping or tracking. Again, the size of the school and its philosophy and financial ability will be major factors in the determination of the number of tracks it can afford. In general, the foreign language pupil population, with its usual college admission aspirations, has required fewer differential groupings than, for example, mathematics or English programs which may encompass a far wider span of abilities and career intentions. The present emphasis upon some experience in foreign language learning for a wider range of the population will tend to increase this span of abilities. Currently two tracks (not including Honors or Advanced Placement) would seem to be adequate.

It must be observed, however, that two tracks or levels may not be feasible in the limited enrollment of the smaller school or even within certain languages with small enrollments in a larger one. The problem then becomes one of utilizing a method of instruction which allows for different rates of progress and different standards of attainment within the same classroom. While this latter approach may not be as attractive to many educators as the more easily structured tracking solution, it should be noted that there were elements of learning within the old one-room schoolhouse which were singularly productive and that modern technologies, tapes, programs, texts, and the like have greatly enhanced its possibilities. The much maligned "progressive" movement of the past decades also developed valuable techniques as one of its prime objectives in providing for individual differences in schools of limited enrollments.

As an administrative and educationally productive device, the possibilities of including several ability levels or even several grades of language proficiencies within a single class should be considered as an alternative to elminating a language offering for the economic reasons occasioned by small enrollment.

Administrative Functions and Roles

Within a school there exist three major roles—teaching, administration and guidance. It is essential to remember that the latter two exist only for the purpose of servicing and promoting the first.

The administrator is concerned with organizing a school in such a way that the classroom teacher is freed, insofar as practicable and desirable, from the non-academic responsibilities involved in the operation of the school in order to concentrate on the primary function of classroom teaching. At the same time he should provide leadership in the cooperative effort among teachers and in the total educational effort.

There is a delicate balance in this function of promoting continuous growth and cooperative effort and at the same time retaining a high degree of autonomy within the classroom itself. There is an art in providing helpful supervision and necessary evaluation, especially with younger teachers, and still conveying a respect for the ability of the individual encouraging initiative and stimulating experimentation. The over-supervision and domination of a teaching staff in the name of efficiency can produce mediocrity and stagnation just as effectively as the complete lack of organized leadership.

A truly effective operation implies mutual respect, an understanding of objectives, a cooperative effort, and a considerable latitude in role definition. The administrator should be conversant with the basic techniques and ideologies of leadership and management and with the current reassessment and developments in the field.

The role of *principal* will vary considerably with the size of the secondary school. In the medium to large school he will sacrifice a certain degree of personal involvement with teacher supervision, pupil contact, etc., but will be freed from administrative detail sufficiently to exert strong leadershp in structural and curriculum change.

As the intensity and scope of each subject matter discipline increases, it becomes impractical if not impossible for the principal to remain a subject matter specialist. He tends to act as a catalyst in the broad sense but must increasingly rely upon the initiative and expertise of the department chairmen for specific content, curriculum, technological revision, and innovation within any discipline.

His role becomes rather one of referral and encouragement of innovation within departments, and even of arbitration as to what is feasible, both in terms of finances and curriculum.

The demands of the philosophical direction of the school, college admissions considerations, proper apportionment of the budget, superintendent and school board relationships, community considerations, and many other related factors may even place him in a role which seems obstructionist to the department head and the teacher.

At the same time the *department chairman* tends to become more and more of a specialist as the demands of subject matter specialization grow more intense. It has been said that administrators tend to be people (pupil) centered and department chairman tend to be subject matter centered, a generalization which is probably unfair to both, but which contains a germ of truth.

It is almost a truism that a secondary school of excellence will have strong, even aggressive department chairmen. The initial contacts, selection, and attraction of good teachers, the development of a sound curriculum, the unification of a cooperative, forward-looking departmental staff, the development of the less-experienced teachers and the continued enthusiasm of the older ones, will depend primarily upon the leadership and the sound academic background of the department chairman. It is essential to the educational quality of the school that this person be outstanding in personal qualities of leadership and have the time at his disposal to exercise these qualities.

A third administrative figure which will concern the foreign language program, particularly in the larger school system, will be one operating from the *Superintendent of Schools* office. One of the functions of the superintendent's office is to oversee the development and the articulation of curriculum throughout all grade levels. In recent years the orderly development of a so-called K through 12 program in each of the major disciplines has become a matter of particular concern. To this end *city-wide curriculum directors* or *supervisors* have attained added responsibilities and prominence.

There are several methods of establishing the role of the city-wide supervisor, each with its own advantages and disadvantages.

To establish a polarity for the purpose of illustration:

a. The central office may act principally as a servicing, advisory, articulating body allowing considerable autonomy and opportunity for leadership, selection of programs, development of curriculum and techniques in the hands of the secondary school and its department head.

b. The secondary department head, at the other extreme, may operate only as the medium for carrying out programs and techniques established by the Central Office.

Obviously there are many options possible between these two extremes. In any arrangement, understanding and cooperative relationships must exist if the optimal program is to ensue.

This writer, with a firm belief in the development of the individual school as a prime requirement for quality, leans toward all possible delegation of authority and leadership. At the same time he recognizes the importance of bodies outside the school which will provide leadership for the various levels, and services and help which are beyond the resources of the individual school.

The department head within the secondary school must be aware of and establish relationships beyond the immediate ones with his principal and teachers. There is really no such thing as an autonomous school, only schools having various degrees of independence.

Specific Responsibilities of the Foreign Language Department Head. As already stated, the role of the department chairman will vary considerably with the size of the school and the structural framework within which the school operates. It is generally considered fruitful, even in the larger schools, for the department head to teach at least one section in order that he may keep in closer contact with the realities of the classroom. An adage of some merit states that "two years away from the classroom and one has forgotten most of its problems".

The following are some of the primary responsibilities which may come under the jurisdiction of the department head. A fuller development of many of these occurs elsewhere in this chapter:

a. Recruitment and initial screening of applicants for teaching positions.
b. Evaluation of non-tenure teachers.
c. Supervision of all teachers in the Foreign Language Department, with special emphasis upon helping the newer ones.
d. Leadership in curriculum development and methodology, including the arrangement for in-service training and workshops.
e. Annual preparation of departmental budget.
f. Ordering of books, supplies, equipment and hardware pertaining to the operation of the department, generally through the school purchasing department.
g. Meeting with other department heads and the principal on matters concerned with the policies, curriculum, and operation of the total school.

h. Through formal conferences and individual initiative, maintaining liaison and articulation with other levels of the local school system and the State Department of Education.

i. Maintaining relations with professional organizations and with the university level so as to make full utilization of outside authorities and the newest concepts in the field.

j. Maintaining the highest possible degree of morale throughout the department by constant recognition, encouragement, and development of the aptitudes of each individual member of the foreign language staff and the development of common approaches and goals.

k. Cooperating with administration, guidance staff, teachers, and often parents in the placement of pupils and in the just resolution of pupil problems.

Selection and Evaluation of Teachers

The most far-reaching and important function of any administrator is the building and development of a first-rate teaching staff. In this period of expanding school populations, opportunity in other fields, and general economic and geographic mobility of the individual, the selection and retention of able people requires a major effort and considered strategy on the part of all concerned.

The position of the foreign language department head, his contacts and his associations make him a key figure in seeking out and presenting good candidates to the final hiring authorities. His role, in some ways, may be more essential than that of his colleagues in other disciplines, in that the principal and superintendent usually must rely upon him almost completely in assessing the scholarship and linguistic competence of the candidate.

Considerations of salary and facilities undoubtedly are important in the attraction of superior teachers to a school system, but these factors being reasonably equal, the key inducement will lie in an exciting educational climate which promises opportunity for initiative, growth, the introduction of new ideas, and association with stimulating people. Education today presents so many opportunities to teachers that it becomes mandatory for each department, under progressive leadership, to provide an environment which will not only attract but will retain teachers of quality.

To some degree, the administration must make a choice between stability of staff and factors involving turnover. Ideally one looks for able candidates who will remain in the classroom for a fairly lengthy period providing continuity and a large measure of experience to the institution. In point of fact, however, the tendencies of our times toward earlier marriage, geographic mobility, generous fellowships, opportunity abroad, etc., make the calculated risk of limited tenure more and more an integral part of hiring policy. It is suggested that department heads and others concerned with the problems of staffing schools must accept the facts of a changing culture and economic structure and incorporate them into their thinking. There is an increasingly large reservoir of bright, well-educated, young women teachers who will not remain with any single institution for more than a few years but whose vivaciousness and capabilities will enrich and enliven the scene enormously for that period. To ignore this source in an effort to retain the stability of the past decades may result in settling for far less competence. This is not to infer that there will not be a considerable number of dedicated, extremely able people who will remain and furnish the very essential backbone of a school, but rather to observe that a considerable increase in turnover and change is with us to stay and that it is affecting recruitment policies, not only in teaching, but in every business and industry throughout the land as well. The problem is not peculiar to the schools.

In effect, this change makes the personnel function of the department head a much more important and time-consuming one. He must devote considerably more energy toward finding replacements each year and equally important, must realize he is running, in part, a teacher-training institution. He constantly must assist, advise and develop young and relatively inexperienced teachers on a scale which was unheard of a few years ago.

The retention of superior young men similarly presents a growing problem, although for slightly different reasons. The unparalleled opportunities for superior people in this era of exploding population growth and academic revolution constantly entice the outstanding person, particularly the male, from the classroom. Administrative positions, curriculum development and supervisory fields, foundations-sponsored projects, research and development, liberal fellowships, university level teaching, and foreign exchange programs are available in steadily increasing proportions to the exceptional secondary teacher.

Higher salaried opportunities in the more affluent suburban secondary schools constantly beckon the bright young man in these competitive days.

It must be recognized that there is something restricting about the traditional secondary school classroom position, which after a number of years, induces a desire to escape in the minds of many of our abler people. It is not necessarily a conscious dissatisfaction with the job at hand, nor lack of dedication or delight in working closely with young people. There probably are ingredients of status feelings, desire to try out programs of one's own on a more independent basis, adventurousness, freedom of physical movement, escape from the behavioral-disciplinary aspects of the classroom, and others. Salary considerations obviously are important but often are not the primary reason for change. This is especially true as classroom salaries begin to approach levels which provide for fairly comfortable living and security. It is perhaps unfortunate that the very attributes of psychological security, adventurousness, inventiveness, and general capability which make the teacher invaluable in the classroom are the very ones which make him attractive to and attracted by opportunities in other aspects of the educational scene.

A major function of the top administration and the department head must be one of making the educational enterprise so filled with excitement, recognition, freedom for the fullest expansion of potential, and identification with the constant improvement of the academic process that other paths will seem relatively less attractive.

One seeks a reasonable balance on a school faculty between men and women teachers. One of the most important influences in an adolescent's life is identification with, and emulation of, adult figures. It is very important in a school setting, particularly for the developing young men, that there be male teachers on the staff who combine scholarship and erudition with manliness, strength, and calmness. The presence of this type of teacher in any department actually raises the academic interest and attainment in an area, since the student connects the worth and the personal significance of the subject with the stature and the personal qualities of the instructor.

The same principles apply in seeking academically competent women teachers who will represent something fundamentally attractive and admirable in the eyes of the female students.

Aside from any academic consideration, although they are actually inseparable from the total *Gestalt,* youth badly needs constant contact in this important stage of their lives, with faculty members of both sexes who will represent the highest qualities of scholarship, decency, understanding, and strength of character.

It is not within the scope of this chapter to pursue the intricacies of personnel management. One aspect however, which is somewhat peculiar to the classroom and which will be of primary concern to the administrator, is at the opposite end of the spectrum from the discussion of the past few paragraphs. In most professions it is possible for the successful practitioner to taper off gradually in his work as his energy diminishes and retirement approaches, even if it involves a reduction in compensation. In the public school classroom the dedicated teacher must, in most instances, face a full load and the rigors of the classroom right up to the final day of labor. Although the very nature of the school may limit such opportunities, the department head and other administrators have a responsibility to use every practicable device to relieve the burden as much as possible from these individuals so that their final years in service may be as productive and pleasant as possible. Reduction of classroom duties and assignments to part-time supervisory or special projects is a desirable procedure, although the very numbers of individuals involved and the limitations of appropriate alternative positions, as well as budgetary considerations, heavily limit this possibility.

Tenure laws vary in different states, but, in general, protect the teacher's right to continue in a position after a probationary period of a few years, except for flagrant breach of professional conduct. In assessment of non-tenure teachers and recommendations as to rehiring, the department head has a responsibility which may affect the ultimate caliber of his department and the school more than any other decision he will make. He must not only weigh the personality characteristics and the potential for growth of the teacher in question, but must bear in mind that each time he recommends a marginal person, he excludes a more capable one.

In summary, the discovery, development, supervision, assessment, encouragement, and inspirational leadership of teaching talent are very important functions of the department head. In the long run, they will determine the quality of education in a school more than any other factor. Ideally, an individual teacher should be recommended to the School Board for initial hiring or retainment after assessment by and agreement among the department head, the principal of the school and the superintendent's office. Because of the nature of the subject matter, the administrators at higher levels are more dependent upon the expertise of the foreign language department head in this process than in many other disciplines.

Curriculum Research and Development

Again, the size and resources of an individual school (or a school system) and its relationships with the larger state or county structure, are factors in the amount and scope of local curriculum development. In any situation, the department chairman, with the support of the principal, is the moving force. This is true either in original development within a school or in the adoption and adaptation of materials established through outside agencies.

The involvement of the "user" (i.e., the classroom teacher) insofar as practicable in the design of a program, tends to ensure its most productive application. With this desirable end in mind there are several influences in current trends which tend to alter its application. These influences stem from (1) the trend toward larger schools, often by consolidating districts; (2) the demand for articulated programs of study continuing from the lower grades through the twelfth; (3) the increasing rigor and pace of classroom teaching which allows less time and energy for development of new programs; (4) the trend to standardization throughout American education; and (5) the growing interest at the university level, often with government or foundation grants, in the preparation of packaged programs for secondary and elementary level usage.

In many school situations, the direction of programs in classroom development has changed in such a way that the opportunities for involvement have not only increased but involvement has become mandatory. It is the responsibility of the department head to be responsive to this involvment and to make the most of it if he is to retain exciting teachers and promote a strong program.

Much stress is placed upon the reasonable autonomy of the classroom wherever good teachers are found. It must be observed, however, that this desirable autonomy can have a concomitant price in its isolation, even in its loneliness. Constructive feedback, academic dialogue with one's colleagues, critical appraisal, sharing of ideas, reassurance, and recognition too often are lacking at the teaching level. To the classroom teacher, communication with his immediate associates may be more important than with the administrator. The good administrator must make provision for group effort and then, oftentimes, get out of the way. One of the most noteworthy contributions of team teaching to the general educational scene has been in providing a framework wherein such interchange can take place.

What we are saying is that constant reappraisal, at the classroom level, of methodology, curriculum, and content is a primary educational requirement of our times and that it serves an additional necessary function in keeping able teachers intrigued with their task.

Finding the time for such involvement increasingly becomes a problem. The rigors of the modern school day mitigate against finding much of a reservoir of creative effort left at its formal closing. The administrator must make special provision for staff time to engage in curriculum change if he is to expect much creativity without hampering regular classroom progress. Ideally, if major change is expected, budgetary provision must be made. This expenditure may still not be accepted in many systems, but there is a growing understanding that research and development are part of the local educational effort, and financial recognition and support are essential.

Grants from foundations, governmental support through various agencies for summer study, cooperative endeavors with universities, and other sources should be explored by the administrator.

Visits by classroom teachers to schools which have initiated experimental programs should be arranged. In-service courses and workshops devoted to curriculum projects are common practice. If the money is available, there is considerable merit in compensating key teachers for curriculum development in workshops during the summer months. Released time during the school year for certain teachers has some advantages, although absence from classes, even with capable substitutes, can be a drawback from the viewpoint of pupil progress.

The Department Head and the Total School

In addition to the primary responsibility which the foreign language department head has for his own discipline, there is a wider involvement expected in the operation and curriculum development of the whole school. In practically all institutions, he will meet with the other department heads and administrators at regularly scheduled staff meetings, and with special committees, to consider matters which affect the education of all the pupils. In a sense, he is a member of a "Board of Directors" concerned with the operation of the school and its program.

In this role, he must not only promote his own departmental needs, but also must have an understanding of the needs of other departments which often affect his own. Compromise and even temporary sacrifice of his own desires may be necessary for the greater good of the school program. As the rigor and extent of subject matter offerings at the secondary school level have increased in recent years, the department head necessarily has become more of a specialist and less of an expert in general education. An unfortunate loss to the school and, particularly, to the student could result if this lack of involvement in the total aims of education is carried to an extreme.

It is almost universally true that each department desires more time, more staff, and a larger budget to carry out its responsibilities and to increase the quality of its offerings. It also is almost universally true that there are practical limitations to all of these desires at any given time, even though the limitations have become less stringent in recent years as the education gains in stature. No capable principal will wish other than an aggressive group of department heads, each convinced of the indispensability of his own subject in the general scheme of things, but he also will need them to be intelligently concerned with the general education of every student in the school and to have some understanding of the complicated logistics involved.

It might be well to touch very briefly upon a few of the problems of a modern secondary school which will affect the extent of the program offerings, the methodology, content, and time available for each subject matter area, including that of foreign languages:

  a. The length of the formal day in many schools has reached the point of diminishing returns. The academic day for the student in the more rigorous college preparatory programs contains about as much content as can be absorbed within the present framework. The addition of more subjects will require either a reduction in other studies or a new approach to the structure of the school day, such as more independent study, different types of presentations, etc.

  b. The school is being asked to absorb more and more responsibility for many social, psychological, ethical, homemaking, and mechanical areas which once were considered the prerogatives of the home and other outside agencies. There seems to be no present indication that this trend will reverse itself.

c. For the first time in history, practically every youth in the land is in school until age sixteen and the overwhelming majority beyond that age. The school serves both an educational and a custodial function since there are increasingly fewer job opportunities in a technological society for anyone without a high school diploma, and society has often provided no other place for youth to go. The problem is exacerbated by the fact that many of these young people are intelligent but not necessarily "academic" in the traditional sense, and the usual formal schooling often has little incentive or meaning for them. The situation may be less troublesome in the foreign language areas since these generally are elective and usually attract students with at least aspirations for higher education, but this does not reduce the responsibility of the foreign language educator in seeking viable solutions to the problems of general and specialized education for *all* youth.

d. The American comprehensive high school is currently committed to a considerable increase in the depth and scope of each of the subject matter fields and, at the same time, to general education through the twelfth grade. Concurrently there is constant pressure to introduce at least the elements of some additional academics such as economics, sociology, psychology, and anthropology, which have hitherto been within the province of the colleges. In the foreign language field, following the introduction of Russian, there are suggestions that Chinese and other less commonly taught languages be included in the curriculum. To further complicate the problem, the body-of-knowledge explosion in the sciences, the increase in historical subject matter and the necessary addition of statistical, computer, and theoretical mathematics make imperative the constant reassessment of what shall be included—and, equally important, what can no longer be included—in the general curriculum offerings and in the academic life of any student.

e. The technological needs of our society and the upward mobility expectations of our American culture result in community demands that the schools adequately prepare a larger and larger proportion of our youth for continued formal education beyond the twelfth grade. Couple this requirement with a serious lag in the post-secondary provisions for any such expansion, and one finds the publically supported secondary school in a rather precarious dilemma.

Structural Experimentation and its Implication for the Foreign Language Programs

As the problems mentioned in the immediately preceding paragraphs become more intense, secondary and primary education are undergoing continual reassessment and change, and there appears to be no slackening of this climate in the foreseeable future. It is not the intent here to include a summary of the merits or the disadvantages of the various innovations which are taking place in secondary schools. It will serve our purpose, however, if we use a few of these innovations as illustrations of the type of thinking going on in educational circles and the implications they hold for the Foreign Language Department of any secondary school.

The writer has three strong feelings insofar as adoption of any of these suggestions is concerned. First, none of them is equally applicable to all secondary schools. The size of the school, its location, its resources, and the relative success of its present program are all factors which must be considered before the adoption of any new scheme. Second, many structural-methodological ideas of great merit do not necessarily apply equally to all subject-matter disciplines *within* a secondary school. Teaching techniques of the foreign language program, for example, may not be amenable to certain changes which produce exceedingly good results in a science program. Third, many innovations which have proven successful elsewhere in the same discipline may require modification to meet local needs.

Although the foregoing statements may appear to justify the status quo and absence of any movement whatsoever, this is hardly the intention.

Faced with the problem of educating almost every American youth to the reasonable extent of his potential, educators are using, or considering the use of the following innovations. The essential aim in all these devices is to provide structure and methodology wherein individualization of instruction will take place, while at the same time, utilizing the school staff, facilities, and budget to greatest efficiency.

A brief description of some of the current innovations follows:

    a. *The ungraded school* proposes to allow students to advance at individual rates without the artificial boundaries imposed by yearly grade promotions. The handicaps of lock-step progression would be removed from both the very able and the less able student. Provision for individual differences may be made within either acceleration or enrichment, or both.

b. *Continuous learning* is a phrase embodying very much the same principle with or without employing the traditional structure of the graded school.

c. *Large and small groupings* are employed with the idea that some subjects are as well, if not better presented before fairly large groups of pupils, while other subject matter is better grasped in a seminar or small discussion group. Manipulation of scheduling to fulfill this concept allows a considerable degree of pupil involvement in different sized groups, including even a one-to-one relationship with the teacher, employing approximately the same sized professional staff as in the case of traditional classrooms. It should be noted however, that the introduction of large lectures, with the primary intent of increasing the overall enrolled number of pupils that can be handled by a given school staff, often leads to ineffective teaching. It is the experience of the writer that a teacher handling large groups in secondary school instruction must be allowed adequate time to prepare both the audio and the visual portions of the presentation. The prime reason for the introduction of a large lecture system should rest upon the improvement of instruction, not upon the assumption that the staff and money will be saved by such an innovation.

d. *Teacher aides and paraprofessionals* are being employed to reduce the amount of clerical and other non-teaching obligations ordinarily assigned to teachers and thus to free them for more direct teaching contact with their students. Further extension of this concept employs paraprofessionals in the borderline teaching tasks of correcting papers, monitoring classes and giving individual assistance to pupils.

e. *Team teaching* employs the varied backgrounds and specialized interests of a team of teachers in working with a common group of pupils. In addition to the advantages which pupils experience in a variety of teacher contacts, the arrangement can induce a stimulating atmosphere in which the teacher is concerned with providing a spirit of "working together" on a common project, with its sharing of ideas and constructive evaluation which the self-contained classroom so often lacks.

There is also a built-in opportunity for the establishment of a "hierarchy" of teachers, recognition of exceptional talent, and helpful training for the less experienced teacher.

f. *Independent study* implements the theory that most pupils may pursue their studies to a greater advantage than hitherto realized, while operating on their own away from the classroom. (The word "independent" is often either misunderstood or abused here; perhaps the word "directed" would be a better adjective.) Proper materials and planning are necessary for the optimal use of pupils' time in this sort of endeavor. The language laboratory is in a sense a form of independent study, as is programmed learning.

In some fields, the principal obstacles to independent study in the past have been the paucity of textbooks written with self-learning in mind and the natural inclination of teachers to feel that the only efficient mode of academic learning must take place in the classroom.

g. *Audio-visual and other mechanical devices* for the promotion of learning have been untilized far more in the enormous educational effort of the armed services and industry than in the traditional schoolhouse. The use of *imagery* in conveying concepts, facts, attitudes, and skills has been recognized by institutions outside of the educational profession, especially in the world of advertising. as a primary and oftentimes the most efficient means of getting a message across. Of course a major part of this lag on the part of the schools has been due to the fact that the school has not only the responsibility for transmitting certain knowledge, skills, and concepts, but in addition has as one of its most important purposes the responsibility for instilling a high proficiency in the skills of reading and writing, a responsibility not shared by the aforementioned agencies. Undoubtedly, however, we have not explored the uses of media other than the spoken and written work as extensively as we should.

h. *Flexible scheduling* is a necessary prerequisite to the proper employment of most of the techniques mentioned above. This presents a challenge to the administrator and requires a certain tolerance on the part of the teacher. It also presupposes a far greater degree of freedom of movement and independence on the part of the individual pupil than we have heretofore acknowledged. We may not be able to allow this freedom to all pupils but we can no longer afford to restrict the growth and learning of the many for the deficiencies of the few, and must make separate provision within the scheduling for each.

The foregoing is not a complete listing of the innovations being introduced throughout the educational scene. It does illustrate a few which may come within the concern of the foreign language administrator. Adaptation of any or all of them to the local situation is a matter of prime concern. It should be re-emphasized that certain innovations are far more applicable to instruction in some of the major disciplines than in others, and selectivity and adaptation, and even rejection, are necessary administrative functions. The underlying assumption is that education is faced with a challenge unparalleled in its history, and that we must seek new solutions to meet the accelerating change of this era.

Ability Grouping and the Administrator

The academic advantages of *ability grouping* have long been recognized and employed within the curricula of secondary schools large enough to support this division of pupils. There are certain valid arguments based upon the democratic ethos of the comprehensive secondary school against such separation, but as stated earlier in this chapter, there is a powerful trend toward increased academic homogeneity in the classroom. The most enthusiastic adherents of academic ability grouping, however, ultimately must face a realistic appraisal of degree and limit. The administrator must measure the point when additional ability groupings reach a point of diminishing returns insofar as efficiency of the program or the entire school is concerned. This degree will be determined by factors of school size, size of school population and staff, as well as certain philosophical considerations. Teachers as a whole are inclined to desire the most academically homogeneous group possible. Experience indicates that there is no such thing as a perfectly homogeneous group and that there should be provision for individual differences *within any* class of youngsters.

This is not a plea against the employment of ability grouping, since realistically it is with us for the foreseeable future, but rather an expression of a desire for common sense in its application. The variability and the indeterminates in human potentialities and performance preclude any exactitude in the categorization of students into discrete ability groupings. We can hamper growth as well as provide for it if we do not allow for considerable latitude and movement in our placements.

General consensus seems to suggest an advanced placement or Honors grouping at one extreme and a slow-learner category at the other extreme within the normal range of pupils. Between these extremes two or, at a maximum, three ability groupings should suffice; in fact it is doubtful that our measurement and appraisal techniques are accurate even within this scope. One might even suggest, concerning foreign languages, that the Honors and perhaps two other groupings would suffice, since the lower levels of academic ability generally do not elect foreign language study.

Since the basic aim of ability grouping or "tracking" is to provide for individual differences in such a manner that pupils may move at different rates without being hampered by the slower pupil or overwhelmed by the faster one, the proper placement of any individual should take into account at least two considerations:

> *First,* regardless of his mark or grade, in which grouping will the pupil learn more? A pupil does not necessarily learn more in his association with a slower class even though his relative grade may be higher.

> *Secondly,* and most importantly, as he indicates his ability level, will the individual pupil have opportunity to move to a higher grouping as readily as to a lower one? This upward form of progression is often given more lip service than actual accomplishment in curriculum organization.

The above remarks have been concerned largely with curricula based upon collegiate or other continuing formal educational aspirations. Within terminal curricula, such as certain clerical and vocational courses, there also will be a wide range of abilities, some of them equal or superior to many college-bound youngsters. Any groupings in these programs should certainly take these varying abilities into account and not type youngsters' intelligence by career aspirations.

Placement of pupils in the proper ability categories is often a function of the foreign language department chairman, in conjunction with the guidance staff, aptitude tests and records of past performance in foreign languages or allied subjects. In building the master schedule, provision should be made to facilitate the movement of any pupil from one ability grouping to another during the academic year by scheduling different sections of the same course at the same hours.

The Junior High School

While most of the items touched upon in this chapter have relevance to both the junior and the senior high school, some mention should be made of the peculiarities and particular role of the former.

The past few years have witnessed vast changes in the philosophical approach to the purpose of the junior high school. The title has always been troublesome and a number of communities now prefer to organize on the concept of a Middle School in an effort to disclaim the connotation of a smaller, younger, edition of a senior high school. The beefed-up, accelerated, subject-minded climate which has so affected change in the senior high school has had a major influence also on the junior high school. The introduction of added ability groupings, modern mathematics programs, foreign language offerings in the lower grades, and other changes have made articulation with other levels much more mandatory and explicit.

Whether the exploratory and social adaptive functions of the junior high school are being modified in the process is an important matter of debate, although not here. In any event, its role and structure is undergoing change that has particular significance for the foreign language program and its administrator.

The current, necessary state of flux in the determination of the proper age for beginning foreign language study, the vested interest incurred in whatever language is initially offered, the varying proficiencies with which pupils enter or are passed on to various levels, and the major question of which pupils should commence a language at a given grade level, all give administrators new problems to consider and solve.

Staffing problems often are more troublesome than at the senior high school level, especially where the size of the school does not provide a full program for a teacher in a single subject or where two or more language offerings require further adjustments.

The original premise upon which the junior high movement grew was that children at this stage in life had greater variations in physical, emotional, social and intellectual maturity than at any prior or later period. Therefore they need more individual consideration and guidance than at other periods of educational development. There was also a sense that these years should be devoted to a general and common education for all, to an exploratory pursuit without the more arbitrary consequences of failure which may come later, and to the development of leadership and participatory opportunities which may be submerged later in the larger society.

All these considerations still hold, although they face a struggle for relative survival in the current changing emphasis. It is the challenge of the administrator to retain their essence and still accommodate the academic demands of our times.

SUMMARY

The foreign language department administrator, in concert with the administrators in other fields, is faced with a world in which the essence of things involves great change and therefore new problems. He must constantly seek out and evaluate innovations which may help, at least partially, to solve problems occasioned by this change. He must deal with a constantly expanding pupil population whose composition, aspirations, and needs are considerably different than those of the past. The conventional wisdom of the past will not suffice. The education of almost the total adolescent population through the twelfth grade, and the continuance of the majority of these into the upper levels of education, is a new and uncharted task.

The pressures upon educators to assume responsibility for schooling which will at least alleviate many of the current problems facing society, is great and in all probability will increase as the patterns and structure of the family and other units of our culture change.

The basic philosophies of education, the content of courses, the aims and directions of the curriculum, syllabi, techniques, materials, and structure will be continually examined and re-examined as means and ends, and as agents of growth and change. The outside resources of the community, the State Departments of Education, the colleges and universities, federal agencies, grants from government and from private foundations must become part of a cooperative enterprise working toward the ultimate improvement of instruction throughout the school community.

Since the secondary school is involved in the critical years between childhood and adulthood and, to a steadily increasing degree, becomes the primary selecting and sanctioning agency in the lives of youth, the administrator at this level will face increasing pressures and challenges to meet the needs of the times and to find solutions to new and grave conditions. If he regards this as the most exciting and promising period in the history of man and education, he will find great reward and limitless satisfaction in the enterprise.

Bibliography

Note—The following is not intended as a comprehensive listing of the many recent and relevant writings on the topics touched upon in the preceding chapter. Rather, it suggests a small sampling which may lead the reader into a wider exploration of any given phase.

Philosophy, Development and Functions of the American Secondary School

Broudy, Harry S., B. Othanel Smith and Joe R. Burnett. *Democracy and Excellence in American Secondary Education.* (Chicago: Rand, McNally, 1964).

Conant, James B. *The American High school Today.* (New York: McGraw Hill, 1959).

Conant, James B. *Education in the Junior High School Years.* (New York: McGraw Hill, 1961).

Cremin, Lawrence A. *Transformation of the Schools.* (New York: Knopf, 1961).

Dropkin, Stan, Harold Full and Ernest Schwarcz. *Contemporary American Education.* (New York: The MacMillian Co., 1965).

Kimball, Solon T., and James E. McClellen, Jr. *Education and the New America.* (New York: Random House, 1962).

TRENDS IN STRUCTURE AND METHODOLOGY

Association for Supervision and Curriculum Development. *Individualizing Instruction.* (Washington, D. C.: 1964 Year Book).

Beggs, David W. III, and Edward G. Buffie (Eds.). *Independent Study* (Bold New Venture Series). (Bloomington, Indiana: Indiana University Press, 1965).

Manlove, Donald C., and David W. Beggs III. *Flexible Scheduling* (Bold New Venture Series). (Bloomington, Indiana: Indiana University Press, 1965).

Shaplin, Judson T., and Henry F. Olds (Eds.). *Team Teaching*. (New York: Harper and Row, 1964).

ADMINISTRATION AND MANAGEMENT

American Association for Higher Education (N.E.A.) *In Search of Leaders*. Washington D.C. 1967

Bennis, Warren G., Kenneth D. Benne and Robert Chin (Eds.). *The Planning of Change*. (New York: Holt, Rinehart and Winston, 1961).

Gross, Neal, and others. *Explorations in Role Analysis*. (New York: John Wiley and Sons, Inc., 1958).

Lupton, Tom, *Management and The Social Sciences*. (London: Hutchinson and Col, 1966).

McGregor, Douglas. *The Human Side of Enterprise*. (New York: Mc-Graw Hill, 1960).

CULTURAL CHANGE AND GUIDANCE

Association for Supervision and Curriculum Development. *Perceiving, Behaving, Becoming: A New Focus for Education*. (Washington, D. C.: 1962 Year Book).

Mosher, Ralph L., Richard F. Carle and Chris D. Kehas (Eds.). *Guidance, An Examination*. (New York: Harcourt, Brace and World, Inc., 1965).

Wheelis, Alan. *The Quest for Identity*. (New York: W. W. Norton, 1958).

CHAPTER ELEVEN

State Level Administration
of the Program

by

Everett V. O'Rourke

California State Department of Education

A state department of education functions in accordance with established laws, statutes and regulations; therefore, there are clear diversities among the states in the ways they perform their individual tasks. It might be well for us to take a look at a few of the typical state's educational administrative structures and their possible ways of operating, in order to get a clearer focus on the foreign language program as part of the whole process.

Educational administration at the state level is, in most states, divided among three entities—the chief state school officer with the state department of education, the state board of education, and the legislature. Some states have other permanent or temporary groups with special tasks. The three main entities and the other groups have specific responsibilities that should have a coordinated effect on all schools within the state.

In relation to the federal constitution proviso that education is a function of the individual state, it has been necessary for each to develop a plan through which responsibility for and control over schools can be exercised. State constitutions normally relegate such responsibility to the legislative branch of government, since constitutional change is much more difficult than change by legislation. Greater responsiveness to the public will and quicker action can be accomplished when the control of education is in the hands of the legislative body instead of more constrictively mandated by a constitution.

The strength of any educational system within a state emanates from the state level but depends finally on the competence of the local staff, the effectiveness of its administration, the adequacy of its curriculum and instructional methods, the appropriateness of its facilities, the extent and nature of the support of its constituents, and the capabilities and attitudes of its students. The state educational agency has responsibilities to all in the state to see that every school has maximum opportunity to achieve its greatest potential.

The organizational plan in each state is very significant. A plan that allows conflicting educational functions to exist, that does not provide for means of establishing recognition of good organization and cooperation at all levels of education, or that is infected with partisan politics at any phase of educational operation should be corrected. The state legislature may delegate much of the power to entities such as a state board of education and the chief state school officer with the department of education. The designation of power to the legislature through the constitution may grant much flexibility and freedom or it may be very specific concerning administration and organization of the public schools, listing officials to be employed, appointed or elected, and indicating their powers and duties.

> State legislatures, apart from appropriating funds for educational purposes, enact two kinds of legislation that affect the schools: *fiat legislation,* that requires certain subjects to be taught or not taught; and *enabling legislation* that establishes machinery, finances, and facilities by which certain goals can be sought.
>
> ⌐he people of a democracy have the right, working through
> ir representatives, to establish for schools any standards
> believe to be necessary. However, such legislation may
> ⌐erious difficulty, for when additions are made to the
> ⌐m it is generally necessary to eliminate others or
> less time to them. Sometimes such legislation also
> lems for school districts, since it does not specify

how the money needed to employ additional teachers can be secured nor how the materials required to implement the provisions outlined by it can be obtained.

Enabling legislation that (1) encourages worthwhile language programs; (2) rewards schools that develop and maintain good language programs; and (3) helps stimulate the recruiting and training of good foreign language teachers is eminently to be desired.[1]

The legislative statutes, fiat and enabling, should be the basic directives for the organization, administration, operation and financing of the public schools of the state. The statutes may be in broad general terms or extremely restrictive depending upon the will of the legislature as it tends to represent the people of the state. Some of the statutes are directives to school districts and intermediate school units such as counties. Much of the legislative action concerning the schools designates the state school board and the chief state school officer with the department of education to perform the necessary regulatory and service functions.

The State School Board

Every state has a state school board. The great majority of the state school boards have powers and duties relating to elementary and secondary schools. Duties and responsibilities of state boards vary greatly from state to state. Events and trends that will inevitably bring about more similarity in state boards of education are: the increasing complexity of the United States economic, social and political system; quick access in communication and transportation; mobility of population; increasing interest and activity of the federal government in the schools and communities; the national conferences and conventions engaging people from every state in the Union; and many more.

An attempt to effect a change and bring about some similarity in state board responsibilities was recommended by the Council of Chief State School Officers in 1952. Some of the responsibilities recommended were:

1. Formulate policies and adopt such rules and regulations as

1. *Language Instruction: Perspective and Prospectus*, Bulletin of the California State Department of Education, Volume XXXII, No. 4, November, 1963, Sacramento, California.

are necessary to carry out the responsibilities assigned to it by the Constitution and the statutes of the state.

2. Establish standards for issuance and revocation of teacher certificates.

3. Establish standards for classifying, approving, and accrediting schools, both public and non-public.

4. Prescribe a uniform system for gathering and reporting of educational data, for the keeping of adequate education and finance records, and for the better evaluation of educational progress.

5. Submit an annual report to the governor and legislature covering the action of the state board of education and the operations of the state department of education and the support, condition, progress and needs of education throughout the state.

6. Consider the educational needs of the state and recommend to the governor and the legislature such additional legislation or changes in existing legislation as it may deem desirable.

7. Interpret its own rules and regulations and upon appeal hear all controversies and disputes arising therefrom.

8. Publish the laws relating to education, with notes and comments for the guidance of those charged with the educational responsibility.

9. Provide through the state department of education supervisory and consultive service and issue materials which would be helpful in the development of educational programs.

10. Accept and distribute, in accord with law, any monies, commodities, goods, and services which may be made available from the state or federal government or from other sources.

11. Designate the extent to which the board is empowered to exercise supervision over public and non-public colleges, universities, state institutions and public and non-public elementary and secondary schools in accord with the law and sound public policy on education.[2]

964, Truman Pierce in his work on government in education

other responsibilities and powers generally exercised degree by state boards of education are:

cil of Chief State School Officers, *The State Department of* n: The Council, 1952, pp. 14-16.

1. Setting forth ways and means for carrying out adopted
   policies;
2. Maintaining general control over the schools;
3. Determining the curriculum;
4. Providing minimum standards;
5. Developing and adopting necessary means for enforcing
   and carrying out state law pertaining to education.[3]

The Chief State School Officer

The chief state school officer, usually titled superintendent of public
instruction or commissioner of education, is commonly considered to
be the chief administrative officer for state education responsibilities,
functions, powers, and duties. Generally he is the executive officer for
the state board of education. As such, he is in a position, and it is his
duty, to recommend policies and regulations for the welfare and progress of the schools of the state and to keep the board advised concerning the status and operation of the schools. His recommendations
should be based on sound knowledge as well as astuteness and judgment for the improvement of all education under the legal jurisdiction of the board. The board is usually a lay board and therefore has
little if any professional knowledge about education. They need bona
fide information and carefully considered recommendations.

The chief state school officer with the professional staff of the department of education should be responsible for overall leadership
of the public schools of the state, the organization and operation of
the department of education within policy established by the legislature and the board; enforcement of educational standards; approval
and issuance of credentials for teachers, administrators, supervisors,
counselors and other professional school personnel; maintenance of a
retirement system; preparation and publication of curriculum guides;
approval of school building plans; disbursement of funds in accordance with statutes, laws and regulations.

The chief state school officer then administers the state school program within the power delegated to him by the state constitution,
laws and statutes passed by the legislature, and policies decided by
the state board of education. The exercise of a leadership role in
performing the delegated duties is the most important action of the

3. Pierce, Truman M. *Federal, State, and Local Government in Education.* The
Center for Applied Research in Education, Inc. Washington, D. C., 1964.

chief state school officer and the department of education. Even regulatory and operational functions of the state agency can be fulfilled in ways that exhibit state leadership while still promoting local initiative and autonomy. Preserving the heritage of local control of schools is becoming increasingly difficult in these days when small school districts are unifying. The old system of statistical and supervisory activities of state agencies will not do. Leadership and coordination engaging the state educational agency, the intermediate school unit and the school district, even the federal government, are necessary and vital to good education in the classroom.

Foreign Language Leadership

Establishing and maintaining a foreign language program in the public schools of a state, with some semblance of standards, requirements, and continuity of learning, requires that there be a function of supervisory leadership at the state level. This leadership for the foreign language program should be directed by a supervisor and staff who are members of a division of instruction or similar unit within the department. Supervision should encompass all levels and all grades for which the state's public schools are responsible, and there should be no arbitrary division between elementary and secondary, since across-the-board responsibility helps in maintaining articulation. In addition, the foreign language supervisors should not be isolated in policy or operation from other subject matter. The focus at all times in the educational process should be not only on foreign language, but rather on the place of foreign language in the entire learning program for the students. Undue emphasis on any one subject may in the long run serve to defeat, rather than bolster the program in the schools.

The designated responsibilities of the foreign language supervisor and staff should be:

1. Providing service to schools, districts and the intermediate units (county or regional offices) such as assisting in the design of techniques for planning, operating, and evaluating language programs; providing information about research, excellent foreign language instructional practices, guides for teaching various languages, and for administrative and counseling practices;

2. Organizing and directing special committees for writing lan-

guage teaching guides and other curricular, instructional, administrative, and counseling documents to assist schools and school districts in doing an effective and efficient job of foreign language instruction;

3. Providing information about foreign language instruction and curriculum to the chief state school officer and members of his staff, the state board of education, the state legislature and the public;

4. Providing avenues for cooperation between the department of education, teacher education institutions, school districts, intermediate units, and instructional personnel concerning pre-service and in-service education and certification of language teachers;

5. Communicating and meeting with local, state, and national associations of language teachers;

6. Communicating with foreign countries and various United States governmental departments and agencies, as well as with non-governmental organizations, to plan for teacher and student visits and language training in foreign countries, and for teacher exchange programs.

The number of state foreign language supervisors or consultants in any state will depend on:

1. The organizational plan of the state department of education in relation to its policy for leadership and service to schools;

2. The geographical size of the state and means of transportation and communication within the state;

3. The school population of the state;

4. The organization of school district administrative and attendance units in the state;

5. The interest and capability of districts' administrative staffs in all aspects pertaining to superior foreign language programs;

6. The sophistication and competence of the foreign language staffs in the schools, districts and intermediate units;

7. The cooperation established and continuing for consultants in colleges, universities, districts, and counties to carry on organized in-service education;

8. Finances available from federal, state, and local sources to pay salaries, transportation, and subsistence for consultants under number 7, above;

9. Finances available and budgeted for instructors' and super-

visors' salaries at the district level to attract and keep good staff, to purchase and maintain proper teaching materials, equipment and facilities, and to maintain a satisfactory in-service education program.

It is neither practical nor possible in many states to have enough full-time people on the staff to take care of all responsibilities necessary to create and continue a good foreign language program in all the schools, colleges, and universities, and to work directly with teachers of every school system. Schools, school districts, and counties in sparsely settled or small states may receive somewhat direct supervisory leadership service from the state foreign language supervisor and staff. In large, heavily populated states there must be a far different organization to supply the educational needs in the schools. The leadership function may be served by working with *groups* of local districts and intermediate units. It should be feasible for department representatives to meet with groups of county or district administrators, supervisory personnel, and language department chairmen to discuss with them the latest reliable information concerning research and to exchange ideas. Thus, the state agency becomes involved in the in-service education of the professional staff in the schools. An organization in which intermediate units function as extensions of the state department of education allows for the possibility of coordinated planning, without the need for all supervision to originate directly at the top. State organization, too, should make it possible for personnel at the district level to make decisions suitable to the needs of students in the district, but within the state's guidelines, standards, and requirements.

One competent individual with a sense of administrative responsibility, knowledge of how districts and schools operate the total curriculum of the schools, and knowledge about language instruction and curriculum is probably superior as a state supervisor to one who possesses mainly language instruction capabilities with very limited knowledge about the overall curriculum of the schools and the ways to coordinate competencies of specially assigned personnel. This does not indicate that one foreign language supervisor is sufficient for every state. It does suggest that the policy of organization be such that the best talents be used in the most judicious manner to assure superior language programs, insofar as possible, for every language learner in the state.

Some states employ part-time foreign language consultants, by contractual arrangements, to do special assignments such as developing a German language guide with the help of a writing committee, conducting workshops for language teachers, and other special assignments. Advisory committees of language teachers and administrators appointed from all levels of education for short terms to formulate plans for improvement of instruction in foreign languages, are of great assistance to the state supervisor in serving the districts. These practices preclude the necessity of having a large, continuous staff of language supervisors in the state department. The employment of part-time specialists is probably better than increasing the permanent language staff in the department of education.

A state foreign language supervisor must have competence, time and energy to:

1. Sense situations in schools and districts,
2. Devise means or plans that will assist districts to evaluate instructional procedures and curriculum practices in foreign languages and to decide how to organize for improvement,
3. Involve personnel who are to be affected by the processes and the results,
4. Obtain results of latest reliable research and other pertinent information and to share such research and information with school personnel.

Granting that all of these factors are feasible and operable, how does a state foreign language consultant provide service and leadership to personnel in districts and intermediate units? There are usually several ways of setting up and proceeding with a program. In all, it is necessary to have communication established between the districts and the state department of education, and a very important factor in this communication is the rapport between the state language supervisor and the school people. Regardless of the advances of scientific and social technology in communication and transportation, it will always be necessary to work with people.

In order that we may look directly at a problem in state foreign language supervision, let us suppose that the "sensing mechanisms" lead the state language consultant to feel that there is a general need for major state guidelines for foreign language teaching. If there is a strong and able foreign language association in the state, it is helpful first to establish contact with the executive committee of the association for assistance in approaching the problem. A meeting or series of meetings might be held with a statewide *ad hoc* advisory committee representing various levels of education including teachers, administrators, supervisors, counselors, and college and university personnel responsible for education of foreign language teachers. Some members of the state foreign language association executive committee should also be included on the *ad hoc* committee.

One logical second step may be the appointment of short-term or long-term "task force" groups to carry out regional meetings for detailed discussion with school and college personnel. Regional meetings of this type serve two purposes: (1) to alert the education public to the possible need for change, and (2) to obtain information for project development and operation.

The following steps summarize one way of developing and writing a guidelines document for foreign language instruction:

1. Recommend through proper channels in the state department of education that a statewide committe be appointed to develop and write a guidelines bulletin, e.g., in French for elementary and secondary schools.
2. The committee of nine to eleven people, including representatives of the foreign language association, should include representatives from elementary schools, junior high schools, senior high schools, colleges, and universities.
3. The focus of the project is two-pronged:
   a. Develop and write the document.
   b. Involve the teachers, administrators, and supervisors in the schools as well as personnel of teacher education institutions.
4. Meet with committee to plan strategy and procedure:
   a. Prepare rough draft of plan.
   b. Prepare proposed outline of document.
5. Hold regional meetings with people at all levels of education to discuss proposal for document. Ask for suggestions, ideas and reactions.
6. Discuss ideas and suggestions with committee.
7. Write working draft of document.
8. Meet with *ad hoc* groups throughout the state to discuss the document. Submit it to the field; that is to districts, counties, colleges, and universities for reaction.

9. When reactions and evaluations are available, submit them to the writing committee for consideration in rewriting the document.
10. Rewrite document and prepare for publication and distribution to schools and colleges.

There is, of course, another way to get a language guide written, published, and distributed to the schools. This is to have it written by the state foreign language supervisor or a small group of three or four experts working under his direction; then have it published and distributed to the schools.

While the process we have outlined at length is more time-consuming and clearly less efficient, it does engage the teachers, administrators, and others in the procedure, and they are therefore ready to do something with the document when it is finally available. This is in the long run a much more effective means to the desired end.

All means of communication—newsletters, bulletins, radio, television and other mass media—should be utilized to promote good foreign language programs throughout the state. Explaining the needs for learning foreign language is a responsibility of the state department of education as well as that of other educational units. In fact, the state should take the lead. There should be specialized personnel on the state department staff to perform public information functions.

Materials

Whether a state department and state board should actually select and print textbooks for the schools, particularly elementary, has been a debatable question for many years. The exercise of local autonomy seems to get involved in this process as well as in many other aspects of education. Certainly, there can be no objection to a representative statewide advisory committee drawing up criteria for foreign language texts and equipment and submitting such criteria to language instructors, supervisors, and administrators for their reaction prior to publication.

Money to purchase foreign language texts and supplementary materials is a financial responsibility of not only the local school district. Money should be provided from the state level by the legislature upon recommendation of the chief state school officer and the state board of education. Such recommendation should be made on the basis of surveys to discover actual costs of supplying materials to schools and the financial ability of each district.

Teachers and Certification

Probably the most important factor that must be given consideration in state leadership is that of providing a competent teaching staff for all students in all schools of the state. It is true, of course, that teachers cannot teach as they should without proper instructional materials, equipment, facilities, and buildings; capable administrators, supervisors, counselors, and other personnel; sensible scheduling of the programs of study; manageable class loads; suitable salaries; parents who are interested in the education of their children; and students who want to learn. But in the final analysis, the teachers in the classrooms must do the jobs. It is they who are finally responsible for education.

Competent classroom teachers must have opportunities for high quality pre-service and in-service education. Pre-service education, the preparation for certification and for teaching, should be a joint venture involving the state board of education, the state department of education, school districts, intermediate school units, and teacher education institutions within a state. Concerning the state's role, it is probably not desirable for a state legislature to assume the right to legislate all of the details of the licensing process or even to specify the requirements for credentials of various grades, levels, and subjects. This should be the duty of a state board. A state board of education advised by the chief state school officer, who in turn has been advised by representatives of schools and of college and university teacher education institutions, should be able to make the decisions leading to sensible credential requirements for teachers and other professional education personnel.

A state board should be kept aware of valid changes in instructional practices and related curriculum design so that certification requirements reflect the most recent reliable research. The state foreign language supervisor, representing the chief state school officer and the state board of education, is in a position, or should be, to invite a representative group from teacher education institutions and elementary and secondary schools to meet periodically to review requirements for certification of foreign language teachers. In-service as well as pre-service education might well be considered by such a statewide committee. A teacher "Credentials Office" or "Licensing Commission" is a valuable part of any state department of education. There should be coordination between the heads of the credentials office and the state foreign language supervisor to assure exchange of knowledge.

Publications

Articulation (continuum of learning) of instruction and curriculum can better be established if all teachers are properly knowledgeable in the language methodology as well as competent in a language. Recommendations and bulletins from the state language supervisor and from advisory committees concerning ways and means of articulating language programs should be developed and written by a statewide representative committee under the direction of the state language supervisor, then published and distributed by the state department of education.[4]

The state department foreign language supervisor should always maintain a direct consultative capacity with special committees appointed by the state board of education on the recommendations of the chief state school officer to write language curriculum guides. These should not be detailed courses of study but guideline documents that recommend standards for all language levels. These guideline bulletins should be disseminated to the schools at state expense. It should then be the responsibility of districts to write detailed courses of study in keeping with the standards established for learning each language.

Summary

These are but a few of the general activities and responsibilities of foreign language specialists at the state level. Today the state supervisor's job is expanding to include many new areas. Accelerated research in education, data processing, new means of compiling and exchanging data, increasing power of education associations, avail-

---

4. *Blueprint for Greater Foreign Language Articulation.* Indiana Language Program. Indiana University, Bloomington, Indiana, May, 1965.

Language Instruction: Perspective and Prospectus. Bulletin of California State Department of Education. Vol. XXXII, No. 4. Sacramento, California, November, 1963.

ability of federal funds, and unification of school districts with their developing initiative and autonomy, all make it necessary for supervisory personnel to be continuously alert to opportunities to increase their effectiveness. The state supervisor is rapidly becoming a resource person rather than a supervisor per se. He is a super-planner of programs, a disseminator of research and information, a coordinator of state committees, a participant in national organizations, and above all a person with vision to see both the forest and the trees.

Index